Behavior Problems in Horses

All horse owners find from time to time that their animals do not behave in an acceptable manner. In this book Susan McBane shows why a horse's behaviour can fail to reach *our* expectations. She examines the problems from a new perspective and asks us to imagine how the horse might see a given situation and identify it with events in its own past. Above all the necessity to understand the animal can often take us half way to solving the problem itself.

The first part of the book examines the evolution of the horse and the instinct mechanisms it has developed to protect itself in its natural environment. The author evaluates the horse's learning and memory faculties and asks why habits are formed and how they can be changed. The essential differences between intelligence and conditioned behaviour are stressed and methods of scientifically assessing intelligence are set out with the proviso that instinct may impinge on any conditioning process.

There is an informative section giving accounts of problems that have been encountered by other horse experts.

The latter part of the book is a practical problem dictionary – the author does not just cite the various problems that can be encountered but sets out the particular vice or problem, examines the potential causes and then offers sound, corrective action. Her approach is realistic; valuable advice is given on when professional help should be sought, and on when a problem simply cannot be remedied.

Illustrated throughout with practical black-and-white photographs and line illustrations *Behaviour Problems in Horses* is an invaluable handbook for all those wishing to understand and solve their horse problems.

By the same author
Keeping a Horse Outdoors (David & Charles)
Your First Horse
Keeping Horses: How to Save Time and Money

How to Cure

Behavior Problems in Horses

Susan McBane

Cover photography by David Brownell

Melvin Powers
Wilshire Book Company

12015 Sherman Road, No. Hollywood, CA 91605

Photographs, unless specified otherwise, are by the author

Line illustrations by Joy Claxton

British Library Cataloguing in Publication Data

McBane, Susan
    Behaviour problems in horses.
    1. Horses – Behaviour
    I. Title
    636.1   SF281

    ISBN 0-7153-8749-9

Typeset by Typesetters (Birmingham) Limited
Smethwick, West Midlands
and printed in Great Britain
by Redwood Burn Limited, Trowbridge, Wilts
for David & Charles Publishers plc
Brunel House   Newton Abbot   Devon

**Wilshire Book Company has the exclusive
English language trade paperback rights
in the USA and Canada. Printed in the USA.**

Contents

In memory of my friend Jack Fisher's horse
FINN MacCOOL
He was a problem to many people but not to his family

Preface

Horses give us problems in many ways, in both their management and their work. Most of the problems we may come across, and which we may be able to deal with ourselves as opposed to constantly calling in specialist help, involve the way the horse is behaving, and that is specifically what this book is about. Diseases, allergies, misshapen hooves, poor conformation and so on are the province of the veterinary surgeon and farrier and are outside the scope of this work.

Some behavioural problems cannot be dealt with by any but very competent and experienced horsemen and horsewomen, and when it is felt that an expert trainer should be called in, this is recommended. It should be possible, however, for many difficult horses to be greatly improved by the thoughts and actions of any reasonably competent horsemaster, rider or whip, and it is for such a readership that the book has been written. It is not a scientific treatise on equine behaviour but a practical guide on problems with emphasis on the general theme of why horses behave as they do and why bad habits develop.

As Secretary of the Equine Behaviour Study Circle (see Appendix A), I have for several years been able to discuss all aspects of equine behaviour with a wide variety of horse people from all over the world, from scientists to casual riders, and during much of my research for this book I drew on past issues of its journal, *Equine Behaviour*. I asked two of its officers, Dr Moyra Williams, founder and Chairman of the Circle, and Dr Sharon Cregier, its North American Co-ordinator, to make personal contributions, and also asked Mr Dominic Prince to add his observations on the vexed subject of stable vices. These three independent contributions form Part II of the book and bring it a valuable element which I could not personally have provided. Part I is mainly my personal view of equine behaviour as it relates to problems and Part III is a dictionary of problems with reasons for their occurrence, and remedies, mostly acquired from my own experiences and from personal interviews. The answer to every little problem which may arise during training cannot be provided here but many of the more disturbing and alarming behaviour patterns which appear during ridden or driven work and in the stable are covered.

I hope that this book will not only encourage membership of the Equine Behaviour Study Circle but also stimulate more reasoned thought, research and discussion on the important subject of equine behaviour, especially where it relates to the habits and vices which can so mar our association with that magnificent animal, the horse. The subject does not attract the interest it should: after all, we are *all* interested in how our horses behave. The very process of training a horse involves our attempts to influence his behaviour.

For generations, 'horse psychology' has taken a back seat to riding, management, training, driving and many other equestrian and equine topics. Little or no attention was paid to it during, for example, examinations and their preparatory training courses, although this is now changing. Some of the better books did stress its importance but it seems that some of their readers paid no more than lip service to it and there is still, in many quarters, little evidence that its important principles are actually carried through to management and schooling. Indeed, it is probably our lack of regard for all aspects of equine behaviour and psychology which brings about most of the problems we experience.

Susan McBane

PART I
A PERSONAL VIEW

1
What is a Problem?

A problem can be described as a matter causing difficulty, puzzlement, worry or indecision. It may have to be resolved before the status quo can be restored or before further progress can be made. It may cause expense, danger and destruction. Solutions to problems may not be clear cut and can demand the use of thought, intelligence, skill, understanding and time. What appears to be the best course of action might not have the desired result, or at best might be only partially successful. Science is continually solving problems, but often only to create others in their place: for instance, nuclear power may have been harnessed but we now have to find an infallible method for disposing of the waste. Perhaps this problem, like many others in all areas of life, simply has no answer.

What does all this have to do with horses? The fact is that the troubles of mankind are so intricately entwined with those of horses as to be inseparable, and it is usually man who is at fault. Would it be too sweeping a statement to say that there are no problem horses, only problem humans? We associate with them because we want to, whether they are our work or our play, yet because the demands we often make on them are so unnatural, excessive and unreasonable, we create a knot of Gordian complexity for ourselves and for them.

Our horses *can* cause us difficulty, puzzlement, worry or indecision. Problems do have to be solved before the status quo can be restored or before further progress can be made. They can, indeed, cause expense, danger and destruction and we do need to call on thought, intelligence, skill, understanding and the expenditure of time in our dealings with them.

Similarly, many horse problems remain unsolved, either because we do not have the ability, the experience, the know-how or the courage to put things right, or because no true answer exists. For example, as far as I am able to discover, there is no known case of a confirmed crib-biter having been cured. Horses who have newly developed the vice have been stopped in their tracks by special surgical procedures but dyed-in-the-wool cribbers have found a way round them and continue to assuage their craving, even when turned out to grass. (For further views and hypotheses on this and other vices see pages 173–5.)

The 'problem' horse

A problem horse can be described as one who behaves in an undesirable way because he refuses, or is unable, either to do or not do what we want. If a horse is bucking madly, he is (unless he is a rodeo horse) doing what we do *not* want him to do; if he is refusing a jump, he is *not* doing what we *do* want him to do. In other words, in both cases he is refusing to accede to our wishes. His reasons are probably very sound, but we, initially anyway, tend to look on such behaviour as a refusal to co-operate.

If a horse is performing a stable vice, he may truly be unable to stop it. Box-walkers, for instance, although I have met only a few, in some cases simply do not seem to know what they are doing. It is almost as though they are sleep-walking, and just cannot stop. On the other hand, a horse may refuse a jump because he is unable to make the height or width, either due to insufficient training, lack of physical strength because he is unfit, or simply lack of sufficient jumping ability. His 'problem' is inability rather than wilfulness. Telling the difference between 'won't' and 'can't' has long been one of the most difficult questions facing those who associate with horses.

A problem may only be a problem from our point of view, not the horse's. Horses who actually enjoy performing their stable vices cannot be expected to understand why we want them to stop. Reprimanding a horse for, say, crib-biting is absolutely useless. Training usually consists of reward and punishment (although hopefully today the emphasis is tending to be more and more on reward training rather than on punishment training). A horse who is mildly reprimanded for doing something which we consider wrong, such as biting, can often be cured of the trick by being growled at or slapped on the shoulder every time he nips. Often, the horse gets the idea that biting humans is not wanted. Try reprimanding that same horse when he cribs: no

11

amount of 'stop-its' or 'give-ups', and certainly no amount of slaps, will stop him.

Horses who jump out of fields are a real problem to their owners, but not to themselves unless they are injured. They simply want to get to the other side of the fence either because the food looks better there, because company is there (maybe a particular friend), because, in the case of a stallion, there is an attractive mare in the next field, or simply because they love wide open spaces and object to being fenced in a small and perhaps bare pasture. Our concern does not trouble them: we may want to keep them in, but they want to get out and can often do so with little difficulty. (On the other hand, why is it that horses with superb competitive jumping ability will trot along a fence talking to a ridden horse passing by but baulk at jumping out of their field to follow when the surrounding fence is comparatively low?)

Looking at problems from the horse's point of view instead of our own is often the best way of solving them. As with illnesses, treating symptoms instead of root causes is never the answer. It is much more effective to spend some time and thought finding out why a horse is doing, or not doing, something and putting the matter right in the light of that knowledge.

When the problem is a stable vice, we have an additional problem on our hands when we try physically to stop the horse performing it. Horses initially perform stable vices as a release from tension of some kind. When we remove that relief by calling a halt to the physical action the horse will often find another, maybe similar, vice to practise. If we close one door, we must open another for the relief of that tension.

For example, if a cribbing strap is fitted to a crib-biter as a preventive measure, he may well resort to the related vice of wood-chewing instead. (He is unlikely to go on to wind-sucking because the neck-arching movement is more or less the same and is uncomfortable to perform wearing a cribbing strap.) If we stop a weaver by fitting a grille, by hanging blocks of wood or water-filled plastic bottles in his doorway, or by tying him up (positively calculated to make him unhappier than ever), he may simply learn to nod his head up and down instead of from side to side, or weave inside the box instead of in the doorway, or take to box-walking instead. If tied up, he may take to 'weaving' with his quarters instead of his forehand, although this is unusual.

Although some stable vices can be stopped in their early stages by physical means, those that are well established often cannot be prevented entirely. They can be 'controlled' (ie their performance limited) but, when free to do so, the horse once again resorts to practising them.

The equine junkie

Even if the underlying stress and tension are removed, well-established vices have almost always become so ingrained, so much a part of the horse's psyche, so habitual and so irresistible from a chemical point of view, that the horse cannot and does not stop performing them. For recent medical studies show that physical exertion, such as jogging or training for athletic events and other sports, produces the release into the brain of natural substances called endorphins which are chemically similar to heroin, morphine and opium, but which can be a hundred times more powerful. Work done early in this decade at the University of Utrecht in the Netherlands now leads us to believe that the physical activity of performing stable vices also produces these endorphins in a similar manner.

Heroin, morphine and opium belong to a group of drugs, natural and synthetic, called opiates which are used in medicine mainly to relieve pain and other unpleasant sensations both mental and physical; because they can, as is so well known, cause drug dependence and tolerance (necessitating higher and higher doses to be effective until the safety threshold is reached, beyond which life is endangered), their use is strictly controlled. The pattern is that they are taken by patients for their pain-killing effect, and also by drug users for the sense of euphoria they give; if they continue to be taken, the user becomes addicted and, as society knows, it can be extremely hard to break an addiction.

As far as endorphins are concerned, they can be produced in athletes, 'fun' joggers and, it seems, horses and probably any other animals which habitually use up a great deal of physical energy, such as greyhounds, foxhounds, working sheepdogs and the like, and horses and zoo animals who constantly practise a vice no matter how it started. When some such people and animals stop their training or work habit, many become restless and depressed without the activity. Even after retirement, some athletes, boxers, footballers and so on still keep up their running and training activities to some degree as they say it makes them feel better and they like to keep in condition. Horses who have had an active life sometimes do not settle into retirement.

In the light of current research, what really seems to be happening is that these human and animal 'trainaholics' are unwittingly giving themselves a daily 'fix'. They have become addicted to the naturally-produced endorphins in their bodies and feel out of sorts without them. Horses practising vices are, apparently, in the same position. However the vice started, its constant practice has produced an addiction to the endorphins and the horse is on the vicious cycle of dependence. The fact that some vices in some individuals *can* be stopped if caught early may be due to correction occurring before addiction has set in.

This cycle does not appear to happen in all individuals, however, human or otherwise. Not all athletes continue the training habit after they give up competition. Many horses do settle well to a life of retirement. And not all people feel a sense of exhilaration after a training session; many find physical exertion simply exhausting. In all species, at least of the sort we are discussing here, some are athletically inclined and some are not. Perhaps it is only the former who produce endorphins.

It is noticeable that stable vices often appear in those horses who work hardest and are confined most. The hard work produces the endorphins; the confinement, and probably the stress of the work and the unnaturalness of the life imposed on the individual, produce the vices; the vices reinforce the production of the endorphins, and there you are: one equine junkie.

Still on the subject of endorphins and their pain-killing powers, as discussed by Dominic Prince in his contribution to Part II, the discovery of these naturally-produced anaesthetic substances in connection with twitching horses to restrain them is also fascinating and enlightening; and it slots in logically with the fact that the heart-rate of a twitched horse actually drops and the eyes take on a slightly dazed, far-away look. Neither is a sign we would expect in a pain-ridden, panic-stricken animal; they are signs of relaxation. The twitched horse is, in fact, sedated by its own endorphins. The horse in agony has a high heart-rate, 60 beats per minute or more depending on the

14

severity of the pain, and the same applies in situations of panic and fear.

The Dutch team, led by Professor Lagerweij, believes that the upper lip/nose area is, in fact, an acupuncture or acupressure point which the inventors of the twitch accidentally discovered – a shining example of doing the right thing for very wrong reasons. Chinese doctors have for thousands of years induced analgesia while maintaining consciousness by the use of acupuncture and acupressure. They found and used the various points on the body, but we have only recently discovered *why* acupuncture works: endorphins again – produced by pressure on certain points of the body.

Applying a 'neck twitch' to a horse often has a similar effect to the more conventional type and results in control and reasonable quietness. A fold of skin on the neck in front of the shoulder is taken up, pinched and twisted, and in a minute, the horse calms down and becomes amenable. This could be another acupressure/acupuncture point. It could also be that wild animals found these points long before we did. Packs of wild dogs hunting zebras (equidae, of course) often sink their teeth into the upper lip of the zebra and hang on, while a colleague hangs similarly on to the tail. Brian Leith, reporting on this topic in *The Listener* early in 1985, asked 'Could it be that wild dogs have learnt to "twitch" their prey, to sedate the zebra so as to overcome it more easily?' Could the tail also, therefore, be a further acupressure point?

And the story is not quite over yet! How many of us have sustained some injury during the excitement of a sport, or during a traumatic experience such as a car crash or other serious accident, and not felt any real pain for some time afterwards? A few years ago the case of a farm worker whose arm was cut off in a piece of machinery out in the fields was reported widely in the press. He picked up the arm and, although weak from loss of blood, felt little pain as he made his way across the fields to the house. Not until he was in the ambulance did the pain start. Again, it is now believed it could be endorphins deadening the pain, having been produced during the excitement of the game or the trauma of the injury.

The same thing happens with horses. If a horse has the misfortune to sprain a tendon or ligament during a race, for example, he often soldiers on to the finish, possibly in *some* discomfort, but after he is pulled up he becomes more and more lame until he is ultimately hobbling back to the stable area. If the pain had been so great during the race itself, surely the horse could not have continued?

The drug Naloxone is used in the treatment of heroin addicts as when it is injected it blocks the heroin receptor sites in the body and so blocks the effects of endorphins. When injected into a person receiving acupuncture, it blocks the effects of the treatment.

One of the Dutch team, Greg Cronin from Australia, found that when pigs performing their version of stable vices (bar and chain chewing) were injected with Naloxone, they stopped the behaviour and returned to normal foraging behaviour. As vices in horses do not always stop, at least in confirmed cases, when the stressful conditions causing them are improved, this appears to confirm that it is, in fact, an addiction to endorphins which causes this abnormal behaviour in horses and farm animals and that the animals probably could not stop if they wanted to. Could Naloxone prove to be a treatment in helping horses give up their vices (along with improved living and management conditions, obviously)? Only more research on the topic will tell, but veterinary surgeons should be able to keep us up to date with the latest findings and the prospects of treatment by this method.

What causes problems in general?
Stress
Staying with stable vices a little longer, the initial cause of these is surely unnatural and stressful management for the most part. Although it is normal to us to keep horses in stables and to see a row of heads looking out, giving us a feeling that all is right with the world, from the horses' point of view this may well not be so.

Horses were not evolved to live in dens or caves like some other creatures such as dogs or humans, badgers, foxes or rabbits. It is natural to them to live in the open, despite the fact that they must have adequate shelter if they are to feel comfortable and to thrive. In natural conditions, they are free to find their own shelter in woods, behind shrubs, in sheltered valleys and so on – but they are not closed in on all four sides and overhead. They are not forced to live most of their lives, twenty-odd hours a day, confined to an area of about twelve feet square.

If a horse in the wild, or even in a domestic paddock, stayed in one place like this for so long, or even for one hour, it would almost surely be a sign that he was unwell! Yet the domesticated, mostly-stabled horse has no choice.

We tend to feel that because our horses and ponies are domesticated they think, feel and behave differently from their wild, or rather feral, relatives. They are 'tame', after all. They are 'used to' the living conditions we put them into. Indeed, many of them were born in a stable. They are used to being stabled from birth. How can they possibly feel stressed or unhappy when confined?

It is quite true that many horses do love their stables and come to associate them with security. Some do appear to live quite happily in such conditions, giving no sign of neurosis or the claustrophobia inherent in the species as a whole, exhibiting no stable vices and exuding a sense of calm, familiar acceptance of their lifestyles. Such horses are often those who receive a great deal of exercise, far more than most privately-owned animals, who can often count themselves lucky if they are out of their boxes for two hours a day.

Many, many more, however, although maybe associating their stables with security, food, water and shelter, find the excessively long periods of confinement normal in our management methods impossible to bear without some form of release from the tension and frustration – and show it in the various stable vices which are so familiar in many yards up and down the country. It cannot be repeated too often that *each horse is an individual and must be treated as such*. Some horses can take long periods in a stable, provided copious exercise is the normal daily routine. Others, kept in the same way and given the same amount of exercise, *can't* take it. Their natural desire for wide open spaces and dislike, or even fear, of being closed in, are stronger and take precedence over the other advantages of shelter, comfort and security.

As mentioned earlier, it is noticeable that many horses showing signs of stress and tension are those working hardest and being kept almost entirely stabled. Although they may be led out in hand for half an hour to relieve the boredom of being stabled, this is a mere drop in the ocean of their needs. Such horses would do far better if kept on the combined system where they have a significant number of hours out at pasture each day. If this would play too much havoc with their diet, efforts should be made to yard them in a dirt yard large enough for them to kick up their heels and move freely about, canter a bit and buck if they want.

The yard can have an open shed for them to come and go as they please, depending on weather conditions and whether or not they wish to lie and rest (obviously a decent bed, possibly on deep litter, would be a big advantage in the shed). Even a small yard leading directly from their stable is better than nothing and gives them a feeling of at least some liberty and elbow room to move about. Modern waterproof rugs are light and easy to maintain, enabling the horse to be out much of the time, if he wishes – and he probably will. Horses so kept spend most of their time out in their pens from choice.

Anyone who doubts that most horses, not just the neurotic ones, would rather be out than in, except possibly when feed is being given in the stable, only has to open the door and see whether the horse comes out or stays in. We all know what would happen in most cases, and the horse couldn't put it any more plainly if he tried!

It is perfectly possible to give horses more liberty and space without their becoming muddy grass-bags. Yarding on fine

Fig 1 Exercise under constraint is no substitute for liberty

shale, clinker, used bedding from the stables, sand, or something similar, will not result in the horses becoming caked in mud if they roll. These materials brush off very easily. If, when mucking out, the muck is divided into two piles, one droppings and the other used bedding, the used bedding can be used to floor a yard or even a little 'play area' at no expense. The droppings are far more saleable than the normal stable-yard muck, or more use for gardens or vegetable plots than when mixed with about 75 per cent bedding, as most muck heaps are.

'Doctor Green' has for generations been an excellent home cure-all in the horse world, but at least half the credit, and probably more, must go to 'Doctor Liberty'. Not only does horses' mental health improve immeasurably when they are given several hours freedom each day, but their physical well-being does, too. The constant, gentle exercise they take, and also the odd spurt of high jinks, must surely be better for them than periods of concentrated work followed the rest of the time by nothing but standing still.

A common argument against turning a horse on to grass for more than an hour or so is, quite obviously, that the horse will fill himself with bulky, non-concentrated food and will be unable to work. This argument is justified where working horses are concerned, but steps can be taken to ameliorate the effects of pasture. For a start, pasture for horses should never, except in rare cases outside the scope of this book, be rich in the way it is for cattle. Poor to medium quality grazing (but clean and in good order) is what is needed.

As regards the moisture content of pasture it is well known that horses on grass, especially in the earlier parts of the year when the grass is not so fibrous but softer and juicier, do not drink so much water as at other times or as when mainly stabled. The overall water intake, therefore, is not affected. Horses kept out for, say, half a day, particularly *after* their work has been done, on fairly poor pasture are not really at risk of forming a grass belly or of becoming overloaded with bulky food. Their hay/hayage consumption will decrease accordingly, and the concentrates can still be fed at normal levels to ensure required dietary intake.

If yarding facilities are not available, therefore, or cannot for some reason be made, half a day, just about every day depending on exact schedules, out on the sort of pasture described will have virtually no adverse effect on the horse's bulk intake and will do his mind and instinctive needs for activity, space and freedom a world of good.

It should not be beyond today's plant breeders to produce a few different types of grass, which have fairly low nutritional values and which will not appreciably affect the rest of the diet, to formulate into seed mixes for sowing paddocks for athletic horses. In fact, some suitable varieties are already available and advice on this topic can be obtained from The Equine Management Consultancy Service, The Small Hall, The Old School, Shrivenham Road, Highworth, Wiltshire, SN6 7BZ.

Obviously, not all horses should be kept out all the time. However, our horses, in general, could be given more freedom than they usually are and yarding is a management system which we in Britain do not make use of anything like enough. When horses are mentally content, with their instinctive need for and love of movement, space and almost constant activity catered for, problems of all kinds are very rare.

Over-feeding and lack of activity are, together, a prime cause of problems under saddle and in harness, never mind stable vices. All that energy being pumped into the horse has to go somewhere and the exercise given is often too much at once and in too short spells to use it up effectively and in a way which suits the horse's physiology and mentality. Putting a horse on a slightly lower plane as regards dietary energy and giving him more steady work and more liberty, particularly with natural company so he can indulge his social needs with others of his kind, goes further, faster, to solve more problems than any other single course of action.

The equine species has been around on this planet many millions of years longer than we have. Man is very much a newcomer and is only just beginning to become aware of the immense damage he is doing to his own and other creatures' environment. The effects of domestication on horses are plain for all who have eyes and brains to see and analyse. The horse's mental and physical traits and needs have evolved over millions of years and cannot be changed by a mere four thousand or at most five thousand years of increasing domestication. A more natural approach to their management results in horses who are happier, more content, physically more effective and, of particular interest to readers of this book, 'problem' free. Indeed, *we* cease to be so much of a problem to them because we are not the cause of *their* problems. Horses in such a condition do, in practice, work better for us (for the horse is amazingly willing to do our bidding, considering he is not a 'bootlicker' animal like the dog – to use an expression uttered by a friend of mine) and are both mentally and physically more amenable and more capable, indeed, more interested in doing what we ask of them.

So we must find ways of catering more to the horse's requirements to put him in a better condition to work. If there remain problems after that, and after the horse has had time to settle down into what may be a new régime for him, other causes must be considered.

Fear
There is no doubt that many problems, usually those occurring under saddle or in harness, are caused by fear. Horses are under significant stress when confined and, particularly, when restrained. Riding and driving are both forms of restraint, of course; neither is at all natural to the horse, consisting of various straps being placed around the body, sometimes quite tightly, of weight being pulled (which a horse would obviously never do in the wild) or being carried. This latter is particularly frightening to the horse if he has never experienced anything like it or has been scared or hurt in the past. In natural conditions horses do not carry weight. Although a mare might be accustomed to feeling the weight of a stallion on her quarters, or youngsters might rear up and come down onto each other during youthful high jinks, having a weight on the back in wild conditions would mean only one thing, a predator in for the kill.

Many believe there is still an instinctive fear in horses of weight on the back, instilled through millions of years of being preyed upon. It is certainly true that youngsters hurriedly backed are far more prone to trying to buck off their riders than those handled gently but with discipline from birth and very gradually accustomed to having various objects lain across their backs such as a lead rope, a roller, a rug and eventually heavier things such as a saddle, which a human would gradually press on harder and harder. In such youngsters, when the moment

21

actually comes for a human to lie across the saddle it usually causes little or no reaction or trouble. Then the rider can slip a leg over and, still with the upper half of his body bent down, assume a seat in the saddle.

It is often not until the rider sits up normally and the horse sees this unaccustomed sight of a human up in the air instead of down on the ground that a reaction occurs. Even then, if it is done gradually, with much soothing and praising, it usually causes little or no problem.

As long as things go smoothly and the horse is not hurt, confused or frightened while being ridden, either by the rider or by someone or something else nearby, again, problems have no reason to occur. Fear, however, is a very powerful emotion in all creatures. If something alarming occurs the horse may well associate it with the process of being ridden for a very long time, maybe for ever. Horses who have been abused under saddle by rough riding, being jabbed in the mouth by incompetent or insensitive hands, spurred excessively so that their flanks are either bruised or cut, whipped for reasons they do not understand, had a rider with an insecure seat banging about on their loins and been generally pulled about, may be very difficult to 'reclaim', although it can be done by a very competent and feeling rider. However, it often takes only one lapse in the rider's performance for trouble to recur very quickly.

The natural reaction of a horse trying to rid himself of something on his back, whether it be a human or a horse-fly, is to buck. Very few, even expert riders, can stay on a horse who gives several determined bucks one after the other, which may be some consolation to those less expert when faced with this sort of behaviour. It is a very effective 'off-putter' in more ways than one. In fact, the horse-fly is much better at staying put than the human.

Fear can, then, result in various attempts to get the rider off, bucking being a fairly common reaction. A horse who is genuinely terrified, like any other creature in the same condition, can lose all sense and reason. Fear can escalate to panic, or panic can occur almost instantaneously if something very sudden occurs to set it off. Trains are a prime example of objects which can terrify horses. We read in old books, published about the time trains began to appear around the country, of horses bolting in a flat-out panic and killing themselves by running headlong into a building, a tree, a vehicle or whatever, and this danger seems to be returning as trains become more of a rarity in many areas than a normality. Microlight aircraft, hang-gliders and, more rarely, helicopters, these days often unintentionally harass horses and cause the same kind of panic.

Even something as simple as a piece of paper blowing in the road or fluttering in a hedge can cause a sudden shy of fear. Because a horse learns by association of ideas, he may shy at that same spot for ever more, long after the piece of paper or whatever it was has disappeared. An acquaintance of mine had an event horse which she had to stop taking to one particular event because he had an accident at a drop fence there. The visit after the accident, the horse went round the course beautifully till he came to that same fence and, of course, nothing would induce him to jump it even though he had a different rider so, presumably, no nervous 'vibes' were being transmitted from that source. The rider withdrew the horse before a battle ensued.

The following year, the horse's owner once again took him to the event. The offending fence had been dismantled and there was nothing but a hazard, a dip in the ground, where he had had his accident two years earlier, but he would not tackle it, so that was his last visit to that course. Identical drop fences at other events have caused no trouble, so in his case it was association of a painful, frightening experience with one particular place which caused the problem.

Other cases are known where, despite the place, a horse has taken an aversion to a particular object. Umbrellas seem to be notorious for causing fear, usually not great, in horses. The fact that horses may be used to seeing humans carrying umbrellas does not stop them showing signs of considerable uncertainty and timidity if an umbrella is placed on the ground in their paddock (which has been tried as an experiment). In some cases, it seems, fear can be caused by an object or event being associated with a place. In others, the object causes fear no matter where it is. Objects out of their normal position also often cause suspicion.

Both fear and confusion can cause a mental block in the horse, who will probably become rigid and maybe tremble. Only removal of the cause may reverse the situation. If the thing causing the trouble cannot be removed (such as flapping polythene on a neighbouring barn), and the horse is genuinely frightened, probably the only thing to do, especially if alone with no schoolmaster colleague on hand, is gently turn the horse round, not press the point. Returning the way you have come may be the only safe course of action. Remember that the horse is many times stronger than we are; provoking violent actions we have not the strength to control is stupid in the extreme. A horse in such a condition needs calm stroking and talking to, not forcing to go on if we cannot hope to win over the situation. If a colleague is available, a lead can be given and, so, an example set to the other horse. Sometimes, simply trying to lift a foot or steadily push the horse off balance so that it moves a foot itself can help to break the 'block'. Misunderstanding of our requirements on the part of the horse can cause problems if the misunderstanding is allowed to continue or if we worry the horse by not making matters clearer. Most horses do seem to want to please and try hard to understand what is wanted of them. But when given incomprehensible or inconsistent aids a horse has a probably impossible task in interpreting them correctly, and when those aids cause him discomfort or pain, he may well react, according to his temperament, in ways we neither want nor expect.

If the horse has been trained in such a way that he is actually reprimanded or even more strongly punished every time he makes a mistake, he may well almost live in fear of putting a foot wrong and dare not try to obey in case he does the wrong thing. Punishment training of this sort, rather than reward training (where the horse is praised for getting something right rather than punished for getting it wrong) is becoming rarer, although it unfortunately still exists where 'old school' methods are perpetuated. It is quite possible to indicate to a horse that a certain reaction is not what we want by getting him used to the word 'no' in a slightly reproving tone rather than being over-stern or actually physically punishing him when he reacts wrongly. Horses are very sensitive to and quickly understand the tone of the human voice. It is far more effective, and enjoyable for horse and human together, when great praise and fuss are administered for a correct reaction. The horse wants to be praised and will soon associate the aid with the reaction and with the reward.

This way, he remains calmer, too, and so learns faster. An excited, edgy, frightened horse learns little or nothing, except that training means fear, discomfort, pain and confusion so it is little wonder that problems occur with a horse in such a state.

Apart from being generous with rewards during training and mean with punishments, we must ensure that aids whether physical or vocal are given in exactly the same way every time if the horse is to learn what they mean. Many aids must feel, sound or look very similar to a horse who is sensitive to even slight differences. Consistency and exactness are essential if we want a confident horse who reacts as required every time until obedience to that aid becomes more or less automatic.

If a horse is punished for reacting wrongly to an aid or request when he innocently misunderstood its meaning, he will quickly associate that particular aid with pain, injustice and fear. If he misunderstands other aids, and is punished for them, too, he will come to associate all work contact with humans as something to be dreaded and hated. It will be small wonder, then, if he becomes difficult, violent and dangerous to ride, or generally sluggish, unco-operative and sullen. Misunderstanding in the horse is always the fault of the handler/rider/driver. In the case of a horse who is being taught something right from the beginning and knows absolutely nothing of what is wanted, he will probably just stand stock still, trying to puzzle out what on earth we are doing or what that queer sound we are uttering so earnestly can possibly mean. If he reacts wrongly, sensing that something is required although he cannot figure out what, it is not a case of misunderstanding – it is a case of not understanding at all. To punish a horse in such a circumstance would be the height of stupidity. The correct course of action on the part of the handler would be to use the word/s of command and to deliver the aid or physical request in such a way that the horse can only react in the way wanted. He will then quickly link the vocal command with the action and will remember it for ever more, once confirmed in it.

Misunderstanding can easily occur when commands sound very similar. This is one reason why the command 'stop' is not normally used for horses, but 'whoa' in a long drawn-out tone. 'Stop' sounds far too much like 'trot' to the horse unless the two are enunciated quite differently. The actual words, of course, mean nothing to the horse, it is the sound he learns. If 'stop' were required instead of 'whoa', a suitable way to say it might be 'sssstop', with the emphasis on the 's' sound to produce a definite hiss. The word 'trot' could then be sounded as 'ter-rot', stressing the first syllable. These two words are just examples, of course, of how clear our differentiations must be to avoid confusion in the horse's mind.

A true story (which few people ever believe when I tell them) in connection with using similar sounding words illustrates just how quick horses are to react and how willing they are to do our bidding when confident and happy with their handlers. A girl I know was making a very good job of schooling her first pony. She had taught him to pick up his feet in order just by standing by the foot required and saying 'hup'. (Initially she had leaned her weight against the pony to shift his weight and bodily lifted his hoof in the usual way, combining it with the command 'hup'. The pony had quickly progressed to the stage where 'hup' was almost not needed, just an expectant posture with the head down looking at the hoof required being usually enough to elicit response.)

When it came to teaching the pony to jump, which she did with the help of an interested instructor, trotting poles and then cavalletti were used in the usual way, then the cavalletti were built up gradually into a little obstacle. Perhaps feeling a little apprehensive at this stage (although the pony had shown no hesitation so far), almost at the point of take-off the girl gave a definite leg aid and called firmly 'hup'. The pony immediately stopped, despite the leg aid, and obligingly lifted a foot, if rather uncertainly because he did not know which foot was required.

Admittedly, in this case the words were identical, but obey the pony did. 'Hup' did not mean 'up' to the pony; it meant 'lift your foot', which he did without quibble. As mentioned, the word itself does not mean a thing to the horse; it is the sound which the horse links with a particular action.

It is interesting to note that the pony, although progressing well with his work under saddle, responded to the verbal command to lift a foot and not to the leg aid to go on, despite both being given simultaneously and assertively. Driving horses respond easily and quickly to vocal commands, of course, and riders experiencing difficulty in getting a horse to respond to physical aids given by hand, seat or leg often find that when these are reinforced by a spoken command, the horse will obey at once. This illustrates that physical aids often seem to be given in a way not quite identical to the way in which they were given on previous occasions, yet vocal aids apparently sound identical as they usually produce such a prompt response. Perhaps the horse is more geared to communication by sound than by touch. In herd situations, 'body language', as it is called, is used more in visual situations than contact ones. Facial expressions, postures, different body positions, all communicate to other herd members without actual contact.

Horses' vocal range is quite varied, although they are not in the habit of having running conversations with each other. The fact remains that some riders, particularly in dressage tests where vocal commands are not allowed (they are allowed in driving), feel at a distinct disadvantage not being allowed to speak to their horses. Many, however, do cultivate a set smile which enables them to issue vocal commands through their teeth and under their breath to get the required response from a horse – it works very well!

How many times, too, have we seen a novice, either on the ground, in the saddle or on the box seat, having difficulty in getting his horse to understand what he wants and act accordingly; then when he remembers, or someone reminds him, to speak to the horse, the situation is transformed and the horse often obliges without more ado.

Another example of misunderstanding is very common. When a horse or pony is afraid of something and is playing up, perhaps not wanting to go past a certain spot or up to a certain object, the rider, handler or driver may say, among various other soothing noises, 'good boy', and perhaps accompany it with a stroke or pat. 'Good boy' is very widely used to praise horses during training: they quickly come to associate it with doing the right thing and to treat it as a reward. How confusing for the animal, then, who is playing up because unsure or frightened, to be praised (as he thinks) for his actions, when, possibly in the same breath, the human involved also says firmly some word such as 'no', which the animal already well knows is a reproof. The conversation (from the human) might run something like this: 'Easy boy, don't be silly, it won't hurt you, good boy, no, good boy, there then, no,

now then, easy . . .' and so on. Out of all that lot the horse, surprisingly enough, will probably pick out those two phrases he
knows best as they are used often – 'good boy' and 'no' – but
spoken one after the other! One means good boy, the other means
bad boy. What on earth is one supposed to think? No wonder the
horse becomes confused.

It is absolutely essential that consistency and clarity are
adopted as watchwords in all our dealings with horses and
ponies. The same goes for intermittent 'punishment'. If a horse
does wrong and is reprimanded for it, he will understand quickly
that a particular action is not going to be tolerated. However, if
he is reprimanded on one occasion and not on another (probably
because the handler cannot be bothered, which might well
happen if the 'crime' is very minor), he becomes confused. 'Can I
do it or can't I?', he may well ask himself. If he has a propensity
to do it (which he must have or he would not be doing it in the
first place), he will probably carry on doing it.

Horses who are confused feel insecure. They do not know what
to expect and become worried. This is a very short step to fear
and panic, in the right circumstances, and a frightened, panicking horse is a very dangerous animal indeed. By being utterly
consistent and clear to our horses, we, in fact, help them, even
when punishing them mildly, because we are showing them in
no uncertain terms a definite code by which to live. They
certainly have such a code in natural herd conditions. Here,
every herd member knows his or her place according to the herd
hierarchy and knows exactly what treatment he or she can
expect from each other member, in an established herd at any
rate. This is one reason why there is so much upset in a herd
when a new member is introduced without proper introductions
to smooth the path. Nobody knows what to expect. The high-ups
regard the newcomer as a threat to their position and security.
The low-downs regard him or her as yet another boss to be
kowtowed to and respected or even feared. The security of every
herd member is threatened by uncertainty and confusion.

Misunderstanding, confusion, inconsistency and muddled
meaning are all calculated to produce frightened, defensive
animals. Animals with strong personalities might easily take
the upper hand over weak humans who do not know how to
behave according to Nature's rules (consistent herd behaviour),

and those of weaker spirit will become nervous and unhappy and not inclined to co-operate, indeed, defending themselves at every appropriate opportunity.

Wilfulness

When a horse is being downright wilful problems obviously arise. A strong pony can cause immense difficulty for a weak, small or novice child. Although, as mentioned, most horses and ponies are basically willing to please, provided there is nothing stopping them such as ill health, injury or misunderstanding, there are others, thankfully seemingly in the minority, who are not.

There often comes a point during the life of a youngster recently broken to saddle or harness, usually after a period when he has been going quite nicely, when he seems to think he will 'try it on', see how far he can go with his human connections as regards getting his own way. Provided we are sure there is no other cause, such as our having overdone things a little or the horse genuinely feeling off colour, strong, sympathetic riding or driving is what is needed, perhaps with strategically placed help from the ground. The instant the problem is overcome, reward the horse by praising him greatly and putting him away, turning him out or whatever. Youngsters may become tired physically or lose mental concentration sooner than one might think. Being made to work on or think about some strange movement we want them to perform when they are past giving their best is one good way of sickening them of the job in hand and creating resistance or general unwillingness.

Older, experienced horses, especially those who have 'been around a bit' and are well used to the ways of the world can become quite adept at creating problems, either to get their own way or out of laziness or craftiness to avoid doing something, which probably amounts to the same thing. Refusing to be caught is a very common example of this; last-minute running out at jumps, scraping the rider's leg against a wall in an effort to get rid of him or her (or, some experts say, out of sheer vindictiveness) are other ploys. A headshy horse knows full well that if he sticks his nose up in the air, his handler, particularly if short, will have difficulty in getting on a bridle or headcollar.

Pain and physical problems

Unfitness, greenness or poor conformation can all cause physical problems making it difficult or impossible for a horse to do as we want, even though he may understand perfectly well what is required. Even the simple matter of a young horse, or an unfit horse just being brought back into work, having been shod (with the difference this makes to the feel of their feet) can make normal movement strange and difficult, and allowances should be made for this. Carrying weight unbalances a horse not used to it and if we cannot understand why he moves in perfect symmetry round his field yet goes like a camel when we sit on him, we should bear this in mind.

Horses do learn eventually to protect themselves against anything which is causing them discomfort, unpleasantness, difficulty and, certainly, pain. Pain is probably the most potent cause of problems, understandably, to the extent that horses will react involuntarily and instinctively to it. If we feel a sharp prick from a needle or a cut from a knife, we do not think 'Oh yes, that hurt, I'd better pull my finger away'. Our instincts move the finger away for us like lightning. Obviously, the horse being flesh and blood like us, it is the same with him. A nasty jab in the mouth causing pain to gums, lips and, depending on the design of the bit, the roof of the mouth and the chin groove too, will result in the head being thrown up beyond the point of control, free forward movement probably stopped in its tracks and maybe some physical course of action to get rid of the cause of the pain, such as rearing. In the case of a saddle or harness causing pain in the back, bucking is very common, or, if the pain is not extreme, stilted action, kicking out or napping. If the pain continues to be applied, the horse can become more and more frightened until he panics or becomes enraged, resulting in violent reactions of all sorts.

A horse who has rapped his cannons on a pole (or had some foolish human do it for him with a rapping pole) can easily associate jumping itself, not the act of knocking a pole, with pain and fear. Pain in the feet – through neglected, cracked and chipped hooves, hooves pared down too far, shoes left on too long and pressing into the foot, particularly at the heels where corns can be caused, a nail binding against the sensitive structures inside the foot – can make a horse difficult to work and to handle.

Fig 2 Horses are much more impressed by self-inflicted hurt than by punishment inflicted by the trainer. This horse is being 'punished' for continually running back by being allowed to back into a prickly bush

A stallion known to me developed, for no apparent reason, aggression towards his mares during mating. While some stallions are normally aggressive at this time, many are not, and this one was particularly sweet. He became such a liability that a thorough veterinary overhaul was ordered. Brain tumours were suspected, some malfunction of the genital organs, back trouble and so on, until it was found, through watching the horse very carefully, that he seemed to be uncomfortable on his hind feet. When a stallion is mating, of course, the hind feet take much more of his weight than normal. A new farrier had recently started to visit the stud, and it was eventually discovered that he was nailing on the horse's shoes too tight for comfort, although the shoeing was good in every other respect.

This point was corrected and the horse reverted to his normal sweet temperament. He had been taking out the pain in his feet on his mares.

Self-protection from pain or discomfort is not necessarily shown in violent reactions. The horse might simply develop a more stilted way of going, or become unusually difficult during particular movements or on one rein. By holding or using his body in a particular way, he has found that he can avoid the unpleasant feeling which occurs if he uses himself normally. His rider might simply feel that the horse is being unco-operative or that he needs more suppling exercises and schooling. Of course, the more the horse is ridden in this condition the worse the problem becomes. What starts as discomfort can turn to pain, bruising or rubbing to an open wound, strain to sprain, and much more damage is done than would have occurred if more thought had been given earlier to the horse's poor performance.

Damage is also done to his mental perception of being ridden. Although putting the problem right by getting at the root cause will nearly always result in a return to good performance, the unpleasant memories remain and will surface again at the first hint of discomfort.

Association of ideas

Association of ideas applies to every aspect of the horse's life, and their excellent memories make one wonder if horses ever forget anything. There are many instances of horses remembering places they have not visited for years and reverting to a

---

An improvised twitch, with binder twine twisted round the handle of a hoofpick. Despite the new knowledge on twitching, it must be remembered that the practice is still rather uncomfortable for the horse. When applying the twitch, care must be taken to ensure that the edges of the lip are turned under so that the sensitive skin inside the lip does not come into contact with the twitch. The effect of the twitch is much enhanced if it is manipulated and kept moving now and then (in other words, 'twitched' about) as an acupuncturist keeps manipulating his needles to encourage the flow of endorphins. After removing the twitch (which should be in place for as short a time as possible) the top lip should be hand rubbed to help restore circulation and normal feeling

A neck twitch. A fold of skin is simply lifted up just in front of the shoulder, pinched and held firmly (although not excessively so), when it is usually found that the horse quietens down fairly quickly

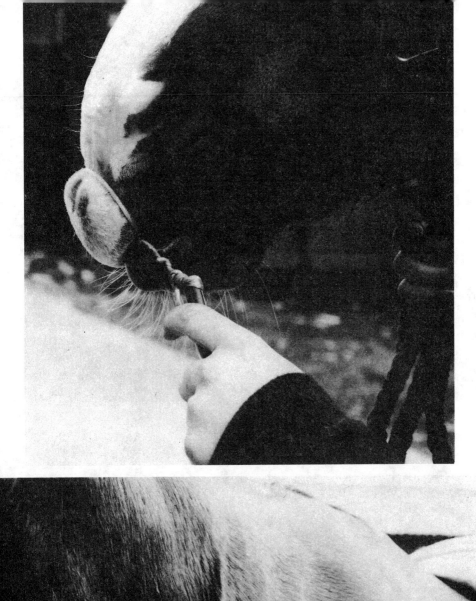

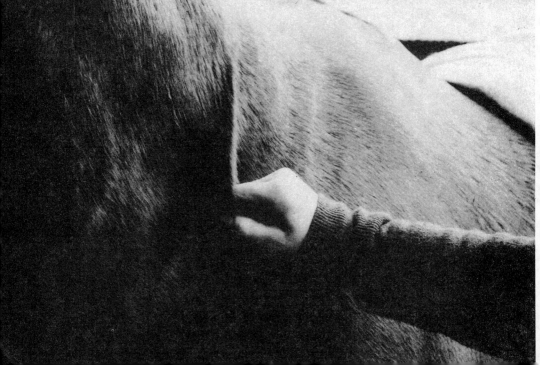

particular behaviour pattern they once showed in that place.

On one occasion when I changed livery yards with my own horse, we had to hack through a certain village, on the way to a show, through which we had regularly ridden when he was stabled near it but which we had not visited for six years since the move. On approaching a familiar part of the route, the horse, never a sluggard anyway, pricked his ears even more and began to prance along the road. We came to the centre of the village where I wanted to turn left through the square. The road to his old stable yard was straight ahead and, well-mannered and obliging though he invariably was, up that road he was going! There was one minor problem. Since our departure from the area, the road had been made one way, and we could no longer ride up it the way we used to.

However, as we had plenty of time I thought I would let the horse have his own way and renew a few old acquaintances. I got round the one-way problem by dismounting and leading him up the road. He plainly knew where he was and appeared to be aiming for his old stable yard where he used to find a good bed and a feed waiting on his return from outings. However, on reaching the entrance to the yard, which had not changed at all in the intervening years, he marched straight past without a glance and on to the end of the road where there was a cross-roads. He then just stopped, all previous animation gone, and looked at me for directions as to which way to go. I remounted

---

These Shires live and work in a busy industrial town, but their management includes several days to a week at grass on the outskirts of the town, every two weeks or so. They are never kept stabled for many weeks or months at a time, or permanently like many others of their kind, and are given hard feeds in the field to avoid sudden changes in diet. The grass on their field is well cared for but purposely kept of poor to medium quality, the best sort for working horses

This racehorse, photographed in full work and at peak fitness, is a stallion but can still enjoy a couple of hours freedom most days with the stable's pony, kept specially to give the racehorses in this yard the company of their own kind and natural social contact. The pony also has a stabilising influence, being very quiet natured and not prone to too much galloping about, so the Thoroughbreds quickly settle down after an initial few minutes play. He keeps them in their place in more ways than one. Not only is he the undoubted boss, but his presence in the paddocks prevents the horses jumping out, which some horses are prone to doing when turned out alone (*Peter R. Sweet*)

and continued on the detour to the show. Although he obviously remembered where he was, I shall never understand why he did not show any desire to enter his old yard. He simply seemed to want to go up the road which had been so familiar years ago.

Changing a horse's job can sometimes have a bearing on any problems experienced. One could scarcely get two more different careers than racing and dressage, but several former racehorses have been successfully converted by competent horsemen. I have been closely connected with two such horses, and in both cases the main problem was getting the horses to accept a comfortable contact on the rein without taking off into the wide blue yonder. 'If you think about it,' said one woman who had bought such a horse, 'racehorses are positively *taught* to take a hold when they are galloping. If you look at it from their point of view, when they feel a rider taking a contact they must automatically think they are required to gallop flat out, so you can't blame them when they do!' The fact that they can be reschooled to such a different way of being ridden says a very great deal for their adaptability and willingness, not only to please but to learn new things even in middle age (one of the horses I mention being twelve years of age when he was retired from point-to-pointing to take up dressage). It is certain they never forget their previous job, yet take to their new, quite different one very well in many cases.

It was a point-to-point horse who really taught me to ride without any significant contact on the reins at all. I used to take him on roadwork for his owner and was told in no uncertain terms never to 'take a hold' no matter what the horse did, otherwise he would be off with me. I was told not to ride him on a grass verge for the same reason. Being a coward at heart, I followed this advice to the letter; and although the old horse obviously wanted to be off on many occasions, and always felt like an unexploded bomb, regularly jigging about with his quarters underneath him, particularly if a tractor was in view, as if he was about to emulate one of the Lipizzaners of the Spanish Riding School and do some airs above the ground, he was, at heart, a perfect gentleman and never actually indulged himself as long as I kept a very light, even contact with hands down and relaxed. The only occasion I forgot myself, when a farm dog ran out at us and he did a little leap, I took a 'normal' contact and he shot off down the lane for twenty yards, until I gathered my jangled wits and let go and suggested he stop, which he did at once. This particular horse did not, fortunately, subsequently develop a habit of repeating the performance at that spot for ever more, which many would have done.

Playfulness

With horses who are mainly stabled we should remember that their work may well be the only outing they get in a day, and in an animal as movement-orientated as the horse it is absolutely to be expected that they will want go into action, and maybe in a way we do not want. They have this urgent need for activity which many people do not fully appreciate. If they play about it is understandable, but can cause problems if we do not control it reasonably or understand what is happening. The following quotation, from a contribution to *Equine Behaviour*, is interesting in that it demonstrates the need and desire to play and shows that, as with humans, some individuals are more prone to playing and 'practical jokes' or exhibitionism than are others. The contribution is entitled 'Frightened, playful or just bloody-minded?' The author, Mrs Ann James, is referring to the first of two horses she once knew but who did not belong to her:

The first was an eight-year-old Thoroughbred gelding that I started riding many years ago when I was young and innocent and believed what I read in books. One of the commandments was 'thou shalt not punish a horse for shying', and it did seem logical that if the horse was frightened by an object he should be coaxed and encouraged to approach it and assure himself that it was not dangerous. The trouble was that Harry appeared to be frightened of everything – cigarette packets on the verge, fertiliser bags in the hedge, fallen leaves blowing in the autumn, large leaves showing a light underside in the spring breezes – in fact, anything that was even mildly conspicuous.

Small things produced spectacular sideways leaps, large things produced really fast sensational whip-rounds from any gait, followed by a gallop away. So I was patient (often frightened, too) and spoke kindly while trying to persuade him to go forward. Sometimes when things were really bad I got off and tried to lead him up to the problem. All to no avail – when I went for a ride I never knew when I would get back. Even the last hundred yards home could take half an hour if there was something strange in the hedge. Local opinion labelled Harry a standard chestnut lunatic, mad and dangerous.

But, gradually, I began to wonder why I never fell off and why he had no scars or lumps on his legs. The more I thought about it the more I realised how careful he always was to look before he leapt and to keep well clear of ditches, deep mud, barbed wire, lorries etc. If I lost my balance and slipped sideways he always stopped and let me recover before rushing off again. Somewhat belatedly, I realised he wasn't really frightened of anything – he was playing. So I changed my tactics and found that by being really angry and using my voice and whip, he would usually pass even major things at the second or third attempt, but I was never able to do more than shorten the game; he wouldn't give it up entirely. He seemed to love an audience and was always at his worst riding out with other horses. Big, elaborate spooks at everyday objects induced near nervous breakdowns in my friends' normal, serious-minded horses, and the chaos he could cause during a lesson in the indoor school had to be seen to be believed, as the other horses got more and more twitchy and up-tight, looking for the dangers which Harry was reacting to so dramatically.

When he was eighteen, he came to live with me and I found he played in the same way when turned out on his own in the field. He would fix on some object, sometimes on the far horizon and apparently imaginary, or at least invisible to the human eye, trot towards it, spin round, gallop away, trot back and repeat, often for hours, until I feared for his legs and/or his heart. However, I needn't have worried; he lived to be thirty-one and, although arthritis slowed him up a bit, he kept on playing right to the end.

Fig 3 Harry would use anything as an excuse for a sny, even fallen leaves blowing about in autumn

Inherited behaviour

Some problems can be inherited and will appear in a particular family. I have known two related horses who both had a fear of entering their stables. On the subject of headshyness being inherited, a contribution by Dr Moyra Williams to *Equine Behaviour*, the journal of the Equine Behaviour Study Circle of which she is Chairman, is most interesting:

> There is no doubt that a tendency to safeguard the head – the control-centre of the individual – is inborn in most animals, but some individuals seem to deal with the matter in a quite peculiar way and, moreover, to pass on their peculiarities to their offspring. I came across this recently in one family stemming from a bay mare, Gem.
>
> Although I did not breed, or know much about, Gem's dam (a chestnut mare; I mention the colour because of the possibility of some temperamental characteristics being colour-linked), I did breed her father, my grey horse, Gamesman; and because Gem's breeder knew

Fig 4 'Once there, she would throw her nose high in the air and rush backwards'

that I was always interested in Gamesman's progeny, she rang me up one day to ask if I would like to buy his three-year-old daughter. I jumped at the opportunity, rushed over to collect her, and started breaking her in the next day.

From the beginning, Gem showed certain difficulties of behaviour I had never met before, and one of them was a very severe reluctance to enter the stable. She could be led up to the doorway without difficulty, but once there, would throw her nose in the air as high as possible and rush backwards. I immediately assumed she must have had a fright at some time in her life, and hit her head on a low roof. However, even after weeks of daily pushing, cajoling, and eventually forcing her inside (where she always received a welcome feed), she was still hesitant at the doorway; and even now, six years later, will 'play up' if a stranger comes into the yard, even though in other respects, she is quite unflappable.

Gem's three offspring to date – all chestnuts – have been extremely headshy from birth, and just like Gem, will occasionally stick their noses in the air and rush into reverse when asked to enter a stable. One filly, when a yearling, also took a strong dislike to being inside the stable, and at one period took to standing with her head over the door throwing it violently up and down and banging her poll against the lintel till it was bruised and bleeding, as if to convince herself of its danger.

The third child is as yet a foal, but a more persistently difficult one to headcollar I have never met. Day after day, he had to be cornered up against his mother in a stable before his head could be touched, and it would take up to thirty minutes of soothing, coaxing and stroking before his jaw and ears would relax or he would begin to look around. Day after day for his first six months of life this continued – and then, two days after he had been weaned and left to run out with a companion of the same age, the battle stopped. Mind you, it is inclined to return if a stranger comes within view!

Perhaps, when purchasing horses, we should ask what problems, if any, the parents had; we might at least be forewarned of the possibility of their occurring in future in their offspring – if we could get an answer to the question!

I know of one mare who, when foaled and in her first home (her breeder's) was all sweetness and light, but who was subsequently ill-treated in two future homes. Her fourth home, where she still lives, is knowledgeable and kind and she has never been ill-treated. In fact, her former trust of humans has to a large extent been restored. However, when it comes to being caught up from the field, she is always uncertain. Although this trait was not hereditary in her, she has taught all her foals to be wary of being caught, and to be just a little suspicious of humans.

2

The Nature of the Horse

If we had to choose just one quality which, in essence, described the mentality or temperament of the horse family, I think it would have to be nervousness. This might be difficult to believe when we think of the many quiet and trustworthy children's ponies and bombproof schoolmaster horses, not to mention the 'plugs' produced by the poorer riding schools, but it is true nevertheless. Horses are also possessed of highly acute powers of observation, excellent and long memories, judgement, natural instincts and a certain level of understanding.

To realise why horses are basically nervous it is necessary to consider their natural, evolutionary lifestyle. The evolution of the horse is very well documented, thanks to the excellent fossil record, and most people know that the most distant, or the earliest, direct ancestor of the various horse types was a fox-terrier-sized mammal, formerly termed *Eohippus* but now more correctly and formally called *Hyracotherium*, which browsed the primeval forests of the Earth during the Eocene roughly 55 million years ago. Its remains are found in Europe and North America, which at that time were joined in the north, whereas what is now Europe was separated from Asia by sea, where the Urals now stand. At that time, the continents had not drifted to their present positions and were in tropical regions: the climate of the whole Earth was warmer and wetter than now.

Hyracotherium in the form it is first recognised had four toes on its front feet and three on its hind. The toes were blunt, more like little hooves than claws, and the feet had dog-like pads. As grasses had not yet appeared on Earth, *Hyracotherium* browsed on leaves from shrubs and bushes and other forest vegetation growing from the swampy floor.

Over many millions of years, various lines branched off from *Hyracotherium* and evolved into different creatures, more and more horse-like in appearance. As the climate changed, forests

41

Fig 5 The horse's ancestor *Hyracotherium* (formerly known as *Eohippus*) was a multi-toed browser more prone to hiding from predators in the dense undergrowth of its primaeval world than to running away

in some parts gave way to grassy plains, and the horse ancestors physically able to adapt to them because of their genetic ability to change, as a species, not only survived but thrived.

The only way animals can adapt to their environment and evolve is through their genes. The environment does not automatically change the animals in it. If a species does not have the genes to produce certain physical characteristics to suit that changing environment, it declines and becomes extinct. Everything is inherited through genes – eye colour, hair colour, size, temperament, constitution, physique and so on – but genes can become altered and are then called 'mutations'.

If a little multi-toed creature like *Hyracotherium* had not produced some offspring with mutated genes, which introduced into the species longer legs for running, harder, high-crowned, more complicated teeth for eating the new vegetation, grass, with its tough silica content, we should not have horses today. Those horse ancestors which did not evolve in that way did, of course, become extinct, because there are none today, yet we have fossils to prove their existence.

Evolution does not continue smoothly at the same rate, like a ticking clock. It proceeds in fits and starts. If an environment is stable, the creatures in it often tend towards stability. Those most suited to flourish in it do so; the others are at risk and often disappear. The fittest, in other words the most suitable, survive.

The horse's ancestors, then, able to adapt because of their genes to the changing environment and climate, gradually evolved into the horse we know today. But other creatures were changing and living alongside *Hyracotherium* and its descendants. These animals did not live on leaves and, later, grass. They lived on *Hyracotherium* and its successors! And, of course, on other creatures. They were carnivorous or flesh-eaters whereas *Hyracotherium* and, as we know, the horse and its antecedents, were and are herbivorous.

Forest-dwelling animals like little *Hyracotherium* had no need for any great speed to escape predators, and it is difficult to run fast in a swamp, anyway. They escaped by 'freezing' and hiding. How often have you been on a country walk or ride and been startled by a rabbit, hare or some other creature, maybe a couple of partridge, which suddenly gets up in front of you and tears away. Because it had been completely still in an effort to 'hide' from you, aided by camouflage, you had not seen it. This is the tactic used by early horse ancestors in the forests. The lush cover of the forests also helped.

When the plains came into being and the horse ancestors living on them had to escape their predators, they could not hide so easily in the scrubby brush (although zebras are very difficult to see, surprisingly, on the African plains against a background of scrub and other animals). They therefore had to develop a different life-saving tactic. They had to be able to run, and run fast and long. But their predators learned and developed running skills and abilities, too.

Why is it that the fastest animal on earth, the cheetah, is successful in an average of only one out of four chases? No horse, zebra or wild ass can run the 80mph or so of a cheetah at full stretch. A Somali wild ass has been clocked at 38mph in bursts, a little less over a distance. Why, then, was the horse family so successful at evading capture, despite their inferior running speed? Because they learned to be constantly on the lookout for predators so that they could get a head start on them. If you can get away quickly while your enemy is still some distance away from you and run as fast as you can (even if it is slower than the predator), and keep on running for long enough, you will escape.

The cheetah, and other hunters, can only keep up very fast speeds for a limited length of time because they are, at those speeds, operating anaerobically. In other words, they are using up more oxygen than they are taking in. In fact, it has been postulated that a cheetah actually holds its breath at top speed. Therefore, after a matter of seconds rather than minutes it is forced to stop; it also becomes uneconomic in terms of energy expenditure for it to keep up the chase on an evasive prey. Therefore, if its prey can get away fast and far enough, and keep going for long enough, the predator has to give up. Antelope twist and turn more nimbly than their predators can, and often get away because of this. Zebras have been seen to do it, but most horse-family animals tend to flee in a straight line and rely on getting an early start, and on keeping going longer than the hunters. Horses and their relatives, when physically fit, find no difficulty at all in keeping up fast paces for minutes at a time, rather than seconds.

(While on the subject of speed, it is interesting to think back to that speed recorded for the wild ass – 38mph – and to compare it with the record time for the Epsom Derby, set by Mahmoud in 1936 at 2 minutes 33⅘ths seconds for the mile and a half, which works out at roughly 35mph. Admittedly, Mahmoud was given a tactical race and was not ridden in a straight line but around Epsom's famous undulating course; he was also, of course, carrying his jockey. However, the British Thoroughbred race-horse has been selectively bred by man, consistently putting the best to the best and hoping for the best, as the saying goes, over 200 years and more, specifically to produce speed. One would have expected Mahmoud's conformation and physical abilities to have surpassed those of what is not much more than a wild donkey! So a speed of 35mph is not astounding in terms of what Mother Nature can produce, left to herself. Traditional training methods as used in most racing stables today do not produce the fastest speeds. American workers in the field – veterinary research physiologists and racehorse trainers – claim that, with correct use of interval training methods, speeds of 45mph are possible.)

So, the horse and his ancestors between them have had two methods of escaping being killed for dinner. They have, in the past, hidden in forests and undergrowth and, more recently, they have run away. What have both these escape mechanisms in common? They both demand that the animals be constantly on guard, watching for danger. The least little sound or unexpected movement, particularly rapid movements such as would occur in a pouncing predator, send them automatically into 'defence mode'. They take off into the distance as fast as their legs can carry them. Today's horses living in feral conditions (and this goes for zebras, wild asses, onagers and feral horses, for it is almost certain that there are no truly wild horses left outside captivity), behave in just that way. Wild asses in particular are very difficult to approach. While you are still a hundred yards or more away, they start to run.

This is the reason for the horse's single overriding mental quality – its nervousness. Horses are jumpy and easily frightened. It all stems from being hunted for millions and millions of years. It is an instinctive reaction which we can do little to change, and if we remember it we shall avoid many of the problems encountered by the inexperienced and the thoughtless who bustle noisily about, move quickly around horses without warning, approach them without speaking and so on. Such behaviour can really frighten sensitive individuals and upset even the calm ones.

While on the subject of predators and prey, it is as well to mention another matter which has an important bearing on the mental security, happiness and ability to thrive of the horse, and that is the herd instinct.

With the exception of occasional solitary stallions who have no herd of their own and cannot find a 'bachelor band' (as herds of stallions without mares are called), it is not normal to find horses living alone in natural conditions. They live in well-structured herds with a well-defined social hierarchy, although their hierarchy is not so obvious as in domestic horses. The reason they developed this social system (along with many other types of animals who are herbivorous) is simply that there is safety in numbers. Horses are relatively defenceless compared with their predators. They do not have sharp teeth or claws; although the strength they can put behind a bite and kick are definitely off-putting these forms of defence do not seriously deter a hunter worthy of the name. And they do not even have horns as do other herbivorous herding animals such as cattle.

If there is a predator with its eye on your particular herd, it is only looking for one kill. A pride of lions or a pack of hyenas (for they hunt as well as scavenge) can live for a few days on one zebra carcass. The numbers idea means that the more in a herd, the less chance there is of that one being you. Horses, therefore, instinctively feel secure in a group. Apart from their learning natural manners if raised in a fairly naturally-structured herd, as described elsewhere, they learn to take their cues from the other herd members and there are plenty of 'lookouts' for danger. So a herd environment has a protective and teaching function.

The role of a schoolmaster horse in training is well known. It is much easier to get a youngster worldwise in the company of an older, more experienced horse than alone. It has a dual benefit. The youngster feels more secure in the company of another horse and so is less inclined to panic (and remember, a panicking horse, or even a mildly frightened one, learns nothing) and he also, as in the natural herd, takes his cue from him, following him where he might otherwise easily fear to tread. Of course, ultimately he has to learn to obey his human trainer rather than his equine mentor but the influence and help afforded by the schoolmaster in the early days, or when reschooling a horse who has developed problems, is invaluable because of this natural herd instinct.

Most domestic horses take to being handled, backed, lunged, long-reined, ridden, put to harness, shod, transported and so on very well indeed. A horse who has been correctly handled all his life and has developed respect, even affection, for his human associates, does come to rely on them for leadership and, if loose and in trouble, may even run to them for help and protection, particularly youngstock. Left to their own devices, however, horses quickly revert to 'wild ways', as evidenced clearly by the mustangs of North America. The wild 'memory' and instincts, always present under the surface, quickly reassert themselves in animals who are either insufficiently handled from birth, or badly handled and who have, therefore, good reason to be suspicious of man. Self-preservation formed those instincts and when that self appears in danger because man is treating the horse in a way which causes pain, fear or suspicion, they come to the horse's rescue. This is the legacy of nature.

Most readers of this book will have heard of the flight-or-fight instinct. It applies to most creatures, not only horses and humans. In nature generally, fighting is uneconomic in terms of energy and gain. Most creatures face up to each other, threaten and test each other but only make aggressive contact if absolutely necessary. Much fighting in many species is ritualised, following a definite pattern. Sheep and goats ram and butt each other, rarely doing any serious harm. Zebras do not ritualise their fighting but use various tactics at random −

Fig 6 Training a young horse in the company of a reliable schoolmaster is not only common sense as the youngster will take his cue from the older horse, but it also makes the job easier

rearing up and coming down with the forefeet on the opponent's body, striking out, biting, running round and round the opponent (he or she doing likewise) kicking out behind, side-kicking and biting the flanks, but fights to the death in the horse world are rare.

The Przewalski horse is different. Przewalski horses have often been observed to fight to the death. Even stallions and mares fight to the death, particularly if kept in enclosures which they consider too small. Unfortunately, it is the mare who comes off worst. The stallion, determined to mate or acquire, as the case may be, will bite the mare's flanks so hard that entrails are torn out and the mare is killed. This trait is not present in all stallions of that race, but many do seem to exhibit it. It could well be a sign of the stress of captivity.

More normal behaviour in other equidae and in domesticated horses is to fight only when necessary. When faced with danger, particularly in the form of a predator or an aggressive human, the favoured response is to run away rather than fight. No matter what the temperament of the horse, if he conceives of danger he normally tries to remove himself from it. It is only when there is no room to move around, no space to flee, that he will put up a fight, except where we have 'taught' the horse prior defence in anticipation of rough treatment.

Competition between stallions for mares is slightly different. Domesticated horses in this situation do fight each other, but one usually surrenders and goes away provided he has somewhere to go to, such as the wilds of Exmoor or the next clearing in the New Forest. Domesticated stallions in a field together are in a very dangerous position because the confinement would result in serious injury, should any breeder be stupid enough to turn out two mature stallions together, particularly if there were any mares nearby. It is not unknown, however, for a mature stallion and a young, very subordinate colt to graze in harmony together, provided there are no mares around.

The significant word here is 'danger'. We must all at some time have entered a field and been molested by one of the occupants who obviously did not perceive us as 'danger' at all. The horse was exerting its believed authority. If we had become suitably aggressive, carried a big stick and used it in self-defence, we may well have come off best, and that particular horse may never

Figs 7 and 8 One way of dealing with a natural bully at grass is to arm oneself with a stout stick, blunt at one end and sharper at the other. One crack on the muzzle with the blunt end as he comes at you will give him something to think about . . . and a poke on the bottom with the sharper end is usually most effective if he turns his quarters on you

have molested us again but kept a respectful distance. However, if it once got the better of us, it would have been much harder for us to exert our own authority in a similar future situation. Unfortunately, although we may feel the flight-or-fight instinct just as strongly as horses, we are quite incapable of running away anything like fast enough to escape an aggressive horse in a field!

The flight-or-fight instinct manifests itself in other ways, apart from the obvious meaning. When a horse refuses a jump he is, in a way, fleeing from the task of jumping it. He is either frightened of pain or the physical effort or knows he simply cannot make the height. When we put off a difficult task, we are fleeing from the problem mentally, if not physically.

Real fear can show itself in temporary seeming paralysis. A horse, human or other animal can be so terrified that it can become rooted to the spot, genuinely unable to move. In horses, perhaps this is a throwback to the behaviour of *Hyracotherium* who hid in the forests of his prehistoric world when faced with danger.

Individual differences

Because horses, like other animals and humans, are individuals, with different temperaments and personalities, they react differently from each other in different situations – not, perhaps, in a herd situation, although even there individual personalities are very apparent to anyone who takes the trouble to observe and study a herd of horses, but in their association with man.

Nervous, timid animals will react more quickly to 'trouble' than calmer, confident ones would do. They will easily become cowed by rough, bullying handling and in such a state of fear will learn nothing except to be afraid of humans and defensive in their company. The horse has a relatively simple mind and cannot easily think of more than one thing at once, especially if one particular emotion is strongly present. All a frightened horse can think of is protecting himself. If someone is beating up the horse for some deed which the human regards as a crime, the horse may not understand that he has done 'wrong'; all he is thinking of is how to stop the pain of the beating. The combination of a timid horse and a bullying handler is not conducive to a harmonious, successful relationship!

50

Horses who have strong, confident characters will react quite differently to a beating. They will not cow to it like a nervous animal. They may well bite and kick back. Again, they will become defensive, of course, but may take to defending themselves first and (perhaps) thinking later. Such horses who meet with rough handling often become confirmed biters and kickers, very difficult to handle and approach in the stable, and with good reason. They have been 'taught' to behave thus by humans!

Inexperienced handling often causes problems which the humans responsible for it neither foresee nor expect. Lack of knowledge of, for example, the correct way to approach a horse (from a point where he can see you, and also speaking to him to give warning of your presence while still some distance away) can cause a serious problem in the form of a kicked, flattened human and a frightened horse. Novices often do not appreciate the value of their own voices when handling horses. They approach a stable in silence, making a sudden appearance over the door, and slam the door-bolt noisily back, frightening to death the occupant who might simply have been rooting around at the back of the box or dozing standing up. The horse's head flies up (a natural and effective way of protecting it), his muscles become taut ready for flight, his hocks gather under him ready to spring away as his instincts demand, but he has nowhere to go because he is literally cornered in his box. The nervous horse may run blindly around his box, knocking over the human and maybe escaping out of the opened door to who knows where. The more aggressive character, more confident and egotistical, may, after his initial couple of seconds' shock, stand his ground and kick out, with feeling.

Nervousness in humans, an emotion more common than many might wish to admit, can have equally different effects on horses of different temperaments. If the horse is the trusting type who follows his handler's example, he may, when sensing our nervousness, simply think that there is something, somewhere, to be nervous about. It will never enter his head that the human is nervous of *him*. 'The human is nervous. What is he nervous about? I'd better be on my guard' is a reaction which produces a level of fear in the horse. His self-preservation instinct begins to surface and his learning propensity recedes to the back of his consciousness. Nervous humans, therefore, rarely teach a horse

51

anything except how to be nervous, especially if that horse is nervous himself to start with or has been conditioned from foalhood to take notice of and trust his handlers. Especially in the latter case, the horse is, again, simply doing what we have taught him to do.

The more self-confident type of horse, particularly if he has an aggressive streak, may take advantage of human nervousness for his own ends. Such a horse may quickly sense the human's insecurity and often does not seem to deal with it in the same way as his more nervous colleague. He does not think that he needs to be on guard; rather, he tends to think 'The human is timid and weak. I'll boss him about and get my own way'. And that is so often precisely what happens.

A relationship with a horse is as personal and individual as with another human. We may say we love horses, but most of us must have come across a few individuals in our lifetimes whom we definitely did not love! Horses in general we love; but, as with people, we are bound to come across some character somewhere, sometime, with whom we just do not get on.

Temperament and personality can be related to breed. It is common when reading breed societies' laid-down standards to see certain qualities quoted for the breed as a whole. Thoroughbreds are generally said to be courageous and intelligent. Horses of more common blood are said to be more tolerant of rough handling than horses of better breeding, with more 'blood', while British native ponies are often credited with common sense.

As discussed earlier on, not all horses are willing and anxious to please their handlers as a matter of course, even when we cause them no problems by making our demands clear and intelligible. We tend to assume that a horse will happily do what we wish provided we make our wishes clear, but this is not always the case. A farmer who worked horses on the land once told me about a horse who was being trained to harness:

He was a fine, upstanding horse. Big and strong and with a lovely nature. He never put up any resistance at all during the whole process. He learned quickly and we had no bother with him, but once he was fully trained to harness he lost all his spirit. We'd never once hit him or been bad to him, but the fact of being in harness seemed to break his spirit for life and he was never the same horse again. He worked well but something seemed to have died inside him.

What was going on in the horse's mind during the process? If he did not like it, despite apparently never being caused any pain or distress, why did he not show the usual signs of resistance? The fact that the horse's spirit seemed to have been broken seems strange considering he was in no way subjected to force. And his attitude to life persisted in stable and field as well as during work; a sure sign that horses definitely think about their work, remember and, presumably, anticipate the next session.

As we have seen, horses of different temperaments react differently to various situations. It is very common for there to be a change in a horse's demeanour when he is moved from one home, job and way of life to another, either for better or for worse. And the new owner concerned can often be heard to remark: 'I get on much better/worse with him than with my previous horse'.

Just like people, horses can be timid, nervous, placid, devious, independent, sulky, aggressive, bullying, extrovert, introvert, leaders or followers, and possess any other quality we wish to bestow on them. These individual qualities are not only the natural result of the horses' characters. Horses take their cues not only from other horses but from humans, too. The way a horse reacts to different handling from different people is an amalgam not only of the horse's character but of his self-protective instincts and how he feels about the way he is being treated by a particular person. Some people have a truly enviable 'way' with horses, who exhibit, in their hands, none of the quirks and problems apparent when they are handled by someone else. This goes for horses and humans who are complete strangers. It is no unusual circumstance for a stranger at a riding school, say, to be given a set of tack and told to 'go and tack up the bay horse in that box there'. In he or she goes, says (we hope) 'hello' to the horse, pats or strokes him, lets him sniff, and sets about tacking up in the normal way, only to be told when the job has been completed without problems that the horse is difficult to handle in the stable. It is said that because the stranger wasn't expecting problems he or she didn't get any.

This has happened to me on several occasions, and readers will doubtless have had their own experiences. At a large centre where I ride sometimes I was given a horse I had never ridden before, although I had seen him about the place. The horse was brought into the indoor school, ready tacked up. I had a very pleasant ride, not under instruction but pottering about doing what I pleased. The horse was active, responsive, comfortable and sensible, if very alert.

After the ride, the weather being warm and the horse likewise, I off-saddled him and led him about a bit, then proceeded to damp-sponge him down in his box. It is not normally my practice to tie up a horse, so I put up with him wandering about a bit while verbally trying to restrain him. I finished the near side with no problem, but the horse would not tolerate my doing his off side. I was about to tie him up when a student appeared at the door and said: 'Oh my God! What are you doing? We never do anything to him without tying him up, he won't stand for it.' When I explained that I had done his near side with no hassle and showed my handiwork to prove it, she was amazed. But the horse drew the line at the off side!

He was sold eventually because he had become unhappy with life in a riding centre and went to a private home with someone who knew and liked him. This shows compassion and common sense on the part of the centre manager; some riding centres stick to their horses long after it has become plain that those animals are miserable being 'communal' horses. They do not give their best, develop all sorts of problems and become unpopular with clients. It really does pay to keep horses happy!

Horses can become adept at assessing their personal relationships. Some years ago I was interviewing a former international show jumping rider about his past exploits and we got talking about one horse which I had always admired. The rider had jumped this horse for only a couple of seasons or so, then the animal was allocated to another rider. It was surprising to hear this quiet, effective and kind horseman, say: 'I never could do anything with that horse. He had me and he knew it. He was master and he knew I knew it, too. I just had to give up with him.' It is nice to know world-class professionals have their problems too!

So, it is possible to ascribe different qualities to horses to describe their characters with some degree of accuracy, but what about more dubious descriptions such as 'courage' and 'intelligence'? We very often hear Thoroughbreds being described as high-couraged as a breed, and attribute this quality to horses who tackle such heart-stopping obstacles as a *puissance* wall or the Grand National course. Some authorities insist that this is, indeed, bravery; others say it is simply implicit trust in humans and 'blind obedience', while others maintain it to be sheer stupidity.

'All horses are bloody stupid', said another interviewee to me a while ago, another show jumper, coincidentally. 'They have to be thick or else they'd never let us even sit on them let alone jump bloody big fences and gallop till they're knackered.' As for galloping until they are 'knackered', it is well known that horses do, when circumstances are right, gallop until they drop, with little or no urging from man. The herd instinct carries them along, as shown by racehorses who have become riderless during a race. On and on they go with the 'herd', sometimes jumping the fences, sometimes going round them. It seems to be only the experienced ones who purposely look for the way back to the stables and make for it. Many go right past it and stick with their colleagues despite the fact that they are strangers and not a familiar, established herd.

Fig 9 'Come on, we haven't got all day'

Years ago, there was a well-known grey 'chaser called The Callant, who, I believe, was used on a sheep farm by his owner out of the racing season. He was a useful horse, popular with the crowds, not least because whenever he 'lost' his jockey during a race he would stop and wait for him to remount. More than once he was seen wandering back to the unfortunate rider who was still putting himself back together again, and on one occasion, when the luckless fellow was obviously out cold, pushed him with his nose. Would you describe this as consideration for the jockey, as common sense because the horse knew he was supposed to have a rider despite galloping with the herd, as knowledge and understanding of the job in hand and of human relationships – or what? This sort of behaviour is certainly not unknown, but it is unusual, particularly in the heat and excitement of a race and in the company of other horses.

The herd instinct cannot be ascribed to horses who bolt off on their own, of course, and 'stupidly' collide with objects which might cause their death, such as a brick wall or a tree in their paddock. This sort of behaviour usually occurs due to fear and blind panic. This is the nature of the horse family. It is not stupidity.

3

Intelligence in the Horse

It is easy to anthropomorphise (attribute human qualities and feelings to animals) because obviously they do have some feelings similar to those of humans, but certain aspects of emotion and intelligence are difficult to define in relation to the animal world. Humans are simply animals, a form of primate with animal instincts, needs and desires, now known to be much more closely related to chimpanzees than had hitherto been thought. According to anthropologists and zoologists we split from our common ancestor only some five million years ago, not at all long in evolutionary terms. It is said that humans alone are capable of thinking and planning ahead and this is the reason for our supposed superiority over the rest of the animal kingdom.

But is it really only instinct which causes squirrels to hoard food for the winter or birds to build a nest for young they presumably do not know they are going to have – because they cannot see ahead? As for the superior human intelligence, dolphins are showing every sign of being far more intelligent than man in many ways.

But how do we judge intelligence? And what is it exactly? According to the *Oxford English Dictionary*, intelligence is the 'mental ability to learn and understand things; having or showing usually a high degree of understanding.' *Webster's Third New International Dictionary* describes it as, among other things, 'the faculty of understanding; to know or apprehend; . . . to learn, to foresee problems, the ability to perceive one's environment . . . and to deal with it effectively, to adjust to it; the ability to use with awareness the mechanism of reasoning.' All this implies the ability to look ahead and to use reasoning power.

We all know horses can look ahead (they anticipate feeding times or an exciting occasion) and can, to some extent, plan ahead ('if I get to the gate first when she comes with the buckets

57

I'll get the pick of the food'), but it is widely held that they do not have reasoning power. Horses can definitely learn, of course, and certainly understand (that if they put their noses in that bucket they will discover whether or not there is any food in it; that if they go into a shed when it is windy and wet they will feel more comfortable, etc) and they can also apprehend and look ahead to foresee problems, if only in the short term. A herd of zebras or wild asses or feral mustangs can plan ahead to the extent that they start trekking to the waterhole in anticipation of finding water. Domesticated horses can look ahead, expecting excitement or alarm when out on a ride, and on approaching home, foresee that they will get rest, water and food on their return.

The 'ability to perceive one's environment' is certainly well within a horse's capabilities. A horse knows if there is grass on the ground, whether a dog or predator is chasing him and whether it is day or night! But can he always deal effectively with it? A horse cannot tell by instinct or intelligence whether a plant is poisonous or not; nor can human children. Human adults know only because some other adult has told them so, unless they have the technical ability and knowledge to analyse the plant for themselves and find out that it does contain poisonous substances.

Horses are said to be able to smell out and, in some cases, dig for water. Zebras have certainly been seen to dig for water. But how good are horses at adjusting to their environment, particularly to changes in it?

Professor George Waring of the Southern Illinois University at Carbondale, on a visit to Britain, spoke to a meeting of the Equine Behaviour Study Circle and told of a group of feral horses which died of dehydration because they could not work out how to get round an open-ended fence which had been erected in front of their normal watering place. The fence was simply in a straight line, not terribly long, across their normal route to the water. All they had to do was make a few yards' detour round either end of the fence to get to their water – but they could not grasp this – and they died.

An EBSC member, in an earlier contribution to *Equine Behaviour*, related how one group of her horses wished to reach a second group in a neighbouring field. The gate at one end of the separating fencing was open so the horses could wander freely in

Fig 10 The mustangs were quite unable to work out how to get round the fence and ultimately died of dehydration

and out of both paddocks, but the first group just stood whinnying to their friends in the second field. They knew where the gate was, having used it many times before when being led from one field to another, but not, apparently, on their own initiative as it was not normally left open. Suddenly, a pony in the group flew down the fence, through the gate and up the other side to the elusive companions. None of his group realised what he had done or experienced a similar brainwave, and they remained separated and even more agitated at the pony's appearance on the other side of the fence.

With the exception of the pony, this behaviour certainly shows a low level of intelligence if adjusting to one's environment is a criterion. Man-made fences may be unnatural in the wild but other obstacles are not.

As regards being chased by a dog or predator of some kind, how good are horses at 'adjusting' to this, to dealing effectively with it? Why do some horses run from the dog, perhaps ending up bolting in fear, while others will stand their ground and kick out with their hind heels or turn on the dog and strike at it, even if not cornered? Difference in temperament (aggression versus timidity again) or intelligence?

And as for 'the ability to use with awareness the mechanism of reasoning', most people with experience of horses believe that they do not, in general, lack reasoning power, though some schools of thought would not agree. The *Oxford English Dictionary* says that to reason is 'to form or to try to reach conclusions by connected thought' and that the noun 'reason' is 'the intellectual faculty . . . by which conclusions are drawn from premises'. *Webster's* gives many definitions, one of which is 'the ability to trace out the implications of a combination of facts or suppositions'. Take, for example, the horse who has learned to open the bolt of his stable door. Letting himself out for the freedom his kind so badly needs would seem to be an intelligent act; yet some will insist that the horse was idly fiddling with the bolt for want of something to do (quite possible) and *by accident* discovered that, if it was fiddled with in a certain way, it could be lifted. Again, quite by accident, we are told the horse discovers that if the bolt is pulled in a certain direction, the door swings or can be pushed open, and he can get out. Having done it once, he remembers, and can do it again.

Can it not be acknowledged, first of all, that a horse's lips are equivalent to our fingers, and as sensitive, and also that he cannot see beneath his chin any more than we can? So could he be investigating the bolt blindly with his 'fingers', not just fiddling with it? He can feel the structure of the bolt with his lips and, by trial and error (not accident), he discovers how it works, whips it back and achieves his objective. That is reasoning power and intelligence. Once the horse has undone the bolt he can remember how to do it for ever more, as some owners may know to their cost.

A simple way of stopping the horse opening his bolt, provided it is a standard stable-door type which slots down over a projecting piece of metal with a hole in it, is to snap a dog-lead type of spring clip through the hole and over the handle of the bolt. This completely prevents the horse's escape act. But it is the horse's anatomy which prevents him opening the clip. He is physically incapable of manipulating it. He is, of course, quite strong enough to get the clip, bolt and all, between his teeth and wrench the lot off the door, achieving his object of liberty that way – but he doesn't. Is that stupid of him, or does he simply not realise he is strong enough to do it?

And how about this for an undeniable example of reasoning power? A close acquaintance of mine has an elderly mare of fairly placid nature but 'not particularly bright'. She was turned out with her companion in her paddock one afternoon. During the morning, the top strand of the wire fence had been broken and was hanging down in a loop at one point. The mare's owner had not bothered to move the wire, thinking it unlikely that the horses would became entangled on this one occasion (the fence was being mended that evening) but, horses being horses, they duly found the loose wire.

The mare got one hind leg inside the loop and, as she walked forward, realised her leg was not free. She attempted to move the leg two or three times but felt the wire on it each time. Her owner was about to go out and extricate the mare when she noticed her stop and stand quite still for a few seconds. The animal looked back to the left, then to the right (it being the left leg that was caught). She then lifted her off hind leg and, feeling for the wire carefully, put the hoof down on the loose wire, pressing it to the ground. This left the near hind leg free. The

61

mare then stepped slowly and carefully forward with the near hind, released the wire by lifting her off hind and moving that forward a step, too, looked round again and finally walked off to graze elsewhere; a clear example of connected thought and the ability to work out the result of certain actions.

At a do-it-yourself livery yard where I once kept my horse, we had managed to buy cheaply a supply of plastic buckets for feed or water from a baby-ware manufacturer. The buckets had been designed for nappies and had lids. We had been using them without lids, obviously, but for fun tried an experiment to test reasoning power. The idea was to feed the horses from their buckets in the usual way but to put the lids on to see if any of them reasoned that to get at the feed (which they knew was there) they had to remove the lids first.

The results were so varied as to be amazing. Six animals were involved (four horses and two ponies). They were fed at exactly the same moment by their owners at the normal time and the buckets were in the usual places on the floor, but with the lids on. My own Anglo-Arab had a quick sniff, dislodged the lid with his muzzle and proceeded to wolf down his food as usual. His neighbour, a Thoroughbred, just stood looking at the bucket in puzzlement, sniffing at it but not making any attempt to remove the lid. Eventually his owner took it off and the horse ate as usual.

Fig 11 'This is a fine mess I've got myself into'

The next down the line, a 'mongrel' pony of quick wit and crafty nature, attacked the bucket with a forefoot until it tipped over, the lid fell off and the food was exposed. He ate up. The next guinea-pig was a supposedly dim-witted, cold-blooded cob-type fellow who stood looking at the bucket, not sniffing or anything, for twenty-five seconds (his was the only owner who timed the response). Then he took the handle of the lid between his teeth, picked up the lid and stood with it in his teeth looking at the feed for eight seconds before seeming to realise that he had to let go of the lid before he could eat the food. He let go of the lid, which obviously dropped to the ground, and began eating.

The next was the other pony, a nervous Welsh/Arab type, young and green, schooling on well and learning quickly, but easily upset. She backed away from the bucket and started pacing worriedly back and forth along the back of her box, eyeing the bucket and lid suspiciously. Her owner had to remove the lid after five minutes (to prevent further consternation) but the pony still would not approach the bucket. A few handfuls of feed given from the bucket induced her to eat, but she was obviously put out by the whole experience.

Last of the six was a very fit three-quarter Thoroughbred one-day eventer, with a fairly bland personality, not noted for being brilliantly intelligent but sensible enough to get himself out of trouble across country. He sniffed all round the lid, got hold of the rim in his teeth and tried to lift the lid off. However, he had hold of the bucket too and lifted the lot. He immediately put (not dropped) the bucket down again and had a few more sniffs. Then he fiddled at the lid with his top lip, as my horse had, until it dislodged, pushed it completely off with his muzzle and began to eat.

So, out of six horses and ponies four appeared to realise that they had to get rid of the lid before they could get at the feed. Three (the Anglo-Arab, the cob and the eventer) appeared definitely to make a clear attempt to remove the lid. The mongrel pony seemed to be bashing away at the lid with his forefoot more out of frustration than in a proper attempt to remove it; he seemed to know the lid was the problem but appeared to feel that any action at all would do the job rather than a thought-out plan. We decided that the three showed clear reasoning power, and the mongrel pony showed promise!

As a matter of interest we repeated the experiment the next day at the same time. The Anglo-Arab did the same thing quickly as if to say: 'I've done this before'; the Thoroughbred went to the door of his box looking for his owner to come and remove the lid; the mongrel pony smashed away with even more gusto than before; and the cob picked off the lid as previously, put it immediately and carefully down on the floor and began eating with no delay. The nervous Welsh/Arab filly stood in the middle of her box staring worriedly at the bucket and, again, had to have the lid removed for her, when she approached and began to eat gingerly; and the eventer abandoned his attempt to remove the lid by the rim with his teeth, obviously remembering that this method had not worked the day before, but quickly fiddled off the lid with his muzzle, like the Anglo-Arab, and began eating.

The funniest thing was what happened on the third day when we fed the horses *without* the lids. The Anglo-Arab stood looking amazedly at the bucket for a few seconds as if wondering where the lid was, then began to gobble normally; the Thoroughbred 'copied' him exactly. The mongrel pony just attacked the bucket without looking to see if it had a lid on (something he never did prior to the experiment); the cob pricked his ears expectantly, saw there was no lid and just began to eat without any ado; the little filly approached the bucket timidly, stretched out her nose and sniffed and, seemingly relieved, began to eat; the event horse blew into the top of the bucket as if wondering where the lid was, and finding no lid to manoeuvre off he nuzzled the rim of the bucket until it fell over (not normal for him) and began to eat.

The horses had, incidentally, been fed at breakfast and lunch in the usual way – buckets without lids. It was only the tea-time feed which we used for the experiment, but the horses seemed to associate this feed with the lid problem, showing a certain amount of acuity. We felt the experiment had, apart from the Thoroughbred and the little filly, shown not only reasoning power but quick learning and acceptance of a new situation, plus the ability to adapt to it – all, according to the dictionaries, signs of intelligence.

It is common practice among scientists involved with animal behaviour to test the intelligence of the animals they are working with by means of various ingenious tests. Laboratory rats are used extensively as they are supposed to be very intelligent. Rats, birds and other creatures learn fairly quickly to press a lever or push a button to release food into a container or to open a barrier which enables them to get at food (the food being their reward, of course). The few papers I have seen which involved horses in such experiments showed them to be slow at learning this type of thing.

A common form of intelligence test among scientists is the maze test. Food is placed in the middle of the maze and the animals (of all sorts) are timed as to how long it takes them to find the food. Then they are timed again at the next feeding session to see how well they have remembered their way through the maze. Again, horses seem to be poor at this, as shown already by the example of the mustangs dying because they could not work out their way round a simple straight-line fence (although, remember the pony who cottoned on that to get to his friends in the next field he had to go down the fence, through the gate and up the other side of the fence – he was the only one of his group who worked it out).

It is obvious that horses, like people and other animals, vary considerably in their ability to solve problems and in their individual IQs. But by whose standards are we judging these animals? Most devised tests seem to be setting human standards on non-human animals. The type of intelligence a human has cannot be the same as that of a horse, a dog, a laboratory rat etc.

A good definition of intelligence might be a creature's (human or animal) ability to survive in *its own* environment, with all that involves. What, then, is the point of confronting non-human animals with tests geared to assessing human intelligence? In natural conditions, a horse would never have to negotiate a maze to get at its food, a rat would never have to press a lever nor a hen a button, although blue-tits in the wild learned to do this very quickly to release nuts. Physical factors apart, we could never survive in a dolphin's environment, nor the dolphin in ours, yet, as mentioned, some scientists maintain the dolphin is more intelligent than we, using our criteria.

The horse family has evolved and survived in a changing environment to the present day, although losing to extinction many branches along the way. Many species of animals survive in the world today because they are super-effective at doing so. Others survive only because man has permitted it – and it is widely held that the horse family comes under this heading. There are still asses, onagers and zebras in the wild, although some have to be protected to ensure their continuance. Wild horses are probably no more, despite the occasional sighting of Przewalski horses in remote parts of China. Other feral horses roaming in the new and old worlds – the North American mustangs, the Australian brumbies, the British native ponies, the white horses of the Camargue, the reconstructed tarpans of Poland and so on – are there only because of man and have, in the past, had their natural lifestyles and breeding activities influenced and controlled by humans.

It would seem, therefore, that on this basis the horse family is not super-intelligent. It would seem, also, that man is the most intelligent animal as he appears to have control of all the others

---

When horses or ponies are brought up in a naturally structured herd like this one on Exmoor, they receive natural discipline and are taught herd manners from their superiors. The artificial segregation by sex and age practised on domestic studs in many countries, after a similarly artificial (and usually highly stressful) weaning, does not help instil natural social graces. Animals brought up in mixed herds and frequently handled by humans are much more easily disciplined and trained later in life (*Mike Roberts*)

Horses feel more secure in the company of their own kind and this instinctive need for company can be used to advantage when we provide a schoolmaster animal during the training of a youngster. This feral herd of ponies on Dartmoor are doing what comes naturally – following one another in single file from one grazing area to another. In wild or feral conditions, equidae only gallop in a grouped herd when frightened. A youngster undergoing training will often follow directly behind a schoolmaster in this natural way through a tricky place or over a little obstacle (*Mike Roberts*)

These Przewalski horses are part of a private collection in England being conserved specifically with the hope that they or their descendants can eventually be re-released into the wild. Their enclosures (with shelters which they readily use) open into large paddocks where they graze in completely natural herd conditions. The stallions are kept with the mares, foals and youngstock all the time, as in the wild. The horses are not handled unless absolutely necessary (for veterinary attention or hoof trimming, for example) and are anaesthetised for such purposes. This policy is to avoid their becoming 'humanised', which could be detrimental to their welfare in a wild existence

to his own ends. But just how intelligent is man at real survival? He is, after all, the only creature to have damaged this planet to the extent of threatening existence as we know it.

It is known that, on an individual basis, a creature has to be taught to maintain itself in the wild if it has been reared in captivity. Some authorities believe that, from the point of view of an entire race or species of animal, it is impossible for the truly wild intelligence and instincts to be regained to the level which occurred before domestication, or, if not domestication as we think of it in terms of pet dogs and dairy cattle, at least insofar as the species has been interfered with by having been kept in such artificially restricted environments as safari parks, zoos or fenced-in areas of natural country. In such situations, animals are protected from predators to preserve their numbers, and they are usually fed by humans. They are not, therefore, living a natural life and may, as individuals, lose the instinct to hunt or forage for food and to protect themselves from predators by fighting or fleeing, as circumstances dictate.

The animals are, however, usually free to breed (if they will, in captivity – some do and some don't) but because there is no natural selection taking place for individuals most adept at hunting/foraging or avoiding/overcoming predators, it is just as likely that animals not so good at these skills will survive to breed and pass on their inefficiencies to the subsequent populations. In the wild, these individuals would be eliminated by natural selection and their genes would die out with them, leaving those genetically fit to survive in a given environment to prosper and pass on those very genes which have made their survival possible. If natural selection and breeding ceases in

---

The most common way to restrain a normally amenable horse is by head-collar and lead rope. It is safer and less stressful to the horse to be held like this, where convenient, while being worked on. If something does frighten him he does not have the rigid restriction of being tied to something firm, which can frighten him even more and create one problem on top of another, especially if he starts to pull back hard to try and free himself. Here, the handler can simply calm him while moving about with him, so the horse feels relatively free and more secure (*Peter R. Sweet*)

If you can possibly spare two people, it is better to have one hold the horse like this for a job which needs two hands, rather than tie him up

'domesticated' preservation, there is as much chance of those genes being lost as kept; therefore, we shall not know how fit for survival a species is when it is returned to the wild until it happens.

Workers observing the American mustangs, however, note that these feral horses revert quickly, as individuals, to wild ways and the herds, in fact, have prospered so well that they are increasing beyond the numbers supportable by the space available to them. Rather than let nature control them by harsh methods of starvation (there being no natural predators in most areas, other than man), various animal welfare and environmental bodies in America have introduced 'adopt-a-wild-horse' schemes to bring these horses back into domestication!

It is very difficult to draw the line between instinct and intelligence. Particularly with domesticated animals, much of their behaviour is learned because we have taught them to behave in a certain way. Foraging for food and searching for water, for example, are restricted behaviours in domestication because these items are provided by man. In the cases of domesticated or farm animals living a relatively 'wild' life, such as sheep on the hills and ponies on the moors, foraging behaviour surfaces,

Fig 12 'I know there's some grub under here somewhere'

although in extreme weather supplies are often again provided by man in the form of hay drops from tractor or helicopter.

When horses and ponies are turned out on snow-covered paddocks, it is interesting to note that some of them will paw down through the snow to get at whatever grass there may be, but others will not. If hay is taken out, the pawing tends to stop. The mongrel pony mentioned in the 'bucket lid' experiment was noted for pawing for grass in snow, and used the same technique to get the lid off his bucket.

Instinct can be described as an involuntary response to a stimulus resulting in a predictable, fixed behaviour pattern. A foal first seeking its dam's udder after birth is responding instinctively to the stimulus of hunger, although how it knows that its mouth is connected with relieving hunger, having never in the womb received nourishment by mouth, defies explanation. A foal is, in fact, in danger of sucking almost anything in its instinctive search for the udder, and will not uncommonly latch on to the mare's elbow. It usually takes only one lesson in the form of guidance in the correct direction for the foal to learn where the milk bar is. The sucking action appears to be reflexive in response to hunger and is part of the whole phenomenon of the urge to relieve hunger.

Foals born to maiden mares often get no directional guidance at all from their dams – it is a case of the blind leading the blind. The foal has never been born before and the dam has never had a foal before. In domestication, at least on managed studs, human help will be on hand to guide the foal if really necessary and to encourage and maybe restrain the mare if she is not showing any signs of connecting the questing foal with her full udder and her desire to have the fullness relieved.

In the wild, human help will not be available. However, the first-time mare will have had the benefit of seeing other mares and foals giving birth, learning to stand, finding the udder, pushing the foal gently to the udder, etc, and so will have some idea how to carry on. This is naturally learned behaviour combined with instinct.

We tend to call horses intelligent when they learn our requirements quickly, just as we tend to call children intelligent when they learn their lessons quickly at school. Slowness to 'cotton on' is invariably felt to be lack of intelligence. Yet academic brilliance is no guarantee of being able to survive and prosper in our society. Entrepreneurs who have no scholastic record to speak of can live on their wits and often become enormously successful; but any number of university graduates live on the dole because they cannot find employment and, it seems, do not have the entrepreneurial bent to make their own opportunities. Perhaps we should be thinking of a whole different definition of intelligence.

Opportunism, both in our society and in wild populations of creatures of all sorts, plays a large part in survival, plus the personal qualities which enable one to rise up the hierarchy of the herd and secure the choicest patch of grazing, the shadiest or most sheltered spot on the plain or in the paddock, or the best mares to keep in one's herd. Intelligence in the natural sense can therefore perhaps best be defined as the ability to adapt to one's environment. We may say that a horse is intelligent if he adapts quickly to a new job (for example, becoming a dressage horse after being a hunter), or settles into a new home quickly, or is not completely put out by an overnight snowfall (which completely changes his environment) which meets him on being brought out of his box in the morning.

But how intelligent are the horses of a friend of mine who have a perfectly good drinking trough which they use in preference to a pond in their paddock but who, on finding the trough frozen hard during a cold spell, refused to use the freely-available, clean and still liquid pond, forcing their owner to cart buckets of water out to them? It must be admitted, they were not showing much of a tendency to adapt to *their* environment.

Memory and learning

It is well known that horses do have exceptionally good and very long memories. Most horsemen can quote several instances from their own experiences which prove this.

Horses, whether or not they really do become affectionate towards their human handlers, do not always appear to re-member people as well, at least after a longish separation. They certainly do, of course, remember them when they are in fairly regular contact with them. An acquaintance of mine, for instance, has two homes, one in the town where she works during the week and one in the country where her horses are kept (and cared for by staff) and where she goes at weekends. Her mare always makes a tremendous fuss the instant she recognises her owner's car engine, or hears her voice in the yard or, of course, sees her. She will nuzzle the woman's face persistently and stand in front of her to prevent her leaving the loose box.

People who keep their horses at livery often have the thrill of an enthusiastic reunion with their horses perhaps after several days separation; it is particularly gratifying to them to be told by the staff that the horses whinny enthusiastically only when they hear their owners in the yard, not for anyone else. This does not necessarily occur because the horses are expecting titbits, for many people do not make a habit of feeding such goodies; it seems to be purely because the horses associate their owners with a special relationship, perhaps transmitted by some kind of subtle mental communication (ESP?) which tells a horse that this person is special and that he is very special to the person in turn. Maybe the horse does more interesting things with his owner on board, such as attending shows, going for longer rides or drives, and also experiences a closer rapport with him or her than anyone else.

However, horses' memories of people after a considerable separation, say months or years, are either not so good or else horses soon 'get over' the parting and are not particularly bothered about renewing the association. My own horse's breeder came to visit him six months after I had bought him and he showed no sign whatsoever of even recognising her, let alone being pleased (or otherwise!) to see her, yet she had done virtually everything for him, and seen him more or less every day of his life since he was born. Similar happenings have also occurred in other people's experiences.

Horses' memories of each other seem to be more variable. My horse had been particularly friendly with a cob mare at one place where he was kept. I moved him to a different livery yard for a year, then to another, where, lo and behold, the mare turned up again. Neither animal showed any recognition of the other despite their having been quite close during their first relationship. They behaved like complete strangers, sniffing heads and tails, squealing and stamping, but once they had got to know each other again they did strike up another friendship.

There have, however, been other instances where horses have

renewed a contact or friendship after years of parting. Horses meeting at a show showed obvious, keen signs of recognition to the extent that their owners were moved to quiz each other about the animals' backgrounds. It turned out that they were half brother and sister, having not seen each other since the older one was sold years before from the stud where they were bred. Foals weaned and sold on have recognised their dams years hence, too, and show jumpers who have been sold on around the circuit have eventually ended up in the same yard together and shown that they very obviously remembered each other from days past.

There is no doubt that the horse's memory for happenings is phenomenal. Take the well-known example of a horse shying for ever more at a particular place where he once had a startling experience.

As schooling takes the form of experience, we can be sure that the horse will remember his lessons for a very long time. This makes it essential that those lessons are pleasurable and interesting, not stressful, painful or frightening, if we want the horse to learn well and quickly and to behave properly.

Horses learn by association of ideas and happenings, hence the shying example. (If you are going along a road and a fierce farm dog runs out at you at one particular spot, it is wise to beware at that spot in future as the dog will probably do it again.) A horse will learn nothing when he is under stress or frightened because the primeval urge to protect himself becomes uppermost in his mind and he cannot concentrate on two things at once. He will learn nothing, that is, apart from the need to protect himself by reacting naturally (trying to run away or, if this is impossible, defending himself) in stressful circumstances or in a place where something frightening once happened to him.

It is a good idea, therefore, to make sure that lessons do not cause stress or fear to the extent that the instinct for self-preservation comes to the fore and becomes more important than what is being taught. It is true that horses can be trained to stand up to very frightening situations. Police horses are the most obvious example of this, but the standard training policy of mounted police branches throughout the country involves never pushing the horse into a frightening situation to the extent that he reacts violently.

Slowly does it is the rule. The horse will be 'pushed' so far and when the trainer feels the horse is *about* to react, the lesson is stopped, the horse praised and turned away from the situation. Next time this lesson is taught, it is invariably found that the horse will approach the object just that little bit closer before the trainer feels it necessary to stop, and so on, until a fully trained horse results. Considerable use is also made, in the early stages, of the schoolmaster horse, bearing in mind the fact that horses take their examples from one another and find great reassurance in the presence of their fellows, particularly those whom they sense are older and more worldly-wise than they.

This follows closely what would happen in a herd environment, natural or otherwise. The older animals in the herd are, maybe unwittingly, guiding lights to the younger members, who learn a great deal from their example. This influence of one horse over another can sometimes work the other way round.

When I first bought my own youngster he had never been near traffic, having been born and reared in a country district. The livery yard at which I first kept him was in a suburban area (although with reasonable hacking facilities nearby) and it was essential to begin traffic-training him as soon as he responded

Fig 13 The idea is to turn the horse away before he starts to object

well enough to the aids. The owner of the yard had an elderly, quiet cob on whom she kindly agreed to accompany us round the shortest, quietest routes. We never decided whether it was the enlivening influence of my youngster on the cob or simply the fact that the cob was feeling full of beans, but he was so playful and skittish during these rides that my youngster, taking his cue from the old horse, abandoned his surprisingly quiet, placid behaviour and began to dance around, too.

The young horse never, in fact, gave any problem in traffic until later in life after a couple of unpleasant experiences with a tractor and a bus, both of which simply made too much noise and came too close for comfort without actually making contact. Probably because, on arrival, he had barely seen traffic let alone been frightened by it, he did not know that it was anything to fear and so reacted not at all to it. Having been startled later in life, however (not until he was ten years old, when both incidents took place within a month), he learned that these motorised creatures could do unpleasant things and so, in future, one had to be wary of them.

Horses' learning ability is helped considerably by their truly remarkable powers of observation. In time, they can be taught to respond to the tiniest movement on our part, even subconscious movements or body positions or even mental attitudes, it seems, in some cases.

Watching horses at liberty in a field or in more natural conditions such as on moorland, it is fascinating to observe their reactions to each other. On many occasions, there seems to be no signal of any kind passed between two individuals, yet a response is elicited. For example, one horse will approach another and not seem to be making communication at all, yet the second horse may move away, either calmly, not appearing coerced in any way, or with a definite submissive attitude such as ears down and to the side and tail in, or even defensively, such as head down and away and ears back and down, and maybe also a switch of the tail. Alternatively, the approaching horse may halt for a few moments, again with no apparent communication taking place, then turn round and walk away again, or the other horse might follow as if summoned. The horses have obviously observed some minute body language or even mental communication which is invisible to humans.

Horses also observe minute movements or attitudes on the part of their trainers and many maintain that they respond more effectively to body language and attitudes than they do to the spoken word. Horses certainly use this form of communication among one another more than verbal communication.

The story of Clever Hans is well known but bears relating here in connection with the discussion on horses' powers of observation. Hans was owned by a gentleman by the name of van Osten and the pair was active in Germany in the 1920s. Van Osten apparently taught his horse to spell, count and do simple calculations, Hans signifying his answers by tapping out a required number with a forefoot, for example 2+2 would produce four taps. Van Osten would set Hans problems either by speaking them or writing them on a blackboard and Hans was taught to use one forefoot for the tens and one for the units.

The pair travelled Germany giving displays of the wonder horse's abilities but accusations of a hoax were made by scholars and an official investigation was launched into the equine phenomenon. It was discovered that Hans would perform correctly even when van Osten was out of sight but that he paid more attention to his audience than to the blackboard or to his questioner's voice. The investigators decided that Hans was responding to his audience's reactions and sensed when to stop tapping by observing tiny alterations in the watchers' postures, eye movements etc. Even a relaxation of body tension was enough for him. When the members of the panel of enquiry warned the audience about this and told them to remain perfectly still in every way so as not to give Hans any clues, the horse was completely foxed and became most upset. He did not know when to stop tapping and completely 'failed' his tests.

Far from accepting good-naturedly that he had been mistaken in his theories, van Osten rejected Hans and, indeed, the idea of equine intelligence of any appreciable kind. Apparently, Hans was disposed of and abandoned to his fate, ending his life as a nervous wreck in cruel hands, the subject of mockery.

This tragic end to his story is double-sided. First, Hans *had*, in fact, been extremely clever to have gathered what was wanted and was only ensuring his own security by pleasing his master, a perfectly understandable thing to do. Humans do it all the time. Second, van Osten did not appreciate this and could not relate

Hans' form of 'intelligence' with that which he, van Osten, *thought* the horse possessed; he was too narrow-minded and bigoted to see the truth and to value Hans for his considerable natural abilities of observation and what amounted to self-preservation. To be fair, at that time behaviourists and psychologists had not developed to any appreciable degree the theories and lines of work and thought which now exist. It is only comparatively recently that a wider acceptance of natural, species-related 'intelligence' has come to the fore: many workers unfortunately do, as mentioned, still use human-orientated intelligence tests on animals, although this is gradually changing.

It is clear, then, from the story of poor Clever Hans that animals certainly can adapt their natural intelligence to help them survive in a changed, artificial or new environment. This is what all our schooling and training of animals is about, from their point of view. Although many horses and ponies do undoubtedly like their work they are basically pleasing us to get what they need out of life to survive. Just as most of us work to earn money to buy life's necessities, rather than obtaining them directly by, for example, growing our own food and keeping sheep to shear off the wool to make our own clothes, so our horses work indirectly to get their life-necessities by pleasing us. The trouble is, horses have no choice, whereas many of us do. We may actually prefer to earn cash to buy what we want instead of going through the perhaps less acceptable toil of physically producing our own necessities.

As far as the horse's powers of observation and learning capabilities are concerned, when combined with his memory we can be faced with a two-edged sword. It is well known that once a problem is established, it can be extremely difficult, if not impossible, to eradicate it completely. The problem behaviour can, often, be lessened to the point where we can live with it. When discussing seemingly addictive stable vices earlier, it was stressed that it appears horses cannot give them up if addiction to naturally-produced endorphins has taken place.

Not all problem behaviours, however, are with us for ever. A horse who has developed a bad 'stop' when jumping, for example, is by no means guaranteed to refuse his jumps for the rest of his working life. He may well remember that he is quite able to refuse if he wants to, but if we can stop him wanting to he may

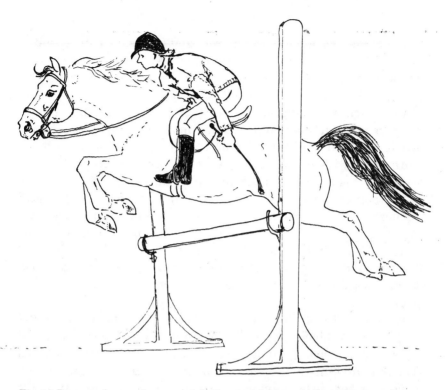

Fig 14 Because horses learn mainly by association of ideas, hitting a horse after take-off, as is often seen like this, will make him think that jumping results in punishment

begin jumping willingly again. A horse who has refused consistently under one rider can easily, on changing homes or riders, begin jumping willingly and fluently again. Perhaps his former rider was too rough with him, habitually socked him in the mouth or spurred him hard or whipped him needlessly.

How many times have you seen a rider whip a horse *after* he has taken off at a jump? This is exactly the same thing as punishing the horse for jumping! We are taught during our equestrian education that we must punish a horse, if at all, instantaneously or within one second at the most, because the horse, unlike the dog, cannot link separated actions, and will otherwise not understand what he is being punished for. Hitting the horse at the point of take-off or immediately after is a sure way of punishing him for taking off. And how confusing for him to be put at a fence knowing he is being asked to jump it yet being punished when he does as his rider asks! Small wonder that so many horses turn into refusers.

If a horse has become used to refusing jumps, he can be said to have conditioned himself to refusing. We have, in fact, conditioned him ourselves by giving him reasons to refuse. Most training is conditioning. If we teach a horse to tolerate a certain action, such as having harness or tack put on, by doing it carefully so as not to make him feel any more uncomfortable than is avoidable, and praising him or rewarding him with food for putting up with it, we have conditioned him to accept it and to feel that this procedure is, in fact, pleasant.

By being completely consistent in our actions, physical requests in the form of aids, verbal sounds linked with particular required movements, we can condition the horse to produce this reaction from that request. Horses can, of course, be conditioned for good and bad, that is, they can learn to associate good or bad things with certain stimuli such as physical aids or verbal sounds.

In the north of England there stands at stud in a highly-respected establishment a Thoroughbred stallion of proven and considerable racing ability. His racing days were spent in 'Geordie-land' in the north-east of the country. British readers will know that people living in that area have a very distinctive regional accent. This horse had obviously had a rough time in his racing life and been harshly treated. When he retired to stud he moved some miles south, to Yorkshire, where the regional accent is quite different. After many months of respectful, sympathetic handling at his new home, his vicious temper improved considerably but he still hated people with a Geordie accent. On one occasion, a gentleman with such an accent forgot the stud owner's advice not to stand too near the stallion's box (they refused to cage him in) because the horse would react violently. The gentleman stood with his back to the stallion, called out in his unmistakeable accent to someone in the yard and found himself with no back to his jacket. This horse will probably associate forever in his mind that particular accent with painful memories, and react accordingly. He had been well and truly conditioned during his racing career!

Horses, then, learn many things in many ways, by associating ideas. They learn obedience if we train them consistently and wisely, but they can also learn to behave badly, by the same principle. It is generally found that horses learn more effectively

80

and quickly by reward-training rather than by punishment-training.

For example, if trying to teach a horse to turn on or about the forehand (depending on your school of thought), it is better to praise the horse profusely and perhaps give him a food reward when he takes but a single step to the side with a hind leg than to crack him across the chest when, from misunderstanding, he takes a step forward. It is better to ignore the step forward and simply place the horse back where he was without punishing him in any way. Try again, probably with a clearer aid (he has, after all, been taught to move forward from the leg) and perhaps help from the ground, and then administer praise or reward for a correct response. In this way, the punishment is non-existent but the praise is obvious and the horse comes to associate training with good things rather than with bad or even a combination of both.

Changing a set habit (rather than an addiction as in the case of a vice) can only be done, if at all, by a consistent course of 'treatment'. Take as an example the horse who habitually pulls back when tied up. Some horses do this without reason, apart from the admittedly excellent one of wishing to get free. There may be nothing frightening them, but they still pull back, quite calmly and premeditatedly, because they have learned how effective this can be.

This particular problem is dealt with in Part III of this book where various methods of dealing with it are suggested. It is one case where praising the horse for standing quietly rather than punishing him for pulling back does not work! The horse has to learn that pulling back causes discomfort, otherwise he will not stop doing it. Here, seemingly 'self-inflicted punishment' works well, particularly if the 'punishment' occurs when no human is near, such as the rope-behind-the-thighs method.

If this, or whatever method is chosen, is consistently administered over a considerable period of time (days/weeks/months as necessary), the habit of pulling back can be changed, in most individuals, into the habit of standing quietly, if resignedly, still; then the corrective equipment can be dispensed with and we have a reformed character. Because of his previous behaviour, however, should anything frightening subsequently happen to such a horse while he is tied up, he will quickly remember that he did in the past get free by pulling, and, if sufficiently motivated, he may revert to his old habit.

The principle of association of ideas as a learning aid can apply in indirect as well as direct ways. For instance, it is a good idea to make sure that a young horse's first outing to a show is as pleasurable as possible. If his first experience of a showground is worrying or frightening as opposed to interesting or even exciting, he may well associate showgrounds and their familiar combination of sights and sounds, with fear and distress, which are not conducive to competent, willing performance in any field. Even bad weather, depressing as it can be for humans and horses alike, can cause the horse to associate shows with unpleasantness if it has to be endured on his first visit. Subsequent bad weather, once the horse has become accustomed to pleasant experiences on the showground, does not matter.

Fig 15 This horse will teach himself that pulling back results in an uncomfortable feeling in a sensitive area, under the tail. The long rope is fixed with its middle under the tail. It is knotted over loins and withers to prevent it falling down, and each free end is passed through one of the side rings or Ds of the headcollar (although they could be passed through the single bottom D under the jaw). The ends are tied together in an easily released slip-knot (a half bow) to a firmly fixed ring

Perception

Like any animal, humans included, horses need to be able to
sense their environment before they can make anything of it.
They have senses of hearing, sight, smell, taste and touch. We
tend to think that horses' senses give them the same facilities as
our own, but this is not quite so.

Hearing

It is known that horses can hear sounds of higher frequency than
humans, and also quieter sounds. We must all have experienced,
during a ride or drive, the horse who suddenly pricks up his ears
and either stops dead or starts to prance excitedly around for no
apparent reason; then minutes later another horse appears. He
has obviously heard its hooves long before we have. Horses can
not only pick up the sound of a familiar car engine some time
before humans can, but are able, like us, to distinguish between
one engine sound and another.

If a horse gets agitated for no obvious reason, then surely we
should give him the benefit of the doubt and consider that he has
sensed something we have not. People who have worked closely
with horses as part of their culture take advantage of the horses'
hearing ability. American Indians, for example, took seriously
the warning of approaching hooves given to them by their horses'
reactions. By placing their own ears to the ground they, too,
could hear the drumming of distant hooves through the solid
medium of the earth, more effective at transmitting sound than
the air.

Horses invariably direct their ears towards whatever is taking
their attention at a particular time. If a distant sound is picked
up, the ears will go towards it and the horse will, if he can, swing
his head towards it, too, so he can try to see what it is. He may
then size it up and make a quick decision to either stay put or
run away. This ability to pick up distant sounds obviously helped
him detect predators, and to counteract it those predators
developed a stealthy prowling gait so as not to cause vibrations
through the earth which the horse could hear or, possibly, feel.

This supposed ability to feel sound vibrations has often been
quoted but I have no personal proof that it exists. I tried it on my
own horse several times; I would go into his field and purposely
approach him from the rear where I knew he couldn't see me. If

Fig 16 Keeping a horse in a stable for many hours a day puts him under unnatural stress, especially if he cannot even put his head outside but is confined to what amounts to a prison cell

he moved his head and caught a glimpse of me, the game was over; if he did not, I stamped forward purposely to see if he could feel any ground vibrations and he never could. I know very well he was not at all deaf, and when he detected me it was invariably by hearing and/or sight, when he would swing round to face me, ears pricked, with that 'She's at it again!' look on his face.

Ears are good indicators of feelings, too. Horses who are intending to bite or kick invariably put their ears flat back and down as a sign of aggression. Ears at half-mast usually mean either sickness, tiredness, boredom or relaxation. Pricked forward, they indicate attention in that direction. Racehorses giving their utmost towards the end of a race when they are tired have their ears flat back, too; a sign of ultimate effort. If a horse is jumping and his ears are not pointed towards the jump, there is a good chance his attention is not fully on the obstacle and he might bump into it, knock it down or refuse, although a horse refusing out of uncertainty or fear will usually have his ears pricked forward at the object of his fear.

Sight

The horse's sight has been the subject of some research lately, and the certainly plausible theory of the 'ramped retina' is no longer held to be valid. The retina is a sort of screen which picks up the light rays entering the horse's eyes through the lens and creating the image. It is on the back of the eye, and it was formerly believed that it sloped towards the bottom of the eye, causing the horse to raise and lower his head to bring objects into focus on it (the lens not being able to change shape so much to focus as in the human eye). Anatomical research now shows that there is no ramped retina. The horse's eyes do not provide him with a round picture in front of him, as do human eyes. Rather he experiences a shallow but very wide panorama of vision almost all round him, although he cannot see directly behind himself or

Fig 17 'She's at it again!'

for about four to six feet in front. The upper and lower parts of the panorama provide long-sighted vision and the central part shorter-sighted vision, which explains the horse's need to move its head around to focus.

The horse's eyes are, in addition, set to the side of his head, giving him wider placement than humans and predators. He needs to be able to see all around him for danger lurking and approaching from all directions, whereas predators need accurate vision in front of them to aim at their prey. Finally, his pupils are not round like ours but more horizontally oval, hence the shallow panorama of vision.

Horses tend to see things with one eye and can see simultaneously objects on both sides, each eye for each side; ideal for them on the plains, but it would be most confusing for us, used as we are to seeing things with both eyes at the same time. A horse, to use the shying example again, will see that piece of paper in the hedge with, say, the right eye but not the left; coming home along the same route, if the paper is still there he will see it afresh with the left eye, perceiving it as a new problem.

When we consider these visual differences, we can more easily understand why horses behave as they do when relying on visual information, and why it is so important for them to have freedom of head and neck so that they can see where we want them to go and are not working blind. The blind area in front of the head makes it all the more remarkable that horses do things like jumping when the jump disappears from view just before take-off, and the horse has to jump what he remembers of its size, shape, spread and exact location. It is also now easy to understand why turning his head away from traffic on a road simply enables him to see the traffic behind him rather than removing it from view, an idea long perpetrated in horsey circles, because the 'away' eye (the left in Britain, right in most other countries) is now angled so that the horse can see in his normally blind rear area. To keep the traffic in view as it pulls to the right to overtake him, he moves his quarters, if permitted, further and further to the right – *into* the traffic – until he may well do a complete circle on the road and end up facing in the wrong direction. The fact that his rider has the outside leg hard on might keep the quarters from performing this circle and so, if the horse behaves, he does so because he trusts his rider, not because he cannot see the traffic approaching. As the traffic disappears behind his quarters, if they stay straight, it then comes into view afresh in the other eye when it is level with the horse – a situation horses often find extremely frightening.

If the head is turned *towards* the traffic, the quarters, if they go anywhere, will turn away from the vehicles, which is much safer, and the horse will be able to trace the progress of the traffic all the way, having no surprises sprung upon him. Some people say that horses are better off if they cannot see the object of their fear, and others feel they are better if they *can* see it. It depends on the individual horse, but during traffic training of a very

Fig 18 Some horsemen advise turning a horse's head *away* from traffic, ostensibly so that he cannot see it. In practice, the horse *can* see this lorry coming up behind him with his left eye and may well turn a semi-circle in the road in an effort to keep it in view. If the rider keeps him straight with her outside leg, the lorry will 'disappear' and suddenly come into view in the right eye as it overtakes the horse. The opposite school of thought advises letting the horse see the traffic with, in this case, his right eye, which is obviously much safer

green horse, schoolmasters to the rear and to the 'traffic' side are a great help!

Driving horses normally wear blinkers to prevent their seeing behind them. While it may be reassuring not to be able to see their vehicle 'chasing' them, some horses do go better without blinkers in traffic, for reasons just discussed. Again, it depends on the individual.

Smell and taste

It seems that just about every animal on earth has a better sense of smell than the human. Dogs, obviously, are renowned for their abilities in this respect. Horses, too, seem to be able to smell things more acutely than humans. It is often recommended that we should not wear perfume around horses as they recognise us by our smell, yet some horses love the scent of hairspray and often nuzzle up to get a stronger whiff of some new aroma which walks into their box on a familiar person.

Horses have long been said to be able to 'smell' fear, and this is not as unreasonable or fanciful as it might seem. Different substances are exuded into the sweat when we experience different emotions, and the sweat is subsequently excreted to the outer world through the skin. The horse is certainly, therefore, able to smell these different substances and can tell how we are feeling, whether we are frightened and nervous or relaxed and confident. In a contribution to *Equine Behaviour*'s Summer 1985 issue, Mr Joe Royds of the Royal MENCAP Riding Fund told how, in the winter of 1982, a Norwegian doctor found unusual peptides (organic compounds which can result from protein breakdown such as during digestion and general metabolism) in the urine of autistic people. 'If in the urine,' remarked Mr Royds 'then in the sweat', and went on to explain how this must be one of the ways horses recognise autistic people at distances of twenty-five yards. (Horses and autists have a tremendous rapport between them and, in the same contribution, Mr Royds said: 'I have heard fourteen autists speak their first words *ever* from the saddle'.)

Horses use their sense of smell in many ways, from detecting in-season mares (which stallions can do, when the wind is right, several fields away) to assessing the suitability of food. Mares and foals recognise each other much more by smell than sight, just one of the reasons why bereaved mares and orphaned foals are introduced largely on this basis. The mare may have Vick or some other strong-smelling disguising substance smeared inside her nostrils, and the orphan frequently has the skin of her dead foal draped over it to encourage her to accept what she would otherwise recognise as an interloper.

Horses in the wild frequently smell their way around a large territory by means of following other animals' tracks on the ground, particularly in uncertain or unfamiliar ground conditions. When strange horses meet, they put nostril to nostril, often on both sides, and squeal and stamp until they decide whether to accept each other or not. This seems to be not only a smelling session but also a form of other communication. Horses also investigate droppings by smell and can tell whether they are friends' or rivals' droppings, and, when breeding is on the agenda, whether mares are in season or not. When a human approaches a horse, it will invariably smell the human, not merely to discover the presence or otherwise of titbits but to see if the human is familiar or strange, frightened or confident, and will react accordingly.

Many humans can smell the difference between their own animals and other people's, and recognise each animal by its smell as an individual, whether horse or anything else, and there is every reason to suppose that horses do the same.

Smell and taste are inextricably linked in horses and other animals, including humans. I once ate cheese and onion sandwiches before being shown round a stud, and almost every horse I met and allowed to smell my hands threw up his or her head and curled up the top lip in the posture known as Flehmen. This does not necessarily mean that the horses found the smell of onion objectionable, for the posture does not mean nausea as was previously thought. The horse has a little pocket at the top of its nose near the soft palate which can be used for detailed smell assessment, and it works better if the nostrils are temporarily blocked off by curling up the upper lip. Notice next time a horse does it how slit-like the nostrils become. At the stud just mentioned, some horses subsequently licked my hands and then did Flehmen again as if fascinated.

Horses often investigate food, particularly new food, by smell, and may decide to eat or not, depending on the resulting aroma. Worming medicines are, of course, often detected in feed, even though we may be able to smell nothing and even though we disguise them with such things as black treacle.

Horses can also taste with their lips as well as their tongues. On a visit to a friend, we offered his cob a tiny piece of ragwort to see what he would do. He smelled it – no Flehmen – picked it up with his lips and promptly dropped it before it made contact with his tongue. His teeth, in fact, remained firmly closed throughout the whole episode. Live ragwort is known to taste bitter which is why horses generally avoid it unless desperately hungry; they subsequently and tragically sometimes develop a taste for it.

Horses appear to have a sweet tooth and normally like to be given peppermints, chocolate (watch the caffeine content if your horse competes formally under any association's rules involving prohibited substances and 'non-normal nutrients'), but they dislike sour, bitter things. If you want your horse to do Flehmen for a photograph, offer him a piece of onion or lemon! Some, indeed most, poisonous growths appear to be bitter, but yew apparently is not, and just a few of the tiny needle-like leaves can be fatal. This must be a serious disadvantage to wild and feral equidae, for they cannot always detect harmful plants.

Fig 19 The attitude known as 'Flehmen'

Touch

The horse's sense of touch is very like our own; he can sense an insect landing on his body even through his coat hair, and feels pain every bit as intensely as we do, something which many people appear not to realise or else to overlook. As mentioned earlier, the horse's very sensitive muzzle is equivalent to our fingers, which is why he investigates nearly everything with it. The nostrils, of course, are right above, indeed part of it, so this entire area is of vital importance to the horse.

The whiskers which grow from the muzzle and around the eyes are, in a way, like an insect's antennae. Their roots are surrounded liberally with nerve endings and they convey to the horse the nature of the objects he is investigating. They also inform him, when nosing around in the dark, of the proximity of various objects, to save collisions. It is common practice, unfortunately, to clip these whiskers off for appearance's sake. Some people feel a horse looks 'smarter' without them. Others, like the author, feel they look deprived, which is exactly what they are.

4

Discipline and Restraint

Discipline

Discipline is obviously necessary with an animal the size and strength of a horse. It is an ever-present part of his life with the herd, in natural conditions. Only one animal can be boss over the whole herd, and then only for that period of his or her life which covers the prime years, for in the wild discipline is meted out by physical means, and dominance is achieved and maintained by physical prowess. As soon as weakness occurs, through injury, sickness or the feebleness of old age, a usurper will be ready and waiting to fill the gap and take over. Perhaps surprisingly, natural discipline by fellow herd members can help us to accustom horses to 'know their place' in their relations with humans. It is noticeable that those animals reared in mixed groups, as in nature, accept discipline from humans much more easily and naturally than those raised in artificial domestic conditions. It is the practice on most studs, except those able to rear animals in vast tracts of country which permit normal social herd relationships, to wean foals at roughly six months of age and thereafter to keep them in age groups, ie all weanlings together, all yearling fillies together, all yearling colts together, all two-year-old fillies together, and so on.

In such management systems, the only 'discipline' met with (and it is not really discipline in the correct sense, only jockeying for position in the herd hierarchy) is from others of the same age and usually the same sex. In the wild, this would only happen in the bachelor groups of young stallions which form when sexually mature males are ousted from the herd of their birth by the reigning stallion. In their case, such a relationship is excellent training for the day when they, too, will fight to take over a herd.

In the case of herd hierarchies in general, the boss of the herd is far more normally a matriarchal mare rather than a stallion, contrary to popular belief, and she will, in fact, boss the stallion

92

about. When mares are in season and mating is occurring, the mare controls the situation, letting the stallion know in no uncertain terms whether or not she is ready to be served. A wise stallion (and wisdom in horses, as in humans, usually only comes with age and experience) will enquire of the mare before mounting and will approach from the safest direction – the side.

Youngstock in natural herd conditions are mixed in all ages with adults and foals and, of course, both sexes. The adults have their own hierarchy and even those at the bottom of it will discipline the youngsters, so they get the brunt of it all the time and develop a healthy respect for their elders and betters. They become used to doing as they are told provided they recognise that the one doing the telling is, indeed, their superior.

It is the same in their relationship with humans. Animals raised in natural conditions (few and far between in most domestic studs in any country) yet habituated to humans, come to hand much more easily (unless they have a particularly independent temperament) than those raised more commonly in artificial conditions. Accepting discipline is a part of their lives already and they accept it, likewise, from humans. Animals reared on studs where they have been segregated by age and sex from an early age are often more difficult to teach, even if they are handled from birth. They are not so used to actual discipline from their superiors. Whatever discipline the dam or other mares may have administered before weaning has been pushed into the past from that time onwards, and although they will surely remember it, it often takes a while for real obedience to human discipline to become a habit.

Undisciplined horses either become nervous wrecks or bullies, if not downright aggressive, depending on their temperaments. Usually, a disciplined horse is secure in his mind as he knows what to expect. Fairness is absolutely essential. Horses are not like dogs; they are not all-forgiving of our failings. Horses bear grudges and recognise injustice when they experience it. Therefore, any discipline administered must be reasonable, fair and, if it takes the form of punishment for something the horse knows is wrong, virtually instantaneous. If you wait more than a second you have waited too long and the horse will not, indeed cannot because of his mental limitations, link the punishment with the 'crime' he has just committed. You cannot take a horse to the scene of that crime and tell him off and expect him to understand that he has done wrong, as you can with a dog. He simply will not know what you are talking about.

Discipline must also be consistent. It is foolish to reprimand a horse on one occasion for doing something wrong but let it pass the next. The horse will never know right from wrong and, worse, will become confused. This in turn breeds insecurity, which leads to nervousness and self-defence.

If a horse has any character at all, we cannot blame him for wanting, and getting, his own way if we are not strong or influential enough to persuade him to do what we want. A horse may 'try it on' once, find he can get away with it, and expect to be able to do so for ever more. Many horses who change homes frequently have to adapt to a whole new set of rules, conditions and relationships and often, after they have been in their new home for a short while, start seeing how far they can go. Just one demonstration of fair discipline will probably nip the tendency in the bud. If the incident is allowed to pass, however, the horse tries with more gusto next time, and so on, until *he* becomes the boss and not the human – a hazardous situation for all concerned, for without the human's judgement of what is safe and what is not the horse is an uncontrolled danger in human society, to himself and all near him.

Discipline together with kindness and understanding is the ideal combination for dealing with horses. Many are very sensitive and even the most wilful can understand this combination and respond to it. The relationship between a stallion and his handler, for example, must be founded on mutual respect. The stallion must, for the most part, behave, and the handler must, on occasion, make allowances.

Horses who are well-trained and fairly disciplined can certainly still retain their individuality. It is noticeable that most of the best horsemen and horsewomen are those who allow their horses to be themselves, to show their individuality, quirks, likes and dislikes, while still getting top performance out of them and enjoying a give-and-take relationship of mutual respect and affection. Conformist automatons are neither necessary nor desirable to a true horseman, who rarely experiences problems in the way the rest of us might. Horses seem to simply slot in with their psyche almost as if they belonged together.

This sort of person, too, pays considerable attention to what the horse himself likes doing and is good at, realising that it is useless to try to force a horse to do something he really does not want to do or simply cannot do in the area of work. The Spanish Riding School Lipizzaners specialise in airs they each have a particular capability for; no horse, or person, can be top class at everything, but most have some special ability which can be brought out, exploited if you like, with sympathetic training and handling.

Many people believe that self-inflicted discipline is more effective in bringing about acceptance and obedience in the horse than any meted out by man. EBSC member Michael Lang said in one issue of *Equine Behaviour*: 'I have noticed horses are much more impressed by self-inflicted hurt than by any conventional punishment applied by the trainer on disobedience, eg the horse that runs back when asked to stand still for the trainer to mount. If, on running back, the horse strikes something painful *by his own* action, he will quickly stop the disobedience.' Another member mentioned how she had prevented and cured a horse from kicking when she tried to pick out its hind hooves by keeping hold of the kicking leg and pushing it into the opposite leg, so the horse effectively kicked itself. It stopped after a very few such injuries.

The subject of discipline was taken up in a later issue by Dr Sharon Cregier, who said:

> Few people with animals recognise the need for discipline or even how and when to administer it. If a horse is the victim of such inept handling, he may be labelled vicious and consigned to auction or slaughter.
>
> A five-year-old Thoroughbred was one such victim. As a foal, he had not had the advantage of living in a herd. No playmates returned nips or kicks. No older, wiser mares had taught him courting manners. No sire had taught him rank and forbearance. Abruptly separated from his dam at weaning, as is the crude custom among the majority of 'horsemen', further problems developed, such as crib-biting and fighting any touch to stomach or legs for cleaning. His handlers showed more fear than understanding. The result was an arrogant, highly-strung, 1,500lb horse that could not be safely handled for medication, grooming or breeding. One of his more spectacular practices was an open-mouthed charge at humans. One farrier had managed to pick up the front feet only to lose shirt and shoulder muscle to the raking teeth.

A man I will call 'D' offered to shoe the animal but requested that no one be present at the first. He asked that the stallion be loose in a corral. The anxious owners protested – as they thought D would surely be killed – but in the end did as D asked. D knew it was no use casting the stallion. That practice taught fight, not manners, where a spirited animal was concerned. He had to leave a horse that was safe for other farriers. With stable and grounds cleared of humans, D entered the far end of the corral. He stood quietly, one hand over the other, knuckles out, and just below his chin. The stallion sighted fresh quarry and charged, teeth bared. At the last moment, D's hand snaked out, clipping the stallion's lips against the animal's teeth. The stallion veered, shook his head, halted, snorting, head up, eyes flaring! There must be some mistake! Again he threatened. D maintained his ground.

The stallion charged. Smack! It was the first discipline the stallion had received from humans that he could understand.

Within the hour, D had fondled the stallion all over and was picking up his feet. When the owners returned, they found D bent beneath the stallion's mouth, tidying up a shoeing job. The stallion held his lips against D's neck as he worked. From time to time, D 'accidentally' bumped the horse's by-now-tender muzzle. The stallion never offered to nip and the shoeing job was completed in front of a wondering audience.

Fig 20 It was the first discipline the stallion had received from humans that he could understand

Restraint

Preventing a horse from moving freely in the way he wants is one of the most frightening things we can do to him. It is a small miracle that it is possible to get horses to accept being led, tied up, ridden, held for various operations such as shoeing, injections, first-aid care and the like. As already stressed in this book, not only do horses need to feel free to feel secure, they need to be aware of space around them into which to escape should the need arise.

It follows, therefore, that keeping a horse confined in a stable, particularly without several hours a day out of it, puts him under unnatural stress. A stable with an open top door at least allows him to look out so that he has space around what he feels is his most important area, his head. The type of stable with a metal grille above the door so that he can see out only through bars is little better than his being shut in all the time behind a solid door. The feeling of confinement and lack of freedom is still there.

It is often necessary for the horse to be restrained for various attentions, apart from everyday routines such as leading about, riding, driving, maybe tying up for grooming and so on. It is a sign of considerable trust of his handler when a horse allows what we might call 'care operations' to be carried out, particularly uncomfortable things such as having a cut dressed, without being tied up or held in any way. Once a horse does trust his human associates, however, he will put up with a surprising number of attentions, many potentially worrying or even frightening, without showing much or any resistance.

When the need arises to physically restrain a horse, it should be done with as little strength and force as is appropriate for the occasion and the individual horse's character. The most simple form of restraint is holding the horse by a top lock of his mane to steady his head while, say, sponging his eyes if he is not too keen on the job. Next comes the usual headcollar and lead rope equipment which is enough for most horses. It is always better to get someone to hold your horse while you work on him, if at all possible, to ensure that feeling of flexibility which the horse cannot have when tied to an immovable object such as a post or tie ring. If this is not possible, the horse should be tied with a slip knot (a half bow) which can easily be undone by a single pull on the free end should the need arise. Many people recommend tying the rope to a ring of binder twine through the metal tie ring so that the horse can break free if he panics. Others maintain this *teaches* him that he can break free and so he is in future never reliable about being tied up.

It is never a good idea, even with a seemingly trustworthy horse, to leave him tied up unattended, even for just a few moments. If anything happens to frighten him and there is no one about to calm him or untie him if necessary, a nasty accident can occur.

When observing a well-schooled horse being led about and gently handled in a simple headcollar and lead rope, it is easy to forget that he had to be taught to accept this simple form of restraint. Most domesticated horses are taught from foalhood to accept wearing foal slips (tiny headcollars) and to being led with their dams. The sooner a foal is used to wearing a slip and to being guided alongside the mare, the better he will learn his lessons. The longer it is left, and the more he is allowed to run free round the mare while she is being led, the more undisciplined he will become and the more difficult it will be for his attendants to school him later on. It is always better to begin handling, and get over any minor differences of willpower, while the foal is still physically weaker than you so that you really can exert physical strength in teaching and restraining him (although never brutally, of course), and any arguments will not become major ones.

Of course, every effort should be made to keep a restrained horse calm. The human voice has a tremendous effect on a horse. Speaking calmly and confidently in a reassuring tone is often enough to quieten down a horse who is beginning to get really worried by something. The touch of our hands reinforces this effect. Again, a confident (neither too light nor too heavy) stroking is calming, and more relaxing than patting.

If it is found that a fairly mild form of restraint is not having the desired effect, it may be tempting to try a stronger method, but this may well have the opposite effect from the one that is wanted. The horse gets more and more worked up; this means more physical resistance, more fear and panic, and against the physical strength of a horse we become powerless and everyone, human and equine, is in danger of being injured. Battles like this

98

also condition the horse to expect trouble, stress and discomfort, not to mention fear and pain, whenever he senses that we want to restrain him. Resistance may then easily become a habit as the horse's instinct to preserve himself takes precedence over his conditioning to obey.

The reason the method of restraint should suit the character of the horse concerned is because individual horses respond differently to the situation. Nervous, green animals will be easily frightened and if permanent damage is not to result to mind and body, very mild physical methods should be used combined with a great deal of reassurance and patience. Mature, well behaved horses similarly should need only mild methods of restraint, but problems can occur with difficult-natured, experienced animals. Often, such horses have always succeeded in evading restraint and have acquired a reputation of being difficult to handle because they have never been made to realise that the human is the Boss in the relationship. Stronger methods of restraint will be needed on such horses, without, of course, any hint of brutality. Rather than allow a 'fight' to ensue, it may be better to have the horse tranquillised by the veterinary surgeon.

A tranquillised horse is, of course, still conscious, although not as aware of his surroundings as normal. Being tranquillised has

Fig 21 A horse has to raise his head in order to rise, so all you have to do to keep him down is press on his head and neck. There is no need to sit on the head or neck, which could cause injury and extreme discomfort. A minute or so of this treatment will make him think twice about throwing himself down to avoid being handled in future

often quietened a horse down enough for him to be handled without trouble yet he fully understands what is happening to him. Once he realises he is not going to be hurt – something which may be difficult to get through to him in his normal state where he is prejudging the situation, perhaps from previous experience – it is possible that, in future, he will give up his difficult ways and be more co-operative.

Any drugs administered tend to interfere with the horse's co-ordination, so it is generally unwise to use this form of restraint when wishing to carry out procedures such as shoeing, where a horse needs to be in full control of his balance to be able to stand on three legs.

Some wily old characters (and some not so old, either, but just determined not to be messed about) develop the habit of throwing themselves down on purpose, thinking this will stop all attempts at handling them. If it is possible and you can reach the part you want to handle, get someone to press fairly firmly on the horse's head or neck (there is no need to sit on him) so that he cannot get up again, and just carry on doing whatever you have to do. The horse has to raise his head in order to lever himself up on his forelegs, so if you keep his head down he cannot do this and is helpless. If this is not feasible, get the horse up again by means of the methods detailed in the Problem Dictionary under *Lying down during work/refusing to get up in stable*, to show him this will not work.

In some countries, it is common practice for a horse to be 'thrown' purposely and rubbed all over with sacking while he is down to show him how helpless he is and that future resistance against humans is futile. This may well work with some animals, and will truly terrify others. It has had the effect of

---

This horse has been tied up to a ring in the wall and left alone while his handler has gone away to get something he has forgotten. This is asking for trouble. Horses can become restless, like this one, and may attempt to break free. If something should happen to frighten the horse and there is no one nearby to calm him, he can, again, pull back on the ring, and break free in panic. A loose, panicking horse is a danger to himself and others. Always stay near a tied horse

One of the mildest forms of restraint is simply to hold a lock of the horse's mane. An amenable horse can be walked along the yard like this and with a hand round his nose

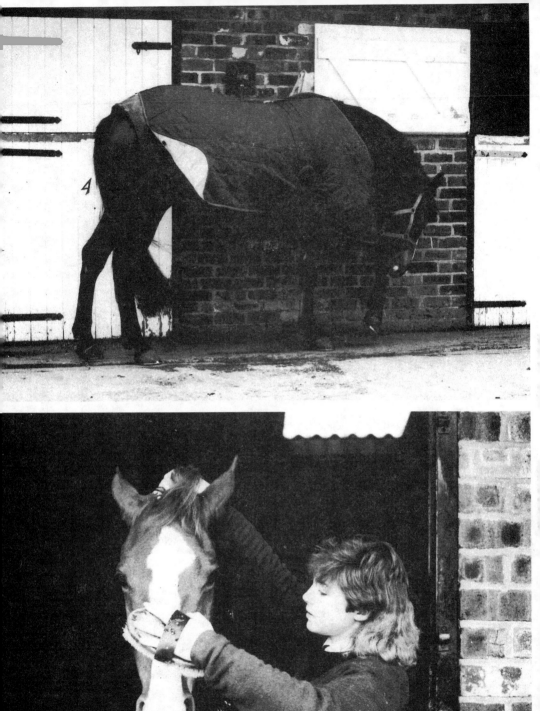

making timid horses into permanent nervous wrecks and wilful ones vicious (an intelligent horse is perfectly capable of getting his own back at some future date). Normal horses should not need this treatment; it is not standard practice in Britain, and we do not seem to have any more 'problem horses' than any other country, so it is a method which can be dispensed with as a matter of course.

Throwing a horse, especially without the use of sedatives of some kind, is most definitely a job for a veterinary surgeon or extremely experienced and competent horsemaster, and should never be attempted by anyone else. There is a risk of the horse sustaining an internal rupture which can result in death, even when expertly done, so it is not a method to be used lightly. One of Britain's best Arab stallions died in this way after being thrown by a vet.

There is not normally anything to be gained by using such strong methods of restraint, active or passive, as to break a horse's spirit. Some people make a habit of leaving horses tied up for hours at a time 'to teach patience and discipline', either leaving them tied normally or put on pillar reins, where a rope or chain goes from both side-Ds of the headcollar or the bridle bit rings to the pillars of the stall (the usual method in standing stalls). The frustration and utter boredom of such restraint must do absolutely nothing for a horse's happiness and temper.

Many people feel that as soon as a horse starts getting really difficult it is as well to twitch him to keep him still and preserve life and limb of all concerned, including the horse. The subject of

---

Even a small foal can be surprisingly strong, and although this handler is purposely showing the wrong way to get a reluctant foal to walk on (staring him in the eye and pulling on the lead rope, which simply cause him to pull back) this sort of situation can easily develop into an unpleasant battle. The foal could rear and come over, causing injury, and also come to mistrust contact with humans as a consequence. The time to begin handling foals is while they are still very young, ideally from birth, so that any 'battle' of strength can be won and the foal be given, from the outset, a knowledge that humans are to be obeyed. We can create problems for ourselves by waiting until the foal is a few months old (see also pp204 and 214)

By spreading out our arms and using our bodies as a 'block' we can make ourselves appear, to a foal not wishing to be caught, much bigger than we are and can overpower it by 'mind over matter'

the current scientific work on twitching is dealt with on pages 14, 15 and 121.

Extra control can be obtained from an ordinary headcollar and rope by passing the rope over the nose and back through the headcollar D, as this places the nose in a firmer grip. A bridle, of course, always gives more control than a headcollar, but the bit should be used carefully and never roughly. In cases where a difficult or green horse has to be led on a road or anywhere where he may be likely to play up (such as passing his friends or through a crowd of people), a well-fitting lungeing cavesson should be put on top of the bridle, a lead rope attached to the front ring and the horse led from both. The reins can be in one hand and the rope in the other, or both can be in the same hand, leaving the other free to hold a schooling whip which can be used behind the leader's back to help control the quarters.

Hobbling a horse (normally by fitting padded leather 'bracelets' to the forelegs and attaching a strong rope, leather strap or chain to them) is sometimes recommended as a means of restricting the pace at which a horse can move and is useful for animals who are hard to catch. Unfortunately, it does have considerable risks and should be used only under expert supervision. Nervous or green animals should certainly never be hobbled as they will probably bring themselves down and be unable to rise again, injuring themselves in their struggles and frightening themselves severely. Horses should be gradually accustomed first to the feel of the bracelets and second to the restriction of movement by being led very carefully round their boxes in the hobbles, then round the yard and finally in the field. Hobbles should be used, if at all, only on solitary horses as, of course, a hobbled horse has no means of defending himself against marauding colleagues.

Tethering is another way of restricting a hard-to-catch horse and teaching him to be approached. However, again expert advice and demonstration is needed. The stake should be hammered very firmly and deeply into the ground and only chains or ropes with swivels on the end used. Alternatively, an extremely heavy weight can be used. If the horse is the type who takes off when you approach, mind you do not get your legs whipped from under you by the chain – dangerous and painful!

In days when Army horses were taken on treks and outdoor

camps, various ingenious methods of tethering or picketing them were used. The horses were normally picketed to long ropes about withers height and, being on the whole well trained and of calm nature, tolerated this without fuss. They were often, in addition, secured at the back end by means of heel ropes and pegs. Stakes were hammered firmly into the ground and a padded shackle fitted to a rear pastern, with a rope from it to the peg. Knee haltering, where a rope passed from the back D of the headcollar and was tied above the knee, was used to restrict the movement of grazing horses. Various other methods are detailed in the Army manual *Animal Management*, which is well worth reading and should be available from any branch of Her Majesty's Stationery Office.

The main thing to remember is that Army horses were worked much harder than privately owned animals, and were rarely in such high spirits that they wanted to play up just for devilment. They were also painstakingly and expertly trained and had the temperament to stand such restraint. There is no reason why 'civvy' horses should not be trained in the same way, provided expert advice is available and the animals are of suitable, calm temperament and not fresh, but it would not be advisable to try it with a hot-blooded type or a green, easily upset horse.

A common and fairly mild means of restraining a horse is to hold up a leg so that he is standing on three legs and will find it difficult to move (except up or down!). If, for instance, you want to treat an injury to the horse's near fore, get a friend to lift up his near hind so the near fore remains firmly anchored to the ground. If a hind leg is being treated, of course, lift the foreleg on the same side. Alternatively, you can lift the opposite leg at the same 'end'. Remember that, particularly in foreleg lameness, you do not want all the forehand weight being supported on the lame leg on which you are working, so lift a hind leg. As two-thirds of the horse's weight is borne by his forehand, this is more important when dealing with the forelegs, although it also applies to the hind.

Sometimes this method is used just to stop a horse fidgeting about, and a foreleg can be held up by a strap put round the pastern and secured round the forearm. If a rope is used, great care is needed to avoid a rope burn. It is much safer and, there-fore, far preferable to have someone hold the strap or rope while you are working so that if the horse does panic the leg can be let down immediately.

I always prefer to give any animal the benefit of the doubt and not restrain it with more than a headcollar and rope until the horse shows me I must. A very simple trick which has worked for me more than once is simply to put an elastic band round the base of the horse's ear just so tight that he can feel some pressure but not so that it is causing pain. It is amazing that many horses do not even shake their heads when you do this, although, as with any method of restraint, it depends on the horse's temperament. Applying a twitch to the ear, as some are wont to do, or twisting, pulling or bending the ear are risky methods. Horses seem to resent them more than other methods and the cartilage and nerve can easily be damaged causing a permanently 'dropped' ear.

A fairly effective and mild method of helping restrain a foal or small animal is to lift its tail under the dock and exert moderate pressure on it without, of course, trying to cause pain. As this often quietens them significantly, it is possible, in the light of the 'endorphin story', that this is another acupuncture or acupressure point. However, certain show horses in tail sets (usually wooden contraptions fixed under the tail to force it, apparently after surgical mutilation of the muscles and nerves, into a most unnatural and ugly high carriage), often show signs of being in great discomfort, not to mention pain, so the acupressure theory is perhaps not accurate as far as tail restraint goes.

In some quarters, restraining stocks are used. These are strong structures of wood or metal which surround the horse and usually fix up a foot. Bars go under and around the horse, making it absolutely impossible for him to move significantly. Apparently some people use them automatically for shoeing or dressing injuries – and surely nothing is more calculated to give a horse a heart attack or at least a nervous breakdown! Restraint in general is anathema to horses and such complete restraint as this must be equivalent to torture.

Passing ropes or, worse, chains, through a horse's mouth and over the top gum are methods practised by some, but they must be used only with great care and by experts. As a jerk on the rope or chain can cause not only considerable pain but injury, too, these methods cannot be recommended as general practice, nor can passing a chain (as opposed to a rope) over the nose. Anything which causes physical pain invariably also causes fear and panic in a horse, which make him *more* difficult to control, not less.

There are at least two makes of 'control' headcollars or halters on the British market at the time of writing, and variations in other countries. These devices do seem to work with some horses but not with others. They appear to be most effective with horses who are 'trying it on' rather than those who are genuinely frightened. They usually work by exerting pressure and constriction round the muzzle and on the poll and, like virtually any piece of equipment, would only cause pain if misused. They certainly have a place in our efforts to control horses, if used wisely.

PART II
AS OTHERS SEE IT

Part II comprises three contributions on topics of so-called problem behaviour in horses by three different authors, each of whom brings both a practical and scientific expertise to his or her subject. These subjects are of particular importance to all connected with horses. They are:

The Recognition of Emotions and Sensations by **Dr Moyra Williams**

Stable Vices by **Dominic Prince**

Transporting the Horse by **Dr Sharon E. Cregier, FIASH** (Hon, Edin)

The Recognition of Emotions and Sensations

by Dr Moyra Williams

Dr Moyra Williams is a clinical psychologist, practical horsewoman and breeder. She is author of many scientific papers, and also of the books Adventures Unbridled *(Methuen, 1960),* A Breed of Horses *(Pergamon Press, 1971) and* Horse Psychology *(J. A. Allen, 1986). In 1978, she founded and is still Chairman of the Equine Behaviour Study Circle, an international group of horse enthusiasts from all disciplines and walks of life, professional and amateur. Her contribution to this book is on the difficult subject of understanding how horses are feeling and so what they are thinking at any one time. The table accompanying her contribution will be of particular assistance in this respect.*

It is not easy to recognise how another individual is feeling. One person, it is true, can describe his sensations to another, but words are as likely to mislead or misdirect as to convey the truth, the latter often being more accurately conveyed by the tone of voice, the angle of the head or the direction of gaze than by the content of what is said. For example, the tone in which a person says 'I am not afraid' may denote near panic, while that in which he says 'Don't you dare' may be an invitation to act.

Every animal species has its own form of language or 'signalling system', some of which is inborn while some is learned at an early age. Animals, it is said, cannot lie, but it is doubtful if this is quite true because mock threats to 'try out the opposition' are very common among horses in a group; and, moreover, are more often given by the underdogs than by the more dominant individuals. Among horses, the first weeks of life seem to be vital for learning horse-language, as horses which have been reared away from others (such as orphaned foals raised by humans) never seem to understand the threats of their elders, or fail to respond with the expected gestures of 'submission', with consequences that can be fatal. Returning to the point

about 'lying', however, a horse, like a human, may gesture submission without actually feeling submissive. He may, like the
gangster who holds up his hands when cornered but at the first
appropriate moment pulls a gun on his captor, be biding his time
to take over mastery of the herd.

Emotional expressions are different from such signals in that
they cannot be faked. This does not mean to say that all horses
respond to the same perceptions or situations in the same way.
For example, a horse which has been with kind, considerate,
understanding handlers all its life may be pleased at the appearance of a strange human being, whereas one that has never
beheld an upright, two-legged creature before, or that has been
ill-treated by one, may be terrified at the sight. Again, a hungry
horse may regard the appearance of food with elation (and be
prepared happily to face pain in order to gain access to it), while
a fully satiated one will regard it with boredom.

As well as the differences which can be traced to existing
physical states or past experience, there are some which seem to
be inherited. For example, although most horses are reluctant to
enter dark, narrow spaces (such as the starting stalls on a race-
track) when first introduced to them, some seem to develop
renewed anxiety later in life for no apparent reason. The same is
true about traffic-shyness. It is usually found that such 'phobias'
appear in generation after generation of the same genetic stock
and are not necessarily caused by the association between a
painful past experience and the visual sensations. It is a matter,
as one very knowledgeable and experienced stud groom used to
say, of 'knowing your horse' and its parental background.

Regarding the way in which emotions and sensations are
expressed, in general *pleasure causes relaxation* and *displeasure
causes contraction* of various muscle-groups affecting the position of the head, the ears, the eyes, the nostrils, the legs and the
tail, while tension further alters the rate of breathing which may
be evident in calls, snorts, squeals and gasps. The names we give
to the emotions, and the signs by which we can recognise them,
are listed in the Table on page 113.

In addition to the signs listed here, which can all be recognised
by the unaided human senses, we know the body makes many
other reactions to alterations of sensation and emotion. For
instance, slight tension of the skin, accelerated heart-rate and

Fig 22 Typical warning that the horse is thinking of biting. Ears are pressed back aggressively, the upper lip and nostrils are wrinkled up and back and the teeth are bared. Altogether an angry and not very welcoming picture!

increased electrical discharges throughout the muscular system accompany all forms of stress as well as excitement. In such cases, too, the sweat glands under the skin begin to discharge and emit their aroma. These signals, as well as the very faint sounds caused by changes in the rate of breathing, although undetected by humans, may be sensed consciously by other horses as well as by other animal species. Moreover, similar signals given off by a human handler or rider may be sensed by horses even when the giver is unaware of what he is doing.

In addition to showing their ongoing feelings by the means shown in the Table, some horses demonstrate previous feelings by developing behavioural habits known to horsemen as *vices* and to the general scientific world as *stereotypes*. Some of these movements involve pressure around or inside the mouth such as crib-biting or wind-sucking (when confined in a stable) or putting the tongue over the bit (when ridden). Others involve movement such as weaving (when stabled), or napping, rearing or bolting (when ridden).

The development of the habits is considered to originate in some form of discomfort, either physical (eg pain in the mouth from a sore tooth or gum, or in the alimentary gut due to colic) or from mental discomfort such as loneliness or the fear of facing the unknown. It is also believed that the activity in which the animal indulges stimulates the formation and circulation throughout the body of endorphins – a form of pain-killer-cum-

Signs of emotion

Sensation	Position of						Muscle tension	Breathing	Voice
	Ears	Head	Eyes	Jaw and mouth	Tail	Legs			
Pain	Back	Flat	Shut	Stiff	Flat	Stiff	Tight	Heavy	Silent
Fear	Back	Up	Wide open directed to cause	Stiff	Flat	Stiff	Tight	Gasping	Squeal
Anxiety	Sideways	Up	Wide open directed to cause	Stiff	Raised slightly	Stiff	Tight	Gasping	Silent
Apprehension	Sideways	Up	Wide open directed to cause	Stiff	Raised slightly	Braced	Tight	Blowing through nostrils	Silent
Anger	Flat back	Pointed out	Looking back	Showing teeth	Whisking	Braced	Moderate	Fast	May squeal
Anticipation	Forwards	Up	Directed to cause	Stiff	High	Moving	Moderate	Moderate	Nicker
Peace	Sideways	Loose	Half closed	Relaxed	Loose	Still	Slack	Slow	Silent
Happiness	Sideways	Up	Half closed	Relaxed	Loose	May move loosely	Moderate	Moderate	Nicker
Enjoyment	Sideways	Loose	Half closed	Relaxed	Raised slightly	May move loosely	Moderate	Slightly faster	Silent
Excitement	Forwards	Up	Directed to cause	Tight	High	Moving	Stiff	Blowing	Silent
Exhaustion	Sideways	Down	Closed	Relaxed	Loose	Flagging	Loose	Heavy	Silent
Submission	Side to back	Pointed out	Half closed	Lips snapping	Flat	Braced	Moderate	Normal	Silent

tranquilliser – which relieves the horse's stress.

As has been shown in laboratory animals, there is a further problem in that the activities so developed tend to become *habits* and to be persisted in even after the stress has been relieved and the circulation of endorphins discontinued. However, by that time, the repetition of the activity has become so automatic that its very prevention causes more stress, and endorphins are once again sought. The cycle is similar to that which is familiar in humans as nail biting, nervous habits and addictions (to tobacco, alcohol or drugs) which may first be taken up to relieve a problem and then cause an even greater problem when attempts are made to give them up.

Stable Vices

by Dominic Prince

Dominic Prince's principal equestrian interests are hunting and racing. He is involved in public relations work in the horse world. Having a particular interest in abnormal behaviour in horses, he undertook, with psychologist Jon Beer, private research funded by the National Race-horse Trainers' Federation. Some of the information in this contribution has appeared in the magazine Pacemaker International.

As a child, I enquired of our veterinary surgeon: 'Why do horses wind-suck?'

'Boredom', he replied. He was older and somewhat wiser than I, so I willingly accepted the fact that all stable vices emanated from boredom. Similarly, one afternoon our farrier was shoeing a particularly troublesome pony who had managed to kick and make life generally unpleasant for several men who were trying to hold her down. Shortly, all parties became bored and tired of playing this rather tedious game and out came the twitch which was fastened to her top lip and tightened. Hey presto, the mis-behaviour stopped immediately. I was told (and had no reason to disbelieve) that the pony had stood still due to the intense pain of the tightening twitch.

At a later date I told my mother of these two explanations for changes in the horses' behaviour. She immediately pooh-poohed them saying, simply, that neither explanation could possibly be true. At the time I preferred to believe the vet and the farrier, and not my mother. This was due partly to an adolescent quirk and partly to my mother knowing very little about horses. She is, however, a very well-thought-of and highly-regarded psych-ologist.

Some years later, having observed stable vices (I use this as a generic term to include wind-sucking, cribbing, box-walking, rug-chewing and weaving) and twitching, I had come to the loathsome conclusion that my mother may well know a thing or two about life that I did not. I grudgingly agreed with her that it

115

was not boredom that induced a stable vice and it was not the pain of the twitch that forbade the horse to play up.

I therefore joined forces with a psychologist called Jon Beer. Jon knows nothing about horses and cares even less for them. My thought was that he would have no 'theories' or prejudices and would treat the subject on a scientific as opposed to an emotional basis. This he did brilliantly.

The problem of vices is a large and expensive one whose existence we, as a nation of horse lovers, are only just beginning to acknowledge. It is a problem that appears to be particularly prevalent in racing yards, and this is where we focused our attentions.

Stable vices cause a great deal of distress, not only to the horse but also to the owner. It is heartbreaking to see a wind-sucker ruin its health. Equally, rug-chewing is an expensive preoccupation that most owners could well afford to live without.

Once a vice has set in, there is very little that can be done. It is, for instance, almost unheard of for a horse to be cured of wind-sucking. Trainers are often reluctant to admit that the stable vice is a problem. One well-known trainer that I visited was loath to accept that any of his horses had a vice. However, after we had been talking for a time it transpired that at least 20 per cent of his horses had a stable vice of some sort. Out of this proportion, he thought that maybe 10 per cent were adversely affected in their performance on the race-track. In other yards I visited, the problem was much greater. Sometimes as many as 35 per cent of the inmates had a vice of some sort.

We do not know what causes these problems, so how can we possibly begin to understand them?

Weaving

Weaving is a bizarre vice in which the horse 'rocks' from foreleg to foreleg, sometimes for hours on end. Again, this is found generally in the stabled horse; I know of no case of a grazing horse that weaves. It is potentially the most damaging of all known vices. Constant swinging on the forelegs causes them to swell, and the animal is, therefore, unable to be put into hard work. In acute cases, the animal will continue to weave even though it is lame. For anyone keeping competition horses the effect on the animal's training programme can be devastating. If

116

the horse is lame it cannot be worked. If the horse is stabled during lameness it will continue to weave which serves to aggravate, not alleviate, the lameness and pain.

If the horse is caught weaving at an early stage it is possible to slow it down and normally in some cases stop it altogether. The horse will start weaving over the stable door. Many people fix an upright plank in the middle of the door, so the horse cannot swing the full length. Alternatively, a brick dangled on a piece of rope often stops the vice, as it swings into the horse every time it is touched. This is rather like employing somebody to stand watch over the horse and hit it on the nose every time it attempts to weave. In extreme cases, the animal will stand in the corner of its box and weave, and there is very little that can be done.

The grazing action of the horse in its natural habitat is to swing from foreleg to foreleg. In this, then, there is constant movement on the retina of the horse's eye and, perhaps more importantly, during its grazing hours it is in constant motion. Stable the horse and it is immediately deprived of the movement natural to it and, perhaps more significantly, the movement on the retina. Clearly, this could answer the question 'Why?'.

Box-walking

Box-walking is perhaps one of the most worrying vices, particularly in terms of danger to humans rather more than any physical damage to the horse. The horse will walk, normally at great speed, round and round its box, irrespective of whether anyone stands in its way or attempts to stop it. The animal, in extreme cases, will continue to walk apace, knocking down and walking over anyone who gets in the way.

The domestic horse will do all it can to avoid treading on a person who is grounded, so why, when it is frenetically box-walking, should it knock people over and tread on them? Perhaps for a short period the horse simply blacks out. This, then, brings an entirely new dimension to vices.

Consider the domestic cat when fed on tinned meat. Although well nourished, it still goes to hunt and play with garden birds and we malign it as being savage. If we try to stop it we are blocking the fundamental secondary drives – its need to hunt, stalk, kill, chew, swallow and digest its prey is not being fulfilled. This occurs similarly with the domestic horse.

Wind-sucking and crib-biting

Many people say that wind-sucking is caused by boredom. One cannot help thinking that it is a very peculiar and specific thing for a horse to do. Boredom would not manifest itself in that way in any other mammal.

Let us consider the feeding behaviour of the horse under relatively natural conditions, that is, grazing in a field. The food available to the horse is coarse and low in nutritional value. The stomach of the horse is small so the animal must eat little and often; virtually all the time (anywhere between 70 and 80 per cent of the horse's time is spent grazing) the stomach is usually well filled.

When the horse is brought into the stable the bulky food is replaced by concentrated, high-energy food. The blood-sugar level of the horse is high without there being a need for continuous cropping by the front teeth, swallowing and distension of the stomach. However, the need to crop, swallow and distend the stomach remains as part of the horse's natural equipment. As with the cat, the actions of natural feeding behaviour will happen autonomously. By feeding the stabled horse high-energy concentrates, we are preventing its secondary drives. Wind-sucking serves to distend the stomach and cribbing can be viewed as a form of cropping with the front teeth. It is no coincidence that wind-sucking usually follows cribbing. It is a natural extension of the secondary drive. Firstly the horse will crop and then the stomach will become distended. We can, therefore, establish a pattern of sorts.

Establishing a pattern to the vice is very important. At first glance there appears to be none, which is hardly surprising as there cannot possibly be a regular pattern in any one yard. It is, however, possible to establish a pattern with a large sample of horses such as in Lambourn or Newmarket.

Once the trainer or owner has recognised that the vice is a problem there are several courses of action open to him. Veterinary surgeons will often recommend an operation on the windpipe of the wind-sucker, but in many cases this is not successful. Again, with the wind-sucker there are several contraptions that can be employed. The muzzle and more popularly the collar, which prevents the horse from flexing his neck to the requisite angle, can be fitted.

But none of these methods eradicate the horse's desire to pursue his vice. Attempting to solve the problem by physical means is rather like pulling out the fingernails of a person who chews them. One cannot blame veterinary surgeons, as they are trained to deal with physical problems, not psychological ailments.

One hard-headed response to the hypothesis just given was that research, however interesting in itself, might not be financially worthwhile. It was, therefore, necessary to inaugurate a pilot survey to assess the extent of the problem.

Assessment

With the assistance of the National Racehorse Trainers' Federation a questionnaire was distributed to fifteen of the country's leading trainers, both flat and National Hunt. Thirteen completed questionnaires were returned, representing 1,033 horses in training. The frequency of the various stable vices is given in Table 1.

Table 1 Frequency of vices

Vice	No of horses	% of horses
Wind-sucking	18	1.7
Crib-biting	26	2.5
Weaving	29	2.8
Box-walking	11	1.1
Rug-chewing	92	8.9

As the figures show, rug-chewing was by far the most common vice – equal to all the others put together. The cost of these vices is harder to assess. The next three questions were designed to find out what, if any, was the financial burden of these vices.

The first of these questions asked the trainers to estimate the annual cost of damage to property caused by horses with stable vices; that is, chewed rugs, splintered stable doors, damage to stalls and so on. The total from trainers representing 755 horses was £4,200 or an average of £6 per horse per annum. Several trainers said most of the sum went on replacing chewed rugs. The cost of the other vices was negligible. Although these figures are only estimates, they seem of the right order. An average of one rug per annum for the 9 per cent of rug-chewers would be in the order of £4–5,000.

Another question asked whether horses with vices were more prone to illness than other horses; increased vet's bills might be another cost. Surprisingly, every trainer reported that there was no difference.

The third question asked whether horses with a vice were more difficult to train. Forty per cent said there was no difference, 60 per cent said that a horse with a vice is more difficult to train – but not much more (an alternative response on the questionnaire). We will return to this difference later.

With the possible exception of this difference in the difficulty of training, it does not appear that the financial burden of a vice is very great – but there is another way of looking at this cost. The final question in the survey asked the respondents to estimate 'the values of a horse with each of the following vices'. Three respondents did not answer this, but the replies of the other ten, representing 755 horses, were remarkably consistent in the relative cost of the various types of vices – the cost of each vice is measured as the drop in value from £10,000. The results are given in Table 2.

Table 2 Drop in value of horses with stable vices

Vice	Average estimated value £
None	10,000
Wind-sucking	5,000
Crib-biting	5,600
Weaving	7,800
Box-walking	6,700
Rug-chewing	9,900

These estimates are remarkable compared to the direct costs of vice as reported in answers to the previous questions. Rug-chewing accounted for the most damage to property and yet produced the least fall in value. (Only one trainer thought the value would be affected at all.) No trainer thought that a vice would produce significantly higher veterinary bills and yet the value of these horses falls between a quarter and a half.

Perhaps the answer lies in the difference in training difficulty reported by 60 per cent of the trainers. In that case we might expect that trainers who considered the training more difficult would give a lower estimate of value for a horse with a vice. We compared the estimates of these trainers with those who reported no difference in difficulty of training.

Table 3 Estimated drop in horses' values according to related training difficulties

Vice	'No difference in training' £	'More difficult to train' £
None	10,000	10,000
Wind-sucking	5,400	5,100
Crib-biting	5,400	5,750
Weaving	7,750	7,800
Box-walking	6,200	7,000
Rug-chewing	10,000	9,800

It is clear from Table 3 that there is no significant difference in the estimates of these two groups of trainers. We are left then with an obvious question. Why does a horse worth £10,000 fall to a value of, say, £5,600 because it crib-bites? The reported damage to property is negligible, there is no difference in susceptibility to illness and any difference in the difficulty of training does not seem to affect the drop in value. There could be (at least) two explanations. First, it may be that the drop in value reflects some large expense in training or upkeep that I failed to encompass in the questions. Second, and perhaps more likely, it could be that these estimated falls in value are not justified on purely financial grounds. It may be that a horse with a vice is a bargain in the light of these findings.

Twitching

During the early 1980s, some revolutionary research took place which proves conclusively that my blacksmith was wrong with regard to the twitch.

Until such time as the research took place (at the University of Utrecht in The Netherlands) it was universally agreed that the pain of the twitch was so intense that the horse had to behave. This explanation did not take into account the fact that the pain in the upper lip should still upset the horse, even if it did distract from pain or inconvenience elsewhere.

The Dutchmen looked at the phenomenon again in the

knowledge that the human brain can manufacture, at will, chemical substances known as endorphins. Endorphins are pain-killers that are one hundred times as effective as morphine. It was found that when a horse was twitched the body furiously pumped endorphins through the bloodstream.

However, this was not conclusive evidence. What was needed was a block of some sort to counteract the endorphins. A drug called Naloxone is often used in the treatment of heroin addicts. The drug 'blocks' the effect of heroin.

Endorphins are also rendered completely ineffective by Naloxone. The next step was to twitch the horse and then inject it with the drug. Sure enough, it was found that if the twitched horse was injected with Naloxone it became agitated again. The implications of the discovery are extraordinary. One might have a reliable guide as to whether or not an animal is unhappy by finding out what happens when it is given Naloxone.

And pigs too

These two matters, stable vices and twitching, appear at first to be unrelated – until one considers the work done with pigs.

Pigs kept in battery farms have a very similar vice to the one we see in horses. They chew and gnaw the bars of their stalls. However, when injected with Naloxone they stop doing it. The implication is that when they chew and gnaw at the bars they are producing endorphins. The Naloxone blocks the endorphins and in turn the bar-chewing stops.

The suggestion, then, is that far from being bored the horse with a stable vice is, in fact, on a constant high. This, of course, is hypothesis and will need to be tried and tested in the field. Whether the theory is correct, I know not. However, one feels that this is nearer the mark than the stock answer of boredom.

With vast sums of money being spent on the purchase of blood-stock and equally large sums lost when horses are returned (precisely because they are found to have a stable vice), it is time that funds were made available for some detailed research.

Transporting the Horse

by Dr Sharon E. Cregier, FIASH (Hon, Edin)

Dr Sharon Cregier has, for the past fourteen years, studied the effects of transporting horses in different kinds of conveyance. Her doctoral disser- tation for an American university was on this very subject. A horse owner herself, she has found that her experience and research concurs with that of independent researchers and horsemen in other countries, namely that conveyances which enable the horse to travel with his tail to the engine, in other words looking away *from the direction of travel, cause the least distress and, therefore, the fewest problems for horses and handlers. Here, she explains why.*

It is a familiar scene around the world. Horses asked to enter a conventional horsebox or trailer often baulk. They show un- willingness by kicking, striking, rearing and head-tossing, to mention a few of the signs of resistance. Once in the trailer, a horse can rush backwards, beneath the restraining bar, to injure itself or its handler. Horses have been known to fall through the rear doors of the trailer and be dragged or trapped.

One horse insurance company in the United States reports that thousands of horses are injured or killed each year on their way to competitive or pleasure events. In Great Britain, a volunteer rescue squad ('Motorway Rescue') under the aegis of the British Horse Society is organised to cope with the increasing number of accidents involving horses and their transport.

My research and experimentation has convinced me that *all* horses, not just a few so-called 'problem' horses, suffer discom- fort and pain when transported in conventional horseboxes and trailers in which they are positioned head-to-the-engine, ie facing the direction of travel.

The horse does not normally, from choice, enter narrow, dark areas such as a trailer or horsebox. This is often when the trouble starts. Even with young horses, patience often runs out and the handlers resort to various forceful means of 'persuading' the

123

horse to load. Buckets of food, titbits and maybe even the previous loading of a friend having failed, first of all a hand may be patted on the tail, then slapped quite hard, firmly spoken commands from the rear are heard and then the whip comes out, just a tap at first but, if that doesn't do the trick, some people have no hesitation in actually thrashing the horse. This, as any thinking horseman knows, will do little except increase resistance and form an association in the horse's mind – loading means fear and pain – compounding trouble for the future. As a last resort, and sometimes before the whip, the lungeing reins are brought out, fastened each to one side of the trailer, crossed behind the horse's thighs and the horse is pushed, normally in terror, inside the vehicle.

More considerate handlers will previously train the horse, perhaps by standing the empty vehicle, ramp down and with the sun shining inside, so that the horse can satisfy his curiosity as to this strange object. Then feed might be given on the ramp and ultimately inside. The horse will be led in and out of the vehicle, taken for short rides and gradually accustomed to the whole process. If the driver is competent and considerate, the horse may simply accept the situation, although disliking it, but, depending on his temperament, he may, for no reason which is apparent to his human connections, begin to play up either during transport or loading, and become a 'bad traveller'.

Travelling problems: behavioural and physical signs
The horse's structure is such that most of his weight and also his centre of gravity are in the forequarters. His hindquarters are his engine, his power source. The horse is, therefore, designed for forward movement. Maintaining that forward movement is the pubio-femoral ligament, which holds the hip joint tightly within the hip socket. When the horse is forced to place a hind leg to one side, as he must do in conventional travel to maintain balance on his hindquarters, an unnatural strain is placed on this ligament, resulting in discomfort and ultimately pain.

The horse's neck weight is maintained during rest at wither level by the tireless elastic action of the ligament running down the top of the neck from poll to withers, the *ligamentum nuchae*. But if he wishes to raise his head much above wither level, as he is forced to do when travelling facing forward, his neck and head must be supported by muscles. These muscles tire without frequent rest.

The horse's ribcage has no bony joints with shoulders or forelegs keeping it in place, but is slung into position by many ligaments and other soft tissues, a structure known as the 'thoracic sling'. This acts very much like the gimbal on a ship, helping the horse to maintain stability over the roughest ground.

In contrast to the forequarters, the hindquarters are comparatively light as they were not intended to carry weight so much as to propel. This is one reason why horses are not expected to perform collected dressage movements, in which the hindquarters carry more weight (plus the weight of the rider) than normal, until their training has gradually accustomed and conditioned the muscles and other soft tissues to do so.

Once a horse is loaded and under way, facing the direction of travel, his instincts and anatomy tell him that he is in danger. He feels as though the ground is being pulled from back to front beneath him, just like a rug pulled back to front from under a person. Although we cannot compare the anatomy of men and horses in this respect, because they are so different, a rough analogy may clarify the abnormality of forward-facing equine transport.

If you are on an escalator but want to stand still, you will have difficulty keeping your balance. Even though the escalator may move smoothly at constant speed, department store management realise the danger and put up notices warning you to 'hold the moving handrail', knowing very well that you might fall if you do not. In a way something like this, a horse is threatened with loss of balance when facing the direction of travel in a moving horsebox or trailer. In response to this sensation, he leans backwards and places an unnatural and stressful amount of weight on the hindquarters. Some horses will try to escape the sensation of falling backwards by leaping ahead of the motion. Thus it is not unusual for horses to be found wedged in the manger or escape door area of a conventional trailer.

In addition, the horse must attempt to protect his head from being thrown, at the original rate of speed of the conveyance, towards the front of the trailer when the trailer brakes or changes direction. He anticipates this impact by holding his head up and back, a cramped, tiring position.

The largest number of horse trailer injuries seen by one Guelph, Ontario, veterinarian are those to the horse's head, throat and chest. To protect the horse during such travel the handler must provide poll guards, tail bandages and leg bandages or protectors.

The strain on the horse's anatomy and physiology is revealed in loose droppings, energetic mouthing activities (orosthenia) such as biting of equine transit companions, rapid snatching at food or chewing wooden fixtures, loss of muscle tone, height increases of 0.2cm (1/10in) to 10cm (4in) and many attempts to see what is behind him.

Also highly significant is the rise in heart rate. Horses travelling facing forward register pulse rates of 56 to 68 beats per minute. As equine veterinary surgeons and experienced horsemen know, this is the pulse rate of a horse close to panic. The normal rate of a horse at ease is about 36 to 44 beats a minute.

Possibly more significant than the risk of physical injury is the constant anxiety which my research and experience show is invariably suffered by the horse when facing the direction of travel. The horse is believed to be the most hypersensitive of large animals, and the effect of such trauma on him can easily be appreciated. Horses so transported are often stiff, exhausted, dehydrated and generally unwell on arrival at their destination. Horses regularly travelled this way suffer trailer fits, laminitis, transport fever, choke, colic, azoturia and hypertension. Often these illnesses are fatal. The muscular effort to maintain balance should be considered a contributing factor to myositis (cramping) of the back muscles and to sacroiliac and sacrolumbar strain.

Blood tests on transported horses reveal significantly increased packed cell volume, a drop in calcium levels, a rise in cortisol and glucose levels and a rise in serum creatinine and a highly significant (five chances out of a thousand of such an increase occurring without the transport factor) increase in creatinine phosphokinase levels associated with muscular exhaustion.

Effect on towing vehicle
The conventional, forward-facing position of the horse is not much good for the trailer driver, either, although the horsebox

driver will have fewer problems in this respect. The horse's attempts to maintain balance actually endanger the trailer and towing vehicle. By throwing his weight towards the rear, the horse can accidentally raise the trailer hitch off its ball, interfere with steering, contribute to jack-knifing and make braking difficult and dangerous. As the horse's centre of gravity is not near the trailer's centre of gravity, the horse's weight cannot help to reduce sway.

Current practice

All the problems mentioned, and more (weight loss, rupture of the uterine arteries in pregnant mares), result from asking the horse to accommodate himself to whatever conventional transport we offer.

Transporters usually respond by treating the symptoms, rather than the causes, of distress. Higher head room is provided in trailers to accommodate the upflung head, coercion is used such as halters with nut-cracker action on jaw or poll specifically developed for the 'hard-to-load' horse, and the use of protective equipment is advised such as padded poll guards, tail bandages, leg protectors, knee pads, hock boots and even chemical sedation.

The solution

The forward weight carriage and the steadying gimbal action of the thoracic sling described earlier are negated in conventional transport. Such transport, as we have seen, forces the horse to balance unnaturally on his hindquarters.

On a world-wide basis, trailers and horseboxes have only recently been purposely designed to help maintain the horse's effortless, natural balance. This is achieved by their being constructed so that the horses face *away* from the direction of travel. The horses so transported arrive at their destination without muscle fatigue or other associated problems. Even after non-stop journeys of 1,930km (1,200 miles), horses entered in endurance trials, cross-country and dressage events have arrived within an hour of their class and ready to compete. And win. In one study, over 500 horses in various stages of competitive readiness have been thus travelled.

The interior front of these conveyances, near the hitch, is left quite smooth and featureless. Its sameness, and the lack of all activity in the area, over the course of introductory rides is a reassuring factor for the horse. And there is no reason to fear sudden stops making a flying missile of the horse's heavy but extremely sensitive head. The horse relaxes his neck muscles and ceases to carry his neck unnaturally high. He leans over his forequarters and maintains his balance naturally. The ground now feels to the horse to be moving naturally beneath him, from front to back.

Such a natural balance leaves the partitions and walls of the trailer free of scramble marks because the horse has no longer any need to scramble to keep his balance. If a sudden stop occurs, he simply leans further forward over his forequarters, away from the point of impact at the front of the trailer. At worst, only his fleshy rump, rather than his fragile and sharp-angled head, will absorb the shock.

Design modifications

To accommodate the weight change of cargo placement in the trailer, the axles are moved about 1.2m (4ft) forward from their position in most conventional trailers. The axle change places the trailer's centre of gravity closer to that of most tow vehicles and directly beneath the horse's centre of gravity as he stands at ease.

The change facilitates emergency braking. The design of the rear-face trailer, in fact, makes it the only horse trailer in the world which can stop on a dry road within 9m at 32kph (30ft at 20mph) with the least probability of jack-knifing the trailer or upsetting the horses.

During transit, the horse maintains his weight over his fore-quarters (which is the normal manner of a sound horse), lowers his head and travels with one or the other hind leg in a resting position. This is quite unlike the straddling and bracing which horses subjected to conventional transport must do. In addition, male horses can comfortably urinate at will during transit.

In one type of rear-face trailer, the horse is led up onto a low-loading platform (level with the floor of the trailer), turned and backed into the trailer. Such a manoeuvre is not foreign or difficult to a horse. It is frequently utilised by knowledgeable harness horsemen when putting their animals to the shafts of a carriage or sulky. In this instance, the horse is brought beneath the shafts from the side, parallel to the front of the wagon, turned, and the shafts are dropped into place as the horse steps back.

Because the horse is backed into the trailer, using non-coercive methods – rather than led in using often forcible methods – the handler remains in a safe position. The horse's instinctive aversion to dark places is not aroused and he has nothing to fear from behind him.

The horse's lead rope on his headcollar is tied to a ring fixed directly opposite his withers. This allows the horse to raise and lower his head, in automatic response to the movements of the conveyance, as he effortlessly balances. In addition, the horse can now readily lower his head to clear his respiratory passages at will, a necessary part of his behaviour to ward off pleuropneumonia (transport fever).

Some horsemen, however, prefer a walk-through type of rear-face trailer. The horses are loaded into the trailer from ramps at either front side. Unlike the platform loading method described above, this rear-face trailer retains some aspects of conventional design. It utilises a restraining bar behind the horses, requiring activity in the horses' blind spot. These designs may retain the windows, now behind the horses. Shadows and lights playing on these windows could increase the nervousness of more reactive animals.

In both types of trailer, horses may be unloaded one or two at a time by one person. The loading platform in the former trailer converts to a ramp for unloading. There is obviously none of the unavoidable apprehension and difficulty that the horse suffers when he is expected to back down the ramp, which, in itself, places an unnatural amount of weight on the quarters. More important than the fleeting weight transfer there is the danger to the horse's pasterns, coronet, and fetlocks when stepping backwards and down a ramp. Veterinary surgeons commonly report trailer injuries to this area.

Conventional conversions
Some conventional trailers can be converted to rear-face travel but it is wise to check the road transport laws of your country before doing so. Generally, trailers at least 165cm (5ft 3in) wide and 284.4cm (9ft 4in) long can be converted to a single entry/exit

balanced transport. The front of the trailer is sealed and rendered featureless. A loading platform which converts to a ramp to unload, and is at least 132cm (52in) long, replaces the conventional trailer's entry system.

The axles of the conventional trailer to be converted are moved forward until a nose weight of between 40.8kg (90lb) and 49.4kg (110lb), with the trailer loaded to capacity, is registered.

Some of the features of the advanced transport can, with care, be utilised by horsemen with conventional transport. For example, horses difficult to load into conventional transport can often be induced to enter provided the conventional ramp is raised level with the entry. The steadiest such improvised platform is obtained by reversing the conventional trailer towards a low rise in the ground and supporting the ramp, at entry level, on the rise. The horse is then led straight in on the level ramp.

A bad traveller can sometimes be travelled in a conventional trailer with the partitions removed. In this instance, the tie-ring at the front is at the roadcrown side of the highway. This allows the horse to stand diagonally in the trailer and to face away from the impact area. The bulk of the horse's weight is maintained away from the soft edge of the road, where such road construction applies.

In virtually all cases, the recommended footing material is 15cm (6in) of slightly damp sawdust. The depth and dampness afford a cradling action to the hooves, increasing the horse's feeling of security.

Driving tactics
The adverse effects of forward-facing transport would be greatly reduced if the horse could be travelled on a perfectly smooth road at an absolutely constant speed with no acceleration, braking or cornering. Of course, this is impossible in practice, but the aim is to achieve such conditions as nearly as possible. The driver should keep much more distance than normal between his vehicle and the one in front so that should the vehicle ahead brake the driver will have sufficient time to also brake gently and so avoid lurching the horse forward. Similarly with accelerating; this should be done very gradually (with extra care taken to ensure smooth gear changes: jerky ones play havoc with the horse's balance) so that the horse's weight is not thrown onto the

quarters. Corners, bends and roundabouts must be taken very slowly to avoid swinging the horse to the sides of the box and back when he straightens up again. The security of the horse is increased where the driver handles the towing vehicle as though it had no brakes. Thinking 'no brakes' produces far smoother traffic manoeuvres.

Smoothness can also be monitored by a glass of water fixed to a level area within eyesight of the driver or his companion. Should the water rise above a 1.27cm (½in) mark above the water level during a steering or braking manoeuvre, the equine passenger has received a rough ride. Expert drivers can complete a journey without the water rising above a 0.64cm line above the water level.

Although a horse can travel comfortably side-on to the direction of travel (provided there is enough room for his head and neck, and he is not cramped into a too-narrow vehicle), this position does not reduce the horse's vulnerability to injury should the transport brake hard or be involved in a barrier collision.

Caution!

It must be emphasised that simply backing a horse into a conventional trailer can be potentially dangerous for the horse. The additional weight over the already rearward axle placement increases the conveyance's potential for jack-knifing and sway. Only the specially designed rear-face trailers are built to accommodate the motor vehicle's, and the horse's, functional integrity.

Note: For the purposes of this book, its author, Susan McBane, contacted thirty British trailer manufacturers to ask if they could, or would, be able to supply or be willing to make to order a rear-face trailer. Very few replied but the following four companies expressed a willingness to co-operate.

Equiluxe, Cherry Tree Farm, Barton Bendish, King's Lynn, Norfolk, PE33 9DJ, tel. Fincham (03664) 229.

J & B Towing Trailer Centre, Cottismore Farm, Kingsclere, Newbury, Berkshire, RG15 8SY, tel. Kingsclere (0635) 298928.

Sinclair Trailers, Wargate Bridge, Gosberton, Spalding, Lincolnshire, PE11 4HH, tel. Spalding (0775) 840442/840640.

Trail West, 3 Mill Lane, Lochavullin Industrial Estate, Oban, Argyll, PA34 4EX, tel. Oban (0631) 63638.

Dr Cregier has provided the names and addresses of these manufacturers in other countries.

About Face, 1975 Bee Canyon Road, Arroyo Grande, California 93420, USA, tel. 805-489-5454.

Taylor Industries, Box 997, Melfort, Saskatchewan, Canada, SOE 1AO, tel. 306-752-9212.

Stratford Motor Body Builders, Stratford, New Zealand.

PART III
PROBLEM DICTIONARY

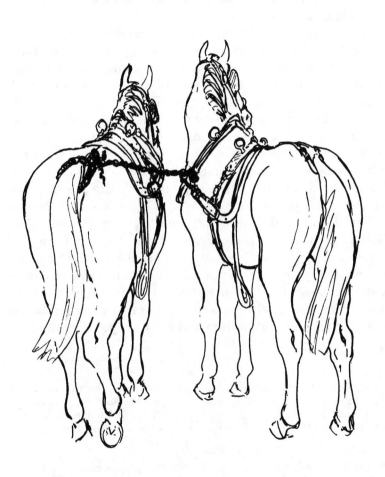

Back, refusing to

Backing is one of the elementary things a horse must learn as part of his general education, no matter what his job in life. Important though it is, many experts believe it should not be taught before the horse is reasonably obedient under saddle – say, about five years of age – as, if taught before then, and before obedience is more or less a habit, the horse may cotton on that it can be used as an evasion.

An equal number of people, however, believe that backing should be taught in very young animals as part of their stable manners, and it seems to be true that a horse who will back readily during stable attentions does not, as a general rule, think of doing so as an evasion under saddle or in harness. If the youngster *is* taught to back on command it will be quite easy to teach him to do so later under saddle.

The following procedure might be followed. Stand in front but slightly to one side of your horse. Put your hand on his breast, push fairly hard and simultaneously say 'back'. He probably will not respond at first but after three or four pushes, each accompanied by the word 'back', he may well take a step back, when you should immediately praise him and ask no more. If he does not react to this, do it again and tap on his nearest front coronet with the toe of your boot. He is almost certain to instinctively raise that leg away from the pressure; while the leg is in the air, push and command again – it would be very surprising if he did not take a step back. Praise him and leave the task for the time being.

(top right)
The headcollar lead rope can be passed over the nose like this for extra restraint, provided one remembers that too much pressure not only causes discomfort but will restrict breathing, horses being unable to breathe through their mouths. Both of these can make horses more fractious, not less

(top left)
An ideal state of trust, when a horse will submit to prolonged and somewhat uncomfortable attentions like shoeing with no restraint at all. The open door was not simply for the benefit of the camera

When leading a difficult horse, a lungeing cavesson over the bridle gives added control by enabling pressure to be exerted on the front of the nose, particularly if the cavesson is fitted a little lower than this one. Two handlers may be necessary, one holding the reins and the other a lead rope attached to the cavesson

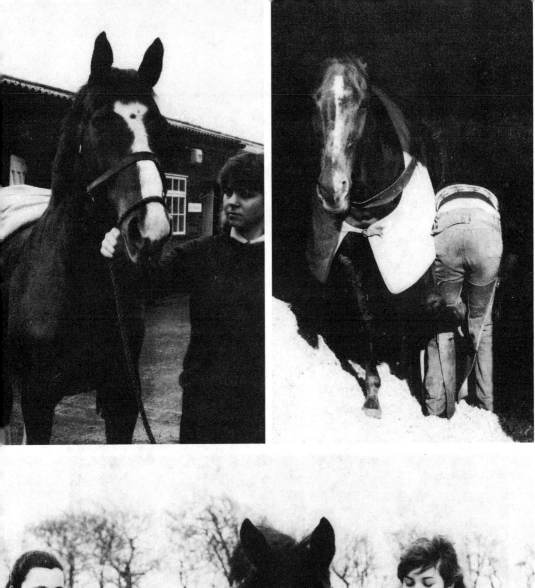
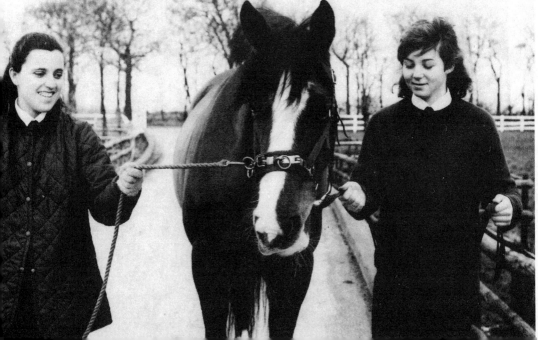

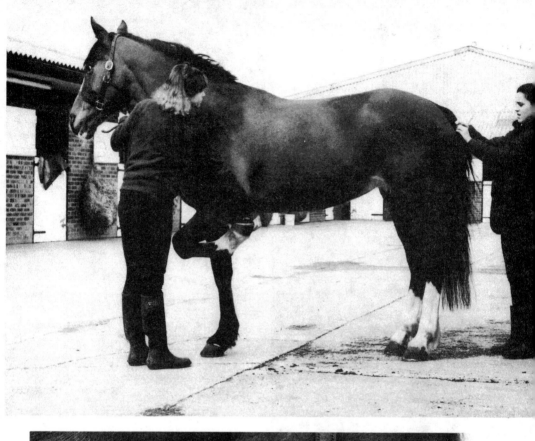

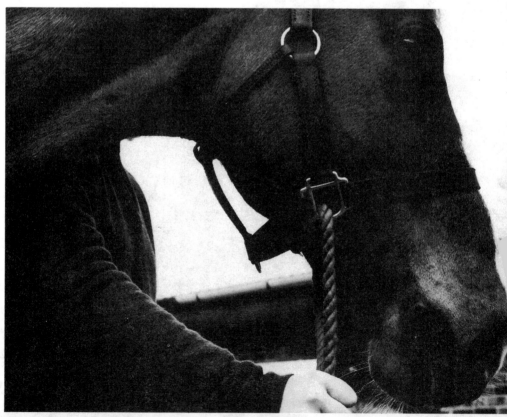

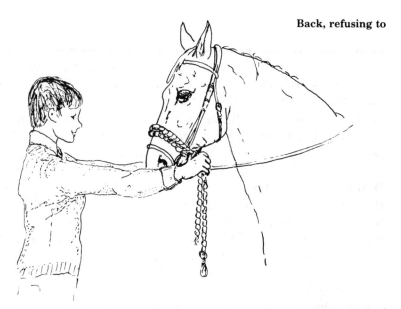

Fig 23 A single or double rope over the nose, pressed backwards and combined with the command 'back', often shows a horse just what you want him to do. The rider should give conventional aids from the saddle

Another method is to stand in front of him and pass a length of rope over his nose mid-way between nostrils and eyes, and, with a gentle sawing motion, exert pressure there, saying 'back', of course, as you do so. Not many horses will put up with such pressure on a sensitive area like the nose and front of the face, and he should instinctively move back away from it. In difficult cases, there is nothing to stop you, if you have an assistant, using all three methods at once.

Obviously, you should make sure that the horse has plenty of room to go back. Let him tilt his head a little to one side so he can see there is nothing behind which is going to hurt him.

If you cannot succeed by the above methods, you must consider the fact that the horse could have some injury, perhaps to the

---

Holding up a foreleg, flexed so that the horse cannot lean his weight on to the handler without discomfort in the joints, is a fairly effective and mild form of restraint for uncomfortable procedures such as having a tail pulled

Another way to obtain slightly more restraint from an ordinary headcollar and lead rope is to pass the rope through one side D, under the jaw and out through the D on the other side. This exerts all-round pressure on the nose and jaw. The effect can be increased by fitting the headcollar with its noseband lower than this one

back, which is making it painful for him to perform the movement. The horse should have his head down and his weight on his forehand to back effortlessly, so if you have his head up in the air and the weight on the quarters he is going to have much more difficulty. Sometimes, lifting a back leg (the one furthest forward) and putting it back for him helps the penny drop, but if all fails, call in the vet for a physical examination.

Bad manners in work

Bad manners in work comprise a refusal to stand still to be mounted, general fidgeting, disregarding rider's/driver's requests, paying too little attention to work and too much to other horses or surrounding distractions, obvious attempts to 'insult' the rider such as brushing him or her against trees etc, and similar behaviour patterns.

Depending on the action performed, bad manners during work can result from poor initial training, weak horsemanship and general lack of discipline. They can also be caused by discomfort and pain such as from tack or harness, or poor riding or driving. Simple thoughtlessness can also cause them; expecting a stallion to go in line behind a mare in season is an example, as is expecting two enemies to work together.

The best cure for general poor behaviour is for the trainer to reschool the animal in a calm, consistent, determined and patient way, reprimanding vocally at first when the horse or pony does something which is not required but, if necessary, physically (probably by moderate use of the whip and never, whatever the offence, by jerking at the bit) should vocal reprimands not work. Not a single instance should go by without it being made plain to the animal that this is not allowed. As in all cases of reward and punishment, it is useless to reprimand a horse when he does something wrong on one occasion but not on another; this simply confuses the horse, who then cannot be expected to know what is required of him.

See also *Handle, difficult to.*

Banging door of stable

This is an infuriating habit for humans to have to put up with but it must be equally infuriating for the horse because if there were nothing bothering him he would not do it. Horses who are content with their management very rarely show signs of annoyance or frustration to any great extent.

Every effort should be made to stop door-banging – and the horse's contentment is only one, if very important, reason. Horses certainly injure their forelegs through this habit. Bruised, swollen and maybe permanently 'big' knees and fetlocks can result, causing lameness. Jarred feet can occur, too. And one must take account of damaged woodwork, strained hinges, loosened door bolts and also severe disturbance to the other occupants of the yard, human and equine.

As with most stable vices and problem behaviour, the mere physical stopping of the practice does not solve the underlying problem, ie why is the horse doing it? Horses bang their doors because they are impatient at feed times, because companions, particularly close friends or even human associates with whom they have a close rapport, are going out when they are not, because they are bored or hungry, because they want attention and because they are of the type who cannot tolerate over-confinement. It has been particularly noticeable to me that many 'bangers' (for want of a better word) mainly bang first thing in the morning and on their days off. Surely this proves that long periods of time without activity or food, such as occur at night and on rest days, can easily drive horses to distraction. Horses, remember, are athletic, nomadic animals needing freedom and movement; they are also, by nature, creatures who eat for about three-quarters of their time and who never, left to their own free will, spend several hours without eating as we often force stabled horses to do, particularly at night. A check in most stables at midnight will show most of the hay gone, yet the horse is not due to be fed again until next morning, a most unnatural state of affairs for him.

The remedy for door-banging is, of course, to remove the cause wherever possible. Tactics such as shutting the top door or fitting a grille to prevent the horse getting close enough to the door to bang it obviously work physically, but they do not alter the horse's state of mind. He might well begin to paw the floor of his box or use his hind feet instead of his front.

If the horse only bangs occasionally under certain circumstances, shutting his door or closing the grille may be resorted to for a short period (eg while his friend is taken out, the door being opened again as soon as the friend is out of sight). If the horse mainly bangs at feed time, feed him first. If he bangs first thing in the morning, ensure that he has more hay at night to last him until the small hours, then he will not get so bored and desperately hungry. If he bangs on his day off, or indiscriminately at any time, his general management is obviously not suited to him as an individual. He needs more freedom, more exercise, perhaps more judicious hard work.

Horses who feel insecure when confined, especially for long periods (and there are more of them than perhaps we appreciate), should only be stabled when absolutely essential. They would probably be much happier, and do better, if yarded with a covered shelter area, or living out, depending on circumstances.

Barging

Having half a ton of horse come charging at you when you open his stable door is no joke, nor is being dragged through the doorway when you try to lead a horse in or out of his stable. Both habits are disconcerting for inexperienced people, dangerous and possibly painful if you get crushed against the door jamb and the horse escapes on to a road. (Stabling should be erected within an inner walled or fenced yard to which the gate is kept closed, then if a horse does escape he will not be able to go anywhere he shouldn't.)

In cases which occur when the horse is being led, he is worried about going through and wishes to get it over with. Such horses have been hurt by banging their hips when passing through the entrance or by banging their heads on the lintel. Some, who have been hurt when, say, going in, have no qualms about going out or of going through other doorways, but others develop a fear of all doorways and even gateways.

Such horses need stables with high, wide entrances; the usual 1.4m (4ft 6in) wide and 2.3m (7ft 6in) high is insufficient for them. Rollers or, cheaper, padding can be fitted down the sides just in case. The handler should also be certain that the horse is led in and out perfectly straight. Where a horse is frightened of hitting his head on the lintel, encourage him to hold his head low by offering a titbit level with his elbows while walking through. These measures often greatly reduce the problem.

Meanwhile the horse must learn that this behaviour is not

wanted. Lead him in and out in a cavesson or bridle as these give more control, although the horse should never be jabbed at with rope or reins as he might throw up his head, injure himself and become more convinced than ever that he is going to get hurt every time he goes through the doorway.

Be calm and firm. Wear leather gloves and hold the rope/reins securely (without, of course, wrapping them round your wrist). Lead the horse expectantly towards the doorway talking in a soothing, confident voice. If he attempts to barge, use one word he associates with calming down, such as 'easy' or 'steady', and tap him firmly on the breast with hand or stick, taking a contact with his head through rope or reins as well. Do this with each step he tries to rush. Do not shout and do not make a big issue out of it or he will worry all the more. Praise him as soon as any improvement is shown. Hitting the horse on the nose is certainly not advocated as it will make him throw up his head, as will jabbing at the bit, and make him headshy or cause an injury on the lintel.

Fig 24 A removable bar placed across the entrance allows the horse to see out when the door is shut but prevents him charging out when it is opened. Just remember to duck under it when you go in!

In cases where the horse barges out of bad manners and bossiness, cajoling is not the answer. He must be shown that he is not allowed to treat you like a stuffed dummy. Again, headgear such as a cavesson, bridle (or both) or a patent headcollar which exerts a tightening pressure round the nose and on the poll (such as the 'Be Nice' headcollar sold by many saddlers) should be fitted. Wear leather gloves and tie a knot in the end of the lead rope. Carry a stick. Act as though he is going to behave but the instant he dives forward pull hard on the rope, hit him *once* but smartly across the breast with the stick and growl firmly 'no' or 'whoa', all at the same time. If you can station someone outside ready to get in his way, with a stick, this combination will be almost sure to stop him, and improve him in time.

Where the horse comes at you when you open the stable door, his head may be the only part you can reach, but one good smack on the side (preferably) of the nose with the stick should stop him and send him back. Again, accompany it with the word 'no'. Provided the horse obeys, there is no point whatever hitting him more than once or keeping on growling at him. Immediately behave normally, otherwise he might simply become bitter and have good cause for coming at you.

Incidentally, many top (not necessarily famous) establishments insist that all horses be taught to stand up to attention at the back of their boxes whenever people enter, usually to a certain command such as 'away' or 'stand up'. This is most impressive (and reassuring to non-horsey visitors) and the horse can quickly be 'stood at ease' again when wanted by general chat, stroking and/or a familiar command such as 'easy'.

See also *Stable manners, bad; Trampling.*

Bedding, eating

Horses who eat their bedding are normally suffering from an inadequate amount of bulky roughage in their diet or from a diet too high in rich, concentrated feed. Any straw bedding is liable to be nibbled at, but if the bed is disappearing in significant quantities the amount, quality and type of roughage fed should be reassessed and the proportion of concentrates probably decreased.

Horses usually stop eating straw if their hay or hayage is of good, clean quality and palatable to them. If a horse has recently been put on to hayage instead of hay for any reason, and the change has been sudden, he may well leave the unfamiliar hayage in preference to straw. Mixing the hayage in small amounts with his hay ration and gradually effecting a complete changeover over a period of two or three weeks often overcomes this problem, apart from being good feeding practice.

It is, of course, easy to stop him eating edible bedding like straw by changing over to inedible bedding like shavings, but this is not the answer. We should aim at stopping him *wanting* to eat straw and in almost every case this will come about by correcting the diet.

Should the horse eat inedible bedding or chew his stable excessively, this can be a sign of severe digestive disorder and veterinary help should be sought. However, youngsters often chew wood when teething.

Bedding, scraping around

Disturbed bedding can be a sign of the horse's feeling cold (insufficient clothing/draughty stable), uncomfortable (rugs which have slipped or fit badly), in pain (colic) or having been disturbed (rats in the stable or other unwanted visitors to the yard at unaccustomed times). It is also a sign of general restlessness, brought about commonly by lack of or inadequate exercise, by strange surroundings or by general unhappiness, lack of friendly company etc, and, indeed, by being stabled next to an enemy.

Horses put on to a different type of bedding material often play about with it for a while until they get used to it and those stabled on earth floors sometimes develop the habit of digging in them.

Generally, horses who have a calm and happy routine, with plenty of activity and interest in their lives, do not disturb their bedding unduly but if the habit seems to be catching hold, look for the cause, as suggested above, and remove it. A disturbed bed with scrape marks up the walls of the stable often denotes a bout of colic or a horse having been cast, so these two circumstances should also be considered if the disturbance is an isolated incident.

Bit, above the

A horse is said to be above the bit when he goes with his nose poking out noticeably and, often, his head held high so that the bit is acting more on the corners of his mouth than anywhere else. In fact, this way of going is unnatural and uncomfortable for the horse. Because of the anatomy of the neck, which is slung into its normal position by a very strong ligament (the *ligamentum nuchae*) attached at the poll, travelling along the top of the neck and attaching at the wither area, the natural propensity for the head is to hang downwards in the position the horse adopts when unhampered by a bridle and bit in use.

Horses only go above the bit when they are afraid of and resistant to the action of the bit in their mouths. They do not adopt this posture from choice because it is uncomfortable. It is obviously, therefore, the fault of the rider or driver, or because of mishandling in the past, if a horse goes in this way out of real or anticipated discomfort.

Apart from tactful handling of the bit, and maybe a change to a different, probably milder one, correct horsemanship is needed, the horse being ridden mainly with seat and legs and a reliably even (not inconsistent, jabbing) contact with the bit through the reins. Keeping up a 'conversation' down the reins, with little vibrations and squeezes aimed at encouraging him to relax his jaw and lower his head, is often the way to help such a horse adopt a more comfortable head carriage. Forcing the head down with standing martingales, draw reins, side reins and other gadgets is not recommended, although the judicious use of such equipment is said by some experts to be useful in the early stages of reschooling simply to get the idea over to the horse that it really is more comfortable to go with his head in a natural position and to reassure him that he is not going to get a painful jab in the mouth when he is working. After the objective has been achieved, however, the equipment should be discarded so that the horse does not come to rely on it (particularly the standing martingale) and so develop the wrong muscles.

See also *Stargazing*

Biting, nipping or 'snatching'

This habit is most common in entire (uncastrated) males as it is one of the ways in which they exert their superiority over rivals

144

and mares. In such horses, it is their way of doing the same to us, on the whole, but in all horses it can also be a sign of aggression or defence. It can be triggered off by rough grooming, or tightening the girth or roller too much and too quickly, causing girth galls, pinched skin etc. Biting is accompanied usually by laid-back ears and a sour expression on the face.

Punishment for biting, as for any other offence, has to be given instantly for the horse to associate the punishment with the action. An acquaintance of mine managed this perfectly by buying two wire dog-grooming mits and sewing them to the sleeves of an old jacket he wore for stable work. When the horse in question turned and made contact, his muzzle received a most uncomfortable prick from the mit and he effectively punished himself instantaneously. He eventually stopped the habit, particularly once he realised he was not going to be hurt by his new owner.

Horses who are nervous rather than nasty should be treated kindly and with understanding but must still be shown that biting is not allowed. Wear protective clothing (a thick jacket rather than a thin jumper or shirt) and leather gloves. When a nervous horse offers to nip, simply say 'no' in a firm but not loud voice and push his head away firmly with your hand – not near the mouth as this gives him something to aim at. Do this every time without fail, and always be sure you do nothing to give him cause to nip, paying particular attention when adjusting his girth or roller.

With a nasty horse, the dog-mit method may well work. Another is to carry a rigid stick (as opposed to a bendy whip) when you enter the stable. If the horse comes at you without provocation, give him one smack on the muzzle so he feels it, but without being brutal, and leave it at that provided he does not come for you again. Laying into a horse for any misdemeanour with several beatings and shouting rarely works and is no treatment, anyway, for an inexperienced handler to mete out.

A firm smack with your hand can be just as good, and some experts recommend a hard pinch (or bite!), if you can manage it, while the muzzle is still turned towards you. Whatever punishment you use, it should be accompanied by a firmly spoken 'no', followed by reassurance in a soothing tone.

Prevention is always better than cure, and it is as well to tie up

145

a known biter for attention, at least the nasty sort, while remembering that this will increase his sense of insecurity and restriction; you must, therefore, be most careful to treat him gently, as you are breeding vicious and justified resentment if you mistreat a horse who cannot retaliate – and one day he will. Each time a tied-up horse tries to turn his head to bite say 'no' firmly, but administer no other punishment. Talk soothingly at other times and eventually you may well find that once he realises you give him no cause for concern he gives up or greatly reduces the habit.

Horses who habitually fly at people with mouths open, ears flat back and a vicious look on their faces have gone further than the general unhappiness and insecurity of the nippy horse, and should be dealt with only by experts. They may be impossible to cure completely. They are dealt with under the heading *Savaging*.

See also *Stable manners, bad*.

Bolting/Running away

A bolting horse is exhibiting a classic case of flight mechanism brought on by fear and panic. He is different from a horse who is excited (perhaps when galloping across country, particularly in company) and who is, as an instructor once euphemistically described it to me, 'getting a bit strong'! Over-excited horses, although perhaps difficult to stop, are easy compared with a true bolter. Indeed, a most experienced horseman once said to me: 'If you ever think you've stopped a bolting horse, you haven't. You've stopped one who has just finished bolting.' In other words, he believed a real bolter is impossible to stop, and many people would agree with him.

Fear concentrates the mind wonderfully, in man and animal, and a horse who is running away in fright seems to be quite unable to hear his rider/driver yelling at him, to feel any but the strongest aids or even to see where he is going. In old books we can read of runaway animals heading straight into brick walls and killing themselves outright. My father witnessed such an incident as a boy, outside his home. This is but one good reason to try to stop a runaway if at all possible. Another is that although it is normally safer to stay with him than throw yourself off or out of the vehicle, unless you have unlimited space to let him run

146

himself out a collision is almost inevitable, resulting in serious injury to the horse, yourself and innocent bystanders.

Horses bolt normally in extreme fear and panic. A slightly less extreme situation is running away or pulling hard due to discomfort or pain – maybe bad riding/driving, incomprehensible aids, harness or tack which is causing pain and, particularly, a painful or badly handled bit. Pulling from excitement is common, especially in animals which are allowed or even encouraged to gallop a lot. Racehorses are an obvious case in point (taught to gallop when they feel a firm contact), as are children's ponies accustomed to 'unofficial races' and some event horses. Polo ponies seem today to be particularly prone to excitement and pulling as their connections resort to varied severe and complicated bitting arrangements in an effort to keep them handy and controllable.

The more horses are allowed to get away with charging off the more they try it on, so whether you have a horse who is really bolting or just running away, here are a few methods to try to resolve this emergency situation.

Under saddle Dig your knees firmly into the saddle and, taking a firm hold, turn the horse in a large circle by hard pulling using intermittent tugs on one rein to bring his head round. Gradually decrease the size of the circles (he won't have much choice if he's looking at his own hip) until he eventually comes to a standstill. Then behave as though nothing had happened and walk on, preferably in the direction opposite to that in which he was running. If he sets off again, repeat the treatment. For horses inclined to this behaviour, a cheek or Fulmer snaffle is advised to prevent the bit being pulled through the mouth.

If you haven't space for circling, shorten your reins and take a firm hold, bring one hand hard onto the withers and bear down on it to steady yourself, then pull upwards, hard and rhythmically on the other rein, alternating sides, if necessary. This usually works quite quickly.

Another method sometimes recommended but which is not always so successful is to take alternately a very firm upward pull on the reins, then release completely, pull and release, and so on; this is said to confuse the horse who doesn't know what to expect and so stops.

Fig 25 Shorten your reins and take a firm hold, bring one hand hard over the withers and bear on it to steady yourself, then pull hard and rhythmically in an upward direction on the other rein

Fig 26 This rider is starting to circle her horse into an ever-decreasing spiral to stop him – a useful method if you have the space

In harness Bolting or running away in harness is even more frightening than under saddle. It is often caused by the noise of the cart or its load in inexperienced horses, those put to an un-accustomed vehicle or given a noisy load (rattling barrels instead of quiet bales of hay, for example). Horses driven without blinkers when they are normally blinkered take fright at the sight of the cart following them, as they feel it is chasing them. The faster they go the faster the cart goes, and the situation escalates.

To cope, take a hard hold on both reins and quickly saw the bit back and forth in the horse's mouth, when he will probably stop quite soon. Keep the vehicle straight to avoid turning it over.

Of course, all the methods mentioned are not going to do the horse's mouth any good, but this is an emergency. Prevention is always better than cure – indeed, as with many equine problems and vices, cure is often impossible. Retraining as if the horse had never even been mouthed certainly helps some horses. If your horse has to be exposed to potentially frightening situations, such as traffic, microlite aircraft, fork-lift trucks and the like, accustom him gradually to them in the company of a ready 'proofed' schoolmaster horse, as police horses are trained.

Do nothing yourself to frighten or hurt him (such as removing his blinkers while he is still in harness so he can see the cart behind when he is not used to doing so, or being heavy-handed on the bit). See his equipment is comfortable and that you ride/drive well so he is not in discomfort or confusion. Avoid excitement by not over-feeding, and give plenty of exercise in work and field, as appropriate (tired horses rarely run away). If running away does occur, act quickly and decisively as the longer and faster the horse goes the more difficult it will be to stop him. It is stupid to punish him after he has stopped – he will think you are punish-ing him for stopping. Also, it is pointless to whip him during the misdemeanour as this will make matters worse. Use your voice, plus the methods described above.

Horses who are confirmed bolters are unsafe for work and should be retired for breeding or as companion animals, or destroyed at home so there is no chance of their being passed on to some unsuspecting purchaser at a sale – not all sale horses go for meat, although many do.

Bolting food

A horse is said to bolt his food when he grabs at it, eats very quickly, usually taking big mouthfuls, and swallows it after hardly chewing. This habit does not make for good digestion. Normal eating comprises contented, leisurely and relaxed chewing to give the grinding teeth at the back of the mouth (the molars) plenty of time to soften up the food and allow it to be mixed with saliva as a preparation for further action by the digestive juices in the stomach. If food is bolted down, this process is reduced and indigestion can result, particularly if whole grain is fed.

Apart from greed, which does affect some horses, rapid eating can arise from great hunger, nervous anxiety or pain caused when the mouth is sore for some reason, either through bit injuries, teething in youngsters or injuries to tongue and cheeks from molars which have not been rasped to remove the sharp edges formed as a natural result of wear. A horse may also acquire the habit by copying a stable companion who bolts food.

Great hunger can obviously be avoided simply by not letting the horse get into that state. It is unnatural for a horse to go without food for long periods. His natural state is to have a little food constantly passing through his digestive tract so he never feels really empty and, with equines living in natural conditions, this is normally possible except perhaps in winter. In domestication, horses on bare paddocks or in dirt yards often feel hungry and try to relieve the feeling by chewing fences, barking trees or even eating each others' manes and tails.

Athletic horses are usually deprived of food before work, and not without reason. A stomach full of food interferes with breathing and digestion when a horse is doing energetic work. Such horses should be given small feeds or a little hay after work to avoid digestive problems, then, once the edge has been taken off their hunger and other ministrations completed, they can be fed normally.

Nervous anxiety should be avoided as far as possible. If a horse is nervous because he does not like his neighbour or is turned out with an enemy who is constantly chasing him around, particularly at feed times, he may well eat in a hurried fashion. The answer is obvious: remove the offending cause. If the horse is nervous because he is in strange surroundings, say at an event or show, there is not a lot you can do except try to calm him by, perhaps, soothing music and a request for a box in a quiet place if at all possible, plus gentle handling by people he knows and trusts.

Sore mouths should be attended to by the vet. Teething is a temporary natural process, but the vet should be asked to check in case the milk teeth have become jammed on top of erupting permanent teeth and, so, are causing more trouble than necessary. Also, horses can, like humans, have teeth coming up too close to each other and causing pressure soreness (although this is rare). Sharp edges should be rasped off as required. Any bit which is causing soreness should be changed for a more appropriate article. (But check that the person at the other end of the reins is not causing pain through bad handling of a bit which itself is perfectly comfortable.) Soft food should be given until the mouth has healed.

If none of the above is the cause of your horse bolting his food, make sure he has plenty of fibrous roughage mixed in with his concentrates in the form of chop (hay and straw cut up small). This forces the horse to chew before swallowing. If you have difficulty buying clean chop, ask for a proprietary brand such as Mollichaff, which is chop mixed with molasses. It is possible to buy small chop/chaff cutters for home use so you can chop up your own good quality hay, and this practice is well worthwhile.

Some people advise putting lumps of rock salt in the manger to force the horse to fiddle out the food from between them. Although this might work in some cases, in others it so enrages the horse as to cause him to wrench the manger off the wall! A divided container may help to prevent the horse from grabbing large mouthfuls.

Try giving the horse a small ration of hay before his concentrate feed. This is not only good feeding practice in a normal routine, as it ensures the presence of some initial fibre in the stomach and intestines, but it also takes the edge off the horse's appetite to the extent that he takes things easier with the meal to follow.

Boring

Boring is allied to pulling except that horses do not do it in fear, panic or excitement, but because they are used to being ridden or driven with a heavy-handed contact, because they are too lazy to balance themselves in a degree of self-carriage, because the bit is too mild and they do not respect it or, occasionally, because the bit causes them some discomfort and they are trying to express their dissatisfaction with it. This may sound contradictory but, as ever, horses are individuals and have their own idiosyncratic ways of expressing their feelings in a given situation.

Horses boring for the first reason should be retrained gradually to accept a lighter contact. Suddenly removing it from them can upset their physical and mental balance and cause confusion; they normally adapt fairly quickly, however, if the change is made in easy stages.

Fig 27 Let him stumble. He has to learn that you won't be his prop

Those boring because they are relying on the bit for support (except green, unschooled horses) should be taught that they are not allowed to use their rider or driver for a prop. A good method, recommended by a champion endurance rider ('I haven't got the energy to travel hundreds of miles a month carrying a horse's head and neck', she said to me) is to take the horse over some rough (not stony) ground, wearing knee pads, and let him go along on his normal contact for a while then, on a particularly rough patch, and particularly if he pecks or stumbles, instantly throw the reins at him so he has no support whatsoever. Be ready to get your weight back so you do not go over his head if he ends up on his nose or his knees, as well he might. Even on level going, a repetition of this sort of treatment will soon and effectively show him that *he* must look after both of you, not the other way round.

Boring is assisted by an even contact on the bit, of course. If you refuse to give the horse this predictable contact, but constantly and quickly give and take on alternate reins and perhaps use a slightly more severe or differently-acting bit, he will learn he cannot rely on the bit for support. Whatever bit is used, it should be comfortable for him when he reacts correctly with it.

See also *Pulling; Raking.*

Box-walking/Stall-walking

This is a sign of a very unhappy horse and is thought by many to be a neurotic reaction to deprivation, normally of freedom. However, a similar action can also be seen in pastured or yarded animals turned out alone. The horse walks round and round his box wearing a trench in his bedding, or the floor if it is soft, or paces up and down the fence or round and round near the gate, in a zombie-like fashion rather than the alert, frantic manner of a horse contemplating jumping out.

Dominic Prince, in his contribution to Part II of this book, explains a very likely and comparatively recent theory that has developed from research work at the University of Utrecht. It is now thought that such useless habits as pacing and head rubbing, bar chewing and other repetitive actions seen in domesticated and zoo animals are the body's way of stimulating the release into the bloodstream of substances called endorphins, similar to the pain-killer morphine, which relieve distress and so

153

help the animal cope with the condition which is so upsetting it.

In the case of the box-walking horse, distress is perhaps being caused by deprivation of freedom, close company, a particular friend or of, quite simply, the right to live a natural life. Although adequate work can relieve the problem to some extent, this is not the same, of course, as freedom, even if only in a paddock, where the horse can exercise himself as he wishes, socialise normally with others of his own species (essential to the mental, and therefore physical, health of most horses and their relatives) and make his own friendships.

There are various methods for stopping the horse box-walking but none of them gets at the root cause, only the physical symptom. Putting bales of straw in his path or tying him up will hamper his progress and distress him even more into the bargain by removing the only release he has, until then, produced against his inner anguish. He will suffer even more and will, eventually, probably find other methods of relief such as weaving or banging.

The real answer is to study the horse closely to see under exactly what conditions he box-walks, and remedy the root cause as far as possible. One thing is certain, the habit will not be cured with keeping. It may be that a particular horse simply cannot tolerate being stabled or kept in small yards. For his health and happiness he should, then, be allowed to live in freedom with proper facilities of shelter, company, clothing and human attention. It is quite possible to have a fit, smart working horse who lives out, if the job is done properly.

Brushing

This is likely to be a conformational problem or one caused by unfitness or immaturity. As the horse moves, he strikes a foot against the opposite fetlock or low down on the leg, causing cuts and bruising. Anyone who purchases a sound, fit horse who brushes may have to accept it and simply work the horse in brushing boots, and ask the farrier's advice on the problem, when probably a feather-edged shoe will be fitted (ie one 'cut away' from the outer edge of the hoof's bearing surface so that at least it is not metal which is making contact but the horse's own horn). In suitably shaped hooves with adequate horn, the farrier might also trim the inside edge of the wall to ease the problem.

Clenches must obviously receive meticulous attention in horses who brush.

Horses who brush because they are weak, unfit or young and green often improve once muscled up and stronger, only to revert again with decreasing condition.

Bucking

Once a horse comes to realise that this is one of the most effective ways of getting rid of his rider (the others being rearing, rolling and, slightly less common, spinning round and dropping a shoulder) whoever rides him is in trouble; it takes an extremely competent rider to stay on a horse who is bucking seriously. It is also a very difficult habit to stop once it has become established.

Why do horses buck? Often, if they are that way inclined, because they simply want to get rid of the people on their backs. Just because a horse has been backed and ridden and is thoroughly accustomed to being sat upon, it doesn't mean he actually likes it, and those who don't may well discover this method of resolving the situation.

Discomfort and pain are obviously other causes and it is perfectly understandable that a suffering horse should try to get rid of the source of distress; in fact, it is a wonder more of them don't. To ride a horse with even a minor back injury, in a saddle that rubs or pinches, or in such a way that the rider's seat does not move in close harmony with the horse's back in all paces, is to cause him discomfort, pain, irritation or anger. A serious buck is, of course, not to be confused with the playful mini-buck or kick of the heels often given by fresh, excited or happy horses, but, if not checked when taken too far, these can often lead on to bucking proper and should not, therefore, be allowed to get out of hand.

As with many problems under saddle, an alert rider can often feel a buck coming. To buck, a horse must raise his back and lower his head; to buck anything like hard he must also be almost stationary. It follows, therefore, that if you keep his head up and keep him going forward he cannot buck so effectively. The instant you feel his back coming up under you and a slackening of pace, and notice the head going down, kick on, pull firmly and *upwards* on the reins and give a sharp vocal reprimand.

Some authorities recommend that you sit down hard and

155

Fig 28 Sit up, get his head up with the reins by using them in jerks (he might use a steady pull for support) and kick on. Forming a bridge with your reins over the withers can also help keep you in the saddle if you get thrown forward

securely in the saddle, others that you lean *slightly* forward, dig your knees into the saddle and use them as a pivot so that the movement goes on beneath you without disturbing your equilibrium. Whichever method suits you personally, one little trick that will be a big help if you do happen to be thrown forward is forming a bridge with your reins as many racing jockeys do, or else tying them together with a knot about a foot down from the buckle end. Then as you go forward your weight is taken by the reins pressing on the horse's neck and your forward progress should be checked.

As for using the whip, hitting the horse behind the saddle is almost sure to make him worse. One, or maybe two, good sharp cracks down the shoulder, if you can manage it, gets through to many horses. If you have to wait until he has stopped bucking before you can use this punishment, maybe you had better not, because you *must* do it no later than one second after he has stopped for the two events to connect in his equine mind. He will be tense after his bucking session and if his rider is stupid enough to lay about him not only will he not know why, but he will probably start bucking again in defence. The best thing to do is soothe him with your voice, stroke his neck and walk off calmly – but keep a contact on the bit in case his head has any ideas of going down again!

Before you resort to any form of relatively harsh punishment such as even a single crack down the shoulder, or firm, upward use of the reins, maybe only one rein if you are unsure of your balance (understandable in the circumstances) it is advisable to get expert help with a bucking horse as it is this very thing – rough treatment – which has made some of them into buckers. The more they experience it the worse they get.

Prevention is always better than cure, so check that the horse is not suffering from a back or girth-area injury, a girth that is too tight, rough or galling him, wrinkled skin under the girth, a folded-up saddle flap or wrinkled numnah under the saddle, or unharmonious riding on your part. Make sure, too, that he is not over-fed and/or under-exercised as this is a very common cause of over-exuberance. If your horse is making a habit of bucking and you are sure he is not in discomfort, reduce the amount of his concentrate food, turn him into a paddock, yard or similar area to let off steam before you work him, and/or lunge or loose school him for half an hour. Tired horses are not inclined to buck!

In the case of children's ponies, some other physical means of prevention may be needed, as even competent children may not have the strength to get a pony's head up. A contraption like the old-fashioned bearing reins for carriage horses is useful. It is simply a piece of strong cord fastened to the front dee of the saddle on each side, passed through the loops of the browband and tied to each bit ring. It should be adjusted so that the pony cannot get his head low enough to buck, ie his ears lower than his withers. (A similar device is also used to stop children's ponies grazing while mounted.) This device can be used while retraining the pony but discarded once he has given up the habit.

If young horses buck, it is often because they do not yet understand what the rider's forward leg and/or seat aids mean, so further reinforcement by vocal commands, which should have been thoroughly learned during lungeing, is needed. At some stage, a youngster will test his rider, maybe by bucking, so vocal reprimand, reinforced only if necessary by physical methods, should be used to nip the habit in the bud.

Catch, difficult to

It always surprises me that some horses are easy to catch even if their owners never give them titbits and their working lives are unpleasant, stressful and maybe even painful, while others, whose owners are known to have pockets full of goodies and/or are kindness and consideration personified, prove extremely unwilling and evasive when it comes to being caught up out of the field. Logically, one would think that horses whose work is to be dreaded would not want to come to those who make it so, or, indeed, any other humans, yet they do, and some who have nothing to fear are a constant headache to their owners or handlers. Although most horses will be trying to avoid the human/s trying to catch them, if they feel cornered some may charge at or past them and there could be a danger of your being kicked or knocked over. Apart from being quick on your feet to

Fig 29 Making a sudden grab for his headcollar is a sure way of startling him and sending him off rapidly to the other end of the field

avoid such a horse it may be considered wise to arm yourself with a stout stick (see Figs 7 and 8).

Past experience on the part of the horse is, of course, very likely to be instrumental in forming his attitude to being caught and if a horse has been mistreated in the past, he may continue to associate this with a new and better owner. Horses, also, are not so stupid as to be unable to realise that being caught usually means work or boring handling or something similar. If the weather and ground conditions are at all bearable they will quite naturally prefer to stay in the field.

Time of day can also have a bearing on whether a horse will come to us or not. If a recognisable routine is adopted and the horse knows he is usually ridden in the late afternoon or early morning, this may be the time when he is difficult to catch. Changing the routine may fox him and improve matters – or it may make him distrustful at *all* times, depending on the individual.

Horses often take their example from other horses; for instance, a mare who is difficult to catch will teach her foal the same behaviour. Occasionally, a horse who is good to catch may become difficult in this respect if turned out with a companion who evades all attempts at capture. This trait can be played upon in reverse. If a bad-to-catch animal is turned out with one or more who are good to catch, so that he is left alone in the field when they are caught up, he often lets himself be caught once he realises he is going to be left in 'solitary'.

Going into a field with some sort of bribe such as a titbit or a bucket of food does, indeed, bring many horses up, but not the inveterate rebel, especially if he knows that being caught means work or something unpleasant. So for this reason it is a good idea to habitually visit horses in the field bearing no gifts and without making any real attempt to catch them. Just stroke them, talk a bit and then leave.

Most horsepeople have their own pet remedies for catching horses and there are so many there is not room here for all those I have heard. However, there are three that I have found particularly useful if you have help and a long rope and/or plenty of time on your hands. They are all 'on-the-day' remedies.

For a start, any horse or pony who is hard to catch must be turned out wearing a headcollar with a short length of rope or binder twine (15cm/6in) hanging from the back ring; this is long enough for you to catch hold of but not so long he is going to tread on it. A brief reminder of the correct way to catch a horse might not go amiss, either. Approach the horse from the shoulder where he is sure to see you, as if you surprise him he may be startled and run off, and suspicion will have been set up. Have a titbit in your hand and tuck the lead rope in your pocket or the waistband of your trousers behind your back so he cannot see it. Put the titbit on one hand and hold the empty hand just in front of it. He will have to reach to your back hand to get the titbit and your empty one will be already under his chin subtly catching hold of the short rope. (Of course, with a horse who is no trouble to catch you do not need to hide the lead rope and may well not need a titbit. He will also not need to have a headcollar on.)

Now for the three remedies. The first is quite common. Take as many friends as you can muster, a long rope or two or three lunge lines tied together and, spreading yourselves out along the rope, advance on the horse craftily with the idea of cornering him – eventually. You obviously all have to work with one accord and fully realise which corner you are aiming at.

The second method often works well. Go into the field and, walking *away* from the horse, start a very large circle round him, completely ignoring him. Keep walking round and round making the circles gradually smaller and smaller so you are spiralling in on him without his realising it. If the horse moves around, adjust your circles so you still go round him. Do not speak to him or look at him, or give any hint that it is he you are aiming at. The idea is for the horse to think you are in the field for some other purpose and to come to regard you as part of the furniture. Before he knows where he is you have come right up to him and caught him when simply walking past him by just catching hold of that invaluable short rope!

Another method (which is all right in fine weather) is to go into the field and sit down with a big, white, rustly bag full of sweets such as peppermints or sugar lumps, and just start eating. (You can stand up if you want but it is more intriguing to horses if you sit down.) Most horses have a sweet tooth and eventually cannot resist the temptation to come up and see what you are doing, especially if they hear the paper and see you eating. Even hard-line evaders usually cannot resist the puzzle, especially if they see all their friends getting sweets. When the culprit approaches don't catch him but give him one sweet as an appetiser then turn and walk slowly back to the gate. He is almost sure to follow – along with the others – making you feel like the Pied Piper of Hamelin. Your problem will then be getting out of the gate with just the horse you want!

It is well worthwhile trying to effect a permanent cure and the following method, which may take a few days or a couple of weeks or so, often works. Even if a hard-to-catch horse or pony decides he can do without food, even on a bare paddock, rather than be caught, one thing he cannot do without is water. Turn the horse out in a field without water or block off the existing supply. Take water to him morning and night in a bucket. Let him drink on the first day so he knows the bucket contains water and will get used to the routine. On subsequent days *do not let him drink* until he has let you catch hold of his headcollar rope. Put the bucket at your side, not in front of you, otherwise you could get bashed in the face if you try to bend down to get hold of the rope. If the horse will not come to you, or will not let you catch him, take the bucket out of the field *without* letting him drink. Grass contains a good deal of water anyway so he will come to no harm at this stage.

If he does let you catch him, praise him and lead him to some plentiful water source as there will not be enough water in one bucket for him. Then return him to his field. (If you want him for work, just let him drink what is in the bucket, of course. However, bear in mind that catching him without working him reinforces the cure as he will not associate being caught with working, as described earlier.)

If he would not be caught the first time, take the bucket back some hours later and try again. Behave quietly and speak encouragingly. Do not grab at him, ever, but wait until he comes to the bucket, then try to get his headcollar. If he shies away, stand and wait for him to come back. Let him get his nose in the bucket so he realises it is full of lovely fresh water, but do not let him actually drink unless he has allowed himself to be properly caught.

If he still will not be caught, be firm and take the bucket away again, but return in about an hour. It will now be about twenty-four hours since he had a drink, so you should pick a time when you can keep returning to the field every hour until he gives in. After all this time without water, he must not be allowed all he wants once you have caught him. Let him have half a bucket and offer another an hour later. Then wait until next morning or evening as the case may be, gradually letting him drink as much as he wants.

Soon the horse will be resigned to the fact that unless he allows you to catch him he will not get a drink and after a few days he will, I almost guarantee it, come trotting up waiting to be caught, particularly if he is denied company and is getting bored with no work to do (although different horses vary in their desire for company and work).

Once he permits himself to be caught fairly readily take him back to his original field or restore his water supply, and try catching him with titbits or even nothing at all. If he gets up to his old tricks again, back he goes to the cure system for a few days. He is almost certain to get into the habit of being caught after this, especially if he is not always made to work but is sometimes just groomed, fussed over, perhaps fed and then turned loose again.

If you cannot avoid having the horse with others, remember that they must not be made to suffer from lack of a water supply. They will have to be caught and led to water twice daily and

Fig 30 A catching pen at the entrance to the field is a big help not only in cornering your quarry, but in preventing the rest of the herd milling about too

allowed to drink their fill. (Horses taking a long draught of water usually raise their heads for a rest after a while. This does not mean they have had enough. Stay still and they will probably drop their heads again for more. They usually move away from the water of their own accord when they have had enough.) The fact that the others are 'going somewhere' may, also, induce the naughty one to let you get your hands on him, although the ultimate aim is, of course, for you to be able to go into any field, with or without other horses, and be able to catch your horse fairly easily.

If the horse will not be caught when the others are taken to water, leave him behind and carry on with the bucket cure. I have known this to work several times with really bad cases, and a permanent cure was effected in all but one case, who is, unfortunately, now only allowed to graze on a tether because of his refusal to be caught. Tethering should not be used as an excuse never to turn the horse out, however. It is a very poor way to keep a horse and all attempts should first be made at a cure.

Because horse-stealing is so common now, you may be reluctant to leave a headcollar on him because it makes it easier for a thief to catch him too. In any case, never use one of the strong nylon headcollars as these break only with great difficulty. It is far safer to leave an old leather one on (kept supple, however, to avoid rubbing) or simply one made out of a single thickness of binder twine, which will snap if it gets caught up on the fence, a tree or your horse's hoof.

If you can discover one titbit which he finds absolutely irresistible, it will be a great advantage, provided you don't tell the whole world about it. When he does come to you, try the trick of walking backwards away from him (out of his personal space and so, therefore, lessening the 'threat' of close presence) but still hold out your hand with the titbit on it. As he finally gets his lips round it you should, especially if he knows there is more, be able to slip a rope round his neck (remember to hold your 'titbit hand' low to facilitate this) and you have got him. Be gentle all the time and chat or sing, and stroke him, and you should succeed.

To summarise, the aim is to make him *want* to come to you. The minimum you should aim at is not to give him cause to object. If he gradually comes to associate being caught with pleasure, you have cured him.

It is well known that punishment, if administered at all, should be administered at the time of, or no later than one second after, the crime. Never, ever catch your horse then punish him for not being caught earlier. You are then, 'sure as eggs is eggs', punishing him for coming to you and allowing himself to be caught! It is also absolutely ludicrous to catch the horse after some effort (or even let him finally come in of his own accord perhaps at a well-known feed time) then lay into him in his box for refusing to be caught when *you* wanted, as I have seen done. The only thing to do when a horse has agreed to be caught is to praise and reward him profusely, no matter how murderous you are feeling. To do otherwise is simply to compound the problem and make life worse for youself.

(The horse to whom this book is dedicated could be very hard to catch. Often the only person who could get to him was the little daughter of the woman with whom he was kept at livery. She would go into the paddock and walk right up to him, and put her arms round his knees. He would then stand stock still and anyone could go up and put a headcollar on, when he would come quietly.)

Catching hold of bit cheek/reins/martingale

It is usually youngsters who develop the habit of grabbing hold of their tack because, when teething, they feel they must have something to hold between their teeth, like a human baby with a teething ring. Although not meant maliciously at first, as horses grow older and lose the need for the habit, they can realise it is an effective way of lessening the rider's/driver's control and may continue to do it. They can get reins or a running martingale caught round their corner incisors or, in male horses, tushes and not only frighten themselves but, in the case of the martingale, unbalance themselves sufficiently to come down.

Apart from smearing the bit cheek (never the mouthpiece) with something objectionable such as old-fashioned liquid bitter aloes or the horse's own droppings, there are remedies for the habit.

Using a bit with no cheek, such as most snaffle bits, is an obvious remedy. If the horse cannot be controlled in a snaffle (which he should be if a youngster) or is being shown in harness classes where a cheek bit is essential, use the well-known and

164

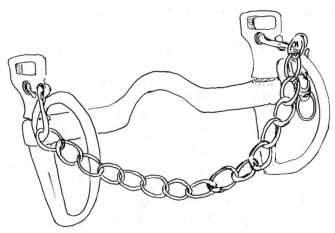

Fig 31 A Kimblewick bit. The curb chain can either be passed inside or outside the bit rings, according to advice or preference. It comes into contact usually only when the rider uses his hands slightly lower than normal, which increases the leverage of the cheeks

usually easily available Army universal reversible port bit, otherwise known as the Army elbow bit or angle-cheek bit. This bit places the cheeks out of reach of the horse. Another bit which gives curb-like control but is basically a snaffle is the Kimblewick, which has no cheeks for the horse to grab.

Catching hold of the reins is easier for the horse provided he can turn his head round far enough – and it is not easy to stop this often very quick movement. Making the reins taste nasty, as described above, is a good remedy, and the same applies for the running martingale, or you can use a bib martingale which has the space between the two branches filled in. The horse can still catch hold of it but it will not become caught round the teeth.

Most horses grow out of this habit when over teething, but it should, in any case, be stopped before this to prevent accidents.

Changing leading leg

Like humans and other animals, horses often show a preference regarding the limb they use for a particular purpose. Most humans prefer one hand to the other for writing, dogs use one particular paw to scratch a door they want opened, horses use a particular hoof for pawing the ground or banging their stable door for attention, to get out or whatever, and it is well known that most of them have a preference for a particular leading leg in canter, the near fore being the most usual.

Most textbooks advise us to school the horse slightly more to the non-favoured side to facilitate the horse's use of the muscles on that side – an aim to make him ambidextrous, in fact. With correct and sympathetic schooling, most horses do become more or less as accomplished on one side as on the other, but some retain a marked preference for leading with a particular foreleg or working on one particular rein all their lives. Horses who have not received good basic training often remain difficult on their non-favoured reins and, indeed, if persuaded to canter with the correct foreleg leading, change legs back to their favourite diagonals even though still going in the direction their riders wish.

Young horses who are still unmuscled and unbalanced under a rider have particular difficulty in maintaining their non-favoured legs or diagonals and may change back unevenly, going with a lateral (disunited) action instead of the normal diagonal canter action.

Even highly schooled and competent horses can change legs when not required if they think they have received signals to do so from their riders. Much depends on the school of equitation in which the horse is being trained. Some rely on a significant bit contact at all paces and, in these, a change of contact, an unevenness or an inadvertent twitch of the rein, even if not accompanied by relevant seat and/or leg aids, can be enough to cause the horse to change legs. Other schools depend much more on seat and legs and very little on the hand; in these cases, a wobble in the saddle from the rider's seat, causing a change of weight from one seatbone to the other, or an unintentional leg movement, can be enough to bring about a change of leg.

Young horses should always be schooled by riders who are in good control of their bodies and aids, otherwise confusion is bound to reign, and the youngsters may never become clear about leading legs. Given a competent rider, however, frequent leg changing in young horses may be expected, depending on the individual, and they should not normally be reprimanded. It is difficult enough for them to canter under a rider anyway and provided their trainers are clear and consistent with their aids, and youngsters are not asked to perform too long in canter, particularly on the non-favoured leg, they will almost certainly gradually improve with experience and growing strength, fitness and maturity. Short, frequent schooling sessions, and short spells on one particular movement such as cantering on a named leg, are better than long sessions which weary the youngster mentally and physically. Indeed, changing leg when not requested can be a sign of tiredness and is often seen in racehorses towards the end of a race.

In mature but poorly schooled horses, the problem can often be cured by paying attention to the aids; it is important to be consistent and 'hold the aid' (in other words, keep your legs and hands in the necessary position for canter-left or canter-right, as the case may be) to stress to the horse that the leg he is on is the one the rider wants.

The position of the seatbones can be very influential in helping the horse maintain canter on a given leg. If, say, you wish the horse to canter and remain cantering with the off fore leading, ensure that your right seatbone is slightly in advance of your left, just as the right side of his body is slightly in advance of his left when cantering on that leg – and vice versa, of course. If you do this consistently, you may well find that in time the simple action of moving your seatbone back again will be enough to bring the horse back to trot. In sensitive, highly schooled horses, flying changes of leg can often be achieved by the rider simply moving forward the seatbone on the same side as the leg with which he or she wishes the horse to lead.

Claustrophobia

It is no surprise to find horses who show signs of fear or intense dislike in enclosed places. Horses were never cave-dwellers in the accepted sense of the word, even though occasionally they might have used caves for shelter. Even humans, who are probably the best known cave-dwellers on earth (and still are although today's 'caves' are far superior in the way of mod cons than were our predecessors') not uncommonly show similar signs in closed-in or crowd situations – wide or wild eyes, tense, jerky movements, taut skin and muscles, patchy cold sweating are all signs of panic and fear, and are shown by humans and horses alike, at least by susceptible individuals. Horses at auctions, when crowded into pens with a herd of strangers, often panic at the enforced intrusion into their personal space, despite being in the open air.

Some horses are so badly affected by claustrophobia that they have to be given a life more or less always in the open and with plenty of space. Some are fine if kept in a paddock and field shelter, but are distressed if stabled behind a closed door, even though only the lower half may be closed. It does help if the horse is given a particularly roomy, high-ceilinged stable, ensuring light and air also, and, particularly, as panoramic a view as possible. When transporting such horses (if this proves possible) it helps if they can see out of their conveyance and, wherever possible, windows and flaps are left open. Even out at exercise, some animals become panicky in 'enclosed' areas such as woodland or if hemmed in a gateway by traffic or other horses.

Some horses improve in time with considerate management: others never do, and have to be treated individually (as should all horses) with their phobia being catered for at every opportunity. It is useless and cruel to force a horse to put up with 'normal' conditions such as a poky stable or small trailer if he is claustrophobic. He will not get better; he will probably get worse. And it should be remembered that a horse in fear and panic is a horse more or less out of control – a dangerous animal indeed.

Climbing over door

The obvious way to stop a horse climbing over his loose-box door is to close the top door, or to fit a grille or at least a single bar to keep him in. Alternatively, he could simply be tied up inside his box.

However, none of these remedies is likely to increase his happiness or peace of mind; in fact, they are more likely to make him more miserable. As with any problem behaviour, we should try to find out *why* he tries to jump or climb out of his stable. Does he do it at any time or only in certain circumstances, for instance when he sees other horses going out when he is not,

---

A familiar stable fitting is an anti-weaving grille like this, the idea being that it allows the horse to put his head out to look around but discourages him from swinging it from side to side. Although this might help in the early stages of the development of a vice, it has little effect with a confirmed weaver. If a horse is going to weave anyway, he will in all likelihood simply start weaving inside the box if he cannot do so with his head over the door

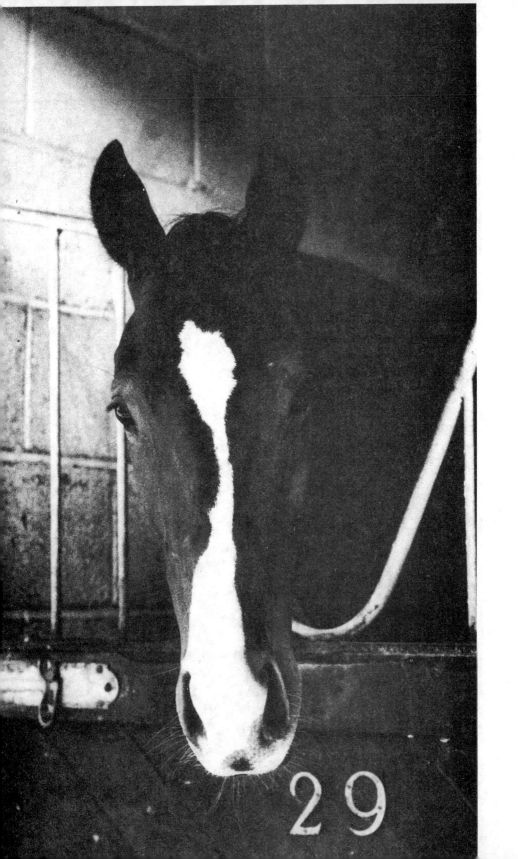

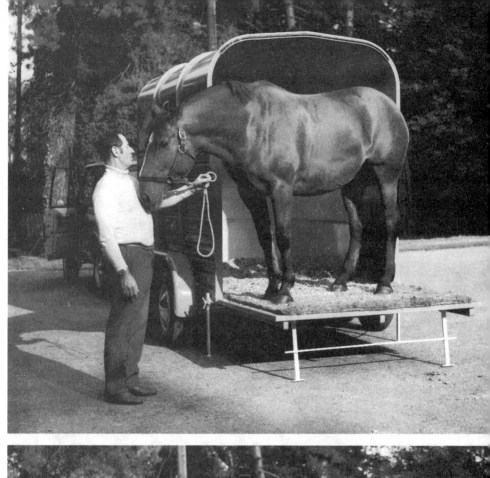

when a certain animal is within sight whom he wants to reach, when he sees his feed coming, when he is the only horse left in the yard, and so on? With some animals, this doubtless occurs because they simply cannot tolerate being stabled and if they feel the height of the bottom door is within their capabilities to jump, they will try to do so. Some try even when it is obviously too high, and injure their heads or withers on the top of the door frame or trip over the bottom door and badly injure themselves in a fall. Sometimes a horse will become straddled over the bottom door.

If the horse only tries to climb out in a certain set of circumstances, try, first, to give him human company in his box, if this is feasible, as a calming, authoritative presence often restrains a horse. If this is not possible and the circumstances are only going to last a short while, resort to closing his door just that long.

If, however, the problem is more frequent and random, serious consideration should be given to not keeping the horse stabled any more than necessary. A box with a small yard leading from it often gives that little extra sense of space and freedom as the horse can wander in and out as he wishes and so loses the sense of constraint that is often the cause of such behaviour. Many of these horses live much happier lives if kept yarded, possibly with access to their stables, or at least overhead cover when conditions make it desirable. They are also often ideal candidates for life outdoors with a field shelter.

Clipping, dislike of
Most working horses need to be clipped at some time during the winter, even if only once in late autumn, and can be very difficult

---

This model of trailer is known as 'The Kiwi'. It is not currently made in Great Britain although the author understands that plans are afoot to make it available in other countries. The horse has been led up on to the platform, a manoeuvre with which very few horses have problems

The horse's quarters have been moved round in a 'turn-on-the-forehand' type of movement, and he has been backed easily into the trailer (which takes two horses). To unload, the platform's stabilising legs are folded down while it is up in its tailgate position, so that, when lowered, it forms a conventional ramp down which the horse can walk in a forward-facing position, obviating the need to back down a slope, which distresses so many horses

to handle if they take a dislike to or develop a fear of it, becoming a danger to themselves and others.

Trouble usually occurs because a horse has been hurt at some time during the process and is naturally frightened of a repetition. Some horses are frightened of the noise of the machine or dislike the feel of the clipper head on their bodies. If the person clipping is not careful or is inexperienced, the horse can easily be nicked with the blades. If the latter are blunt or the horse is damp or dirty, there will be a pull on the hairs which can cause discomfort or pain. If the machine is under strain due to the above, it can overheat which, again, is uncomfortable.

Ensure that the clipper blades are properly sharp and that the tension between the plates is correct. (Turn the adjusting button until it will turn no more and the plates are in full contact, then give it a quarter turn back again.) The horse must be clean and dry and the machine should be allowed to 'take itself' over the coat rather than being pushed too hard by the handler. Of course, the clippers should be earthed properly and the horse standing on a dry surface; a shock can not only frighten the horse more but can seriously injure horse and attendant.

Horses can be accustomed to clipping machines by being groomed with an electric groomer, particularly the rotary brush type. This introduces them to the slight 'pull' on the skin and the sound of machinery near them. A tape recording of the noise can be played in the yard for some days before clipping is due and, during clipping, the horse's ears can be plugged with cotton wool if it is the noise which frightens him. A radio or tape recorder playing soothing music at the same time as clipping can also help.

If the horse still does not improve, resort to hand-operated clippers. For tricky areas such as the head, hairdressers' small hand clippers are useful. If you feel it is necessary to twitch the horse, do so with care having first read the references to it on pages 14 and 15. Your vet could also sedate the horse.

See also *Trimming, dislike of.*

Clumsiness

This often occurs in young and/or unschooled horses simply as a result of physical immaturity, perhaps physical weakness in debilitated horses or those who have been ill and out of work for some time. Bearing in mind that some horses are naturally more agile than others (just as are humans and other animals), the causes can also be too-heavy shoes, an unfamiliar or wrong type of shoe, poor, unbalanced feet which are tender or affect the horse's action, rough going and nervous reaction to strange surroundings or unfamiliar ground. Simple tiredness should also not be overlooked. More seriously, clumsiness can be due to some nervous or muscular disorder, back injury and/or inco-ordination, and this should always be considered if none of the other causes listed above seems to apply.

Given that there is nothing wrong with the horse that requires veterinary attention, points to check are whether the horse is always clumsy or just on certain ground conditions, and whether his feet are unusually thin-soled making him stumble due to discomfort on rough ground.

This condition often improves when a horse increases in fitness and muscular strength and is suitably shod. Work over poles, cavalletti and very small obstacles often teaches a horse to look where he is going, to be handy and to pick up his feet. Well-ridden dressage work can also help, with its sometimes intricate school figures such as circles, frequent changes of direction and lengthening and shortening of stride to teach a horse what his feet and legs are capable of. Some experts recommend work over rough ground to teach the horse to look where he is going and putting his feet but, first, care should be taken that feet and shoes are in good condition and suitable.

See also *Stumbling*.

Crib-biting
This is probably one of the most well-known vices. Horses afflicted take hold of any convenient projection such as the top of the stable door, the manger, the top of the kicking boards or, in extreme cases, even their own knees, arch their necks and gulp in air by making a vacuum in their mouths and then suddenly releasing it. The air which is consequently present in their stomachs and intestines prevents food being digested as effec-tively as it should be and also causes flatulence.

Apart from causing damage to whatever projection is seized, the horse's incisor teeth become excessively and unevenly worn, making grazing less efficient. Because, due to the air present in the digestive tract, digestion of food is also less efficient, it normally takes more food to keep crib-biters in reasonable condition and so costs more money to maintain them. It is also frequently claimed that such horses are subject to colic caused by their vice. However, it is also the case that the vice can be a *sign* of colic and it is sometimes found that when the diet is improved (usually by the addition of more roughage/bulk and the reduction of concentrates) the crib-biting stops.

This is one of the vices dealt with by Dominic Prince in his contribution in Part II of this book, to which readers are referred. It is probably a specific reaction to tension, stress and general unhappiness, possibly caused by over-confinement or unsuitable (for the individual horse) management and work regimes and, as mentioned, can be a symptom of digestive disorder.

When a horse is thoroughly established in this vice it is impossible to stop him performing it. There are mechanical devices such as cribbing straps, which fit fairly tightly round the neck and have a metal projection which pokes the horse in the throat every time he tries to arch his neck to crib-bite, and hollow bits which prevent the formation of the necessary vacuum in the mouth. However, the horse will still try to go through the motions and has the discomfort of permanently wearing these devices except when working. Such horses will grasp any opportunity to crib-bite after a period of prevention, eg when returned to the stable after work they will crib-bite non-stop for several seconds (instead of intermittently, as normal) until a device is replaced.

There are also surgical techniques such as nicking the neck muscles which enable the horse to arch his neck and suck in the air, or making small holes in the cheek to prevent the formation of the vacuum, but their success rate seems very variable. Generally they do not work in horses confirmed in the vice, which appears to become a habit as much as anything.

Some horses stop crib-biting when turned out (indicating that confinement causes the stress responsible for the vice), and if turned out where grazing is available the grass provides a welcome distraction from their habit plus a feeling of fullness (which the horse may seek to obtain by taking in air). However, some horses still crib-bite when out, usually on gates or fence posts, indicating some deep-rooted or long-standing source.

174

It is said that this vice is 'catching' and that afflicted horses should be kept out of sight of others who may subsequently copy the habit. This is certainly not always the case, however, which indicates that the problem arises through mental and/or physical distress or disorder and not simply because the horse has seen another doing it. It is also unlikely that the habit is a natural progression from licking doors or walls, as is sometimes suggested.

It is generally much more satisfactory to try to get to the root cause of the vice (as in all problems) and stop it from there, rather than simply physically preventing the horse, when possible, from performing the vice. A more sympathetic system of management is suggested – more freedom, company rather than solitude, attention to the diet, work the horse is happy doing and does not, therefore, worry about, plus neighbours and attendants he likes and has confidence in rather than those who are going to cause further anxiety or animosity. A veterinary examination as to physical causes – such as inappropriate diet, intestinal ulcers, parasites or other conditions – is also suggested.

It should finally be remembered that this vice may be impossible to cure where it has become firmly established and even if it stops with a change of management, a return to the old conditions will revive it.

Crowding

Crowding can be a very unpleasant habit, and dangerous when a large horse is leaning on you and squashing you against the wall. Young horses who have not learned their manners sometimes do it, but not with the malicious intent of older bully-type horses who wish to exert their authority over their handlers.

With young horses, correct teaching of stable manners, plus a sharp slap on the belly for any who seem to be developing the habit, often does the trick, but with horses established in the habit an old remedy frequently works. This is to take a strong stick just a few inches longer than the width of your body and sharpen one end. Carry the sharp end towards the horse and when he crowds you against the wall jam the blunt end against it and hold the sharp end towards the horse so that he leans on the point. As the stick is longer than the depth of your body, the horse will make contact with the stick, not you, and receive a most uncomfortable poke, which should be accompanied by a verbal rebuke. (The stick must not be *too* sharp, of course.)

Consistent treatment of this sort usually results in a cure, particularly if the voice is also used (as it should be in all cases of disobedience) when ultimately the voice alone should be enough.

See also *Stable manners, bad.*

Dead stop spin-round outside-shoulder-drop!

This manoeuvre is surprisingly common among horses who want to get rid of their riders, either for fun or in all seriousness. Some horses, notably those of Arab blood and those with short backs,

Fig 32 Take a strong, thick stick sharpened (not excessively) at one end. It must be longer than the width of your body so that when the horse attempts to crush you against the wall you can jam the blunt end against the wall and let the horse give himself an unpleasant poke with the sharp end, while you remain untouched

are able to stop dead almost within their own length and this can be enough to get many riders off, but when they combine that with spinning round and dropping the outside shoulder it is almost as certain to deposit the rider as a relentless hard bucking session.

Most horses prone to this habit always do it to the same side, ie they always spin to the left and drop the right shoulder, or vice versa. This at least enables the rider to be ready for it as he knows in which direction he is likely to be ditched. The movement is not always performed as a way of refusing jumps, but sometimes as a form of napping or playing up during flat work or out hacking.

Among experienced riders, the general consensus of opinion about dealing with this trick runs as follows.

First, slightly shorten the stirrup on the side on which you are most likely to come off, ie the same side as the shoulder is usually dropped. This will give you more support when your weight is thrown to that side. Even when jumping (and this manoeuvre is usually performed at a canter), do not ride too far forward and keep your feet slightly forward of the correct position. Keep a firm but not hard contact on the reins and above all be alert and ready for trouble. The instant you feel the horse 'back-pedalling' or even sense that he is going to stop, kick on hard (with suitable verbal encouragement) *particularly* with the leg on the side to which he is going to spin, and pull hard and up on the outside rein in a series of short sharp jerks. This is all calculated to direct the horse in the direction opposite to that in which he wants to go. You must be ready to try and throw your weight in the appropriate direction (ie to the left if he is spinning that way, otherwise you will go off to the right) and slightly back to counteract the forward momentum.

One method suggested as a permanent cure, rather than as a measure enabling the rider to control the movement and stay on, is to pull the horse hard round in the direction of his spin and kick him on and on in a tiny circle in that direction until he is thoroughly fed up. Yet another I have heard, and one which would require a very confident, experienced, not to mention competent, rider is to pull the horse's head up and round in the direction of his spin, throwing your weight in the opposite direction with the object of bringing the horse down. The rider

Fig 33 A common and very effective manoeuvre for getting the rider off. The horse, all at the same time, stops suddenly and drops his outside shoulder (in this case, obviously, the left). Most riders will be deposited over the outside shoulder

Fig 34 Sit up, use your legs hard to keep him going, particularly the left leg (in this case), and jerk the right rein in an upward direction to keep his head up. Direct your weight to the right, too, to counteract the movement

should ideally be quick enough to jump off as the horse goes down. While this method might well eventually make the horse lose his nerve as far as this manoeuvre is concerned, it is only suitable for the expert.

Dismount from, difficult to

A horse who objects when his rider dismounts is much more unusual than one who is difficult to mount, but the problem probably stems from the same cause – either the horse suffers discomfort during the process or has had a bad experience in the past.

The method of dismounting which causes least discomfort to the horse is to quit both stirrups and vault off, supporting your weight with your hands on the pommel of the saddle, as is taught in most British riding schools. Other methods which involve leaving one foot in a stirrup (usually the left) until the rider is half-way off (the old cavalry method) or has the right foot on the ground (the Western riding method) unavoidably cause the saddle to be pulled over somewhat to that side, which must be uncomfortable for the horse. Even with the vaulting method, if the rider hits the horse's hip or croup with his right foot, this again causes discomfort or even pain, and it will be no surprise if the horse becomes difficult during dismounting. Jabbing the horse in the mouth if the rider uses the reins to steady himself during dismounting or on landing, can certainly cause distress. If one stirrup is partly or wholly maintained during the process and the rider's foot sticks in the stirrup, possibly resulting in his falling, this obviously can frighten the horse who might take off and turn a potentially dangerous situation into a disaster, if not a tragedy.

Due to the horse's excellent memory, the problem may stem from an incident from the past in which, as the rider was dismounting, perfectly correctly, something alarming happened nearby – say, a loud bang or the appearance of a tractor – causing the horse in future to associate dismounting with his earlier fright. This association of ideas can, of course, relate to many similar situations.

With a horse from which it is difficult to dismount, it is recommended that the rider uses a lot of patience and soothing techniques such as talking and stroking the neck. Halt the horse, preferably in a restricting location such as a corner of the yard with his nose and off side blocked by walls. Remove feet from both stirrups and run the stirrups up their leathers while still mounted so that if the horse does jig about they will not swing and annoy or frighten him. Make to dismount, talking to the horse calmly, but as soon as he offers to do anything but stand quietly, resume your normal position in the saddle. Keep doing this to gradually get through to him that you will not dismount until he stands quietly.

It is best if you have a single word or phrase to use at any time when the horse does something not required, such as a simple 'no'. Say this now when the horse offers to move about or bite your leg as you dismount. It is initially helpful if you have someone to hold the horse while he is learning. Eventually, if you are careful not to cause him pain, discomfort or fright, and do not dismount until he behaves, you will overcome this problem.

Disunited canter

This is a fault in the canter gait in which instead of the usual diagonal leg sequence (eg near hind, off hind/near fore, off fore) the sequence is, say, near hind, off hind/off fore, near fore, which produces a jarring, rolling, most uncomfortable feel for both horse and rider. It can also cause the horse to fall. It occurs in young horses unaccustomed to manipulating their legs under the weight of a rider (when the horse has to completely readjust his balance, particularly if the rider's weight is unsteady or incorrectly positioned in the saddle), when the horse is learning flying changes and changes only behind instead of in front as well, or when he is having difficulty in striking off into canter to a particular side. He may also become disunited when learning counter canter and, contrary to his rider's aids, tries to change to what he feels should be the 'correct' leg while also obeying his rider's aids to stay on the 'wrong' leg despite having changed direction.

It is a problem which is often overcome by increased maturity. As the horse becomes stronger, fitter and better schooled he learns what is required, and how to position his legs and cope with his own and his rider's weight.

The rider should not allow a horse to continue to canter disunited in the belief that he will eventually right himself. He should bring the horse gently back to trot and, according to which school of equestrian thought he belongs, position the horse correctly, time his aids correctly and maintain the correct position of his own body to assist the horse both physically and mentally to keep up a true canter. Generally speaking, it helps the horse if the rider keeps his inside seatbone slightly in advance of the outside one, in other words, if the canter with the off fore leading is required, the right seatbone should be a little in advance of the left.

Doors/gates, opening

The habit of undoing bolts and fastenings makes some owners marvel at their horses' ingenuity and even creates hilarity in the yard. While one might have a sneaking admiration for the escapee, it can, of course, be very dangerous to have horses escaping from stables and paddocks, especially near traffic, and highly inconvenient, especially near open spaces.

As far as stable doors are concerned, there are various patent 'horse-proof' latches on the market available from most saddlers and equestrian suppliers, any of which would do the trick. If a proper stable bolt is used, (with a metal 'U' at the end of the bolt which slots down over a protruding piece of metal with a hole in it) a simple device like a dog-lead clip taken from an old halter rope and clipped through the hole after the 'U' handle has been pushed down flat works very well.

Methods of overcoming the trick which should *not* be used are placing the bolt down out of reach (if the horse leans over his door he can push it open at the 'loose' end and sprain the hinge) and padlocking or tying up the door (this can cause delay in an emergency such as colic or fire).

Opening gates can be foiled by the same kind of catches recommended above. In any case, particularly where horses are in fields without human supervision, gates should be securely padlocked both ends to deter horse thieves and joy riders.

Drink, refusing to

I can't resist mentioning the old saying that you can take a horse to water but you can't make him drink! It is surprising how long horses and other equidae (zebras and asses) living in wild conditions often go without drinking. Zebras have been recorded as going three or more days without even appearing to try to get to a water-hole. Modern stable practice normally consists of having water always available in stable and field but there are still some superbly-run establishments where horses are watered morning and night only, either by being led to a communal trough or by having water carried to them in their stalls or boxes until they have had enough.

There are several reasons why horses refuse to drink (apart from their just not being thirsty). Sickness is one possibility and if so, other initial symptoms will probably be present and a suspect horse should have his temperature taken and be checked for indications such as dull eyes and coat, patchy sweating, listlessness, hard or loose droppings etc.

Is the horse's water container putting him off? Some horses

181

dislike drinking out of a movable container, especially if they have ever knocked it over and it has splashed their legs. Some do not like containers which rattle when moved. An unfamiliar container, or one that is too small, can also cause a horse to refuse to drink. The noise of an automatic waterer refilling as the horse drinks often puts some of them off until they get used to it – and a few never do. Some sensitive horses are even put off drinking if the container is in a different place from normal or if it is too high or too low.

If a horse is taken away to a competition or for some other reason, the water in the new location may well smell and taste strange to him and cause him not to drink. This is why a large camping container full of 'home' water is usually advised for short trips. Even mixing it with the strange water can help.

If the water is actually contaminated, of course, this is a very sensible reason for the horse to refuse it. Droppings in the bucket leave a lingering objectionable smell even after the bucket has been rinsed out, so if this happens always wash the bucket with some odourless sterilising agent, such as the sort used for babies' bottles. Obviously if the bucket smells of disinfectant, this too will be most offputting.

Horses at grass may be put off drinking if the approach to the source is excessively poached, rough or slippery. If the horse is low down in the herd's hierarchy, he could be kept away from water by 'higher-ups', so take time to stay and watch for this and ensure your horse is getting his fair share. This sort of thing can even happen when horses are lined up to drink at a communal trough in a stable yard; a horse's neighbours should be chosen carefully if he is not to be frightened into taking only a short drink and then moving away, fooling his handler into thinking he has had enough. (Remember, also, that horses usually take a rest during a long drink, then put their heads down for more, so do not pull the horse away if he does this. He will usually come away of his own accord when his thirst is quenched.)

Excited horses often refuse to drink but will do so once they have calmed down. A very tired horse, even a dehydrated one, may well refuse to drink, surprisingly, so if you have worked your horse hard and he refuses water (he may refuse anyway if you have put an electrolyte solution in it), try him with something he likes, such as water in which sugar beet pulp has been soaked – many horses love this, especially if the sugar beet is the molassed sort. If this, too, fails and the horse still does not drink after he has had time to recover from his exertions, call the vet, who will probably administer liquids by means of a stomach tube and give you further instructions.

Droppings, eating (coprophagia)

It seems to be a cause of constant surprise and revulsion when a horse is caught eating its own droppings, particularly when one considers that horses normally find their own and other horses' droppings most objectionable to the extent that they will not graze near them in pasture. In fact, the only time when the practice is normal is when a young foal eats the droppings of its dam to provide itself with the various gut bacteria it needs for digestive purposes. It can also occur in horses treated with anti-biotics, who do it to replace gut bacteria killed off incidentally in the course of the treatment. When performed in other circum-stances, dung-eating denotes a depraved appetite due to severe malnutrition, extreme hunger, indigestion, dietary deficiency, physiological upset of some kind or even sheer boredom.

The root cause should be searched out and the matter put right before it becomes a habit. While the practice continues, extra care should be taken to ensure that the horse always has a ration of good hay or hayage, and to remove his droppings as soon as possible after they are passed. The vice is easy to cure if the correct cause is ascertained and appropriate action taken, and such steps as muzzling the horse or keeping him tied up are not calculated to improve his general contentment and well-being.

(Apart from eating their own droppings, horses may also eat other substances not regarded as normal food, such as inedible bedding, tree bark, afterbirth or soil.)

Dry mouth

A horse is said to have a dry mouth when he does not mouth the bit and produce saliva to facilitate its movement. It is because of this desire to achieve a 'sloppy' mouth that mouthing bits for youngsters have keys for the horse to manoeuvre with his tongue, so encouraging the flow of saliva. Some experts, how-ever, maintain that mouthing bits teach the horse, by encourag-ing him to play excessively with his tongue, to get his tongue

183

over the bit even when it is fitted at the correct height.

A dry mouth often seems to go with a set jaw and produces a horse who does not wish to give to the bit and has a stiff jaw and neck. Often a 'looser' feeling bit helps, eg if the horse has been used to a bit with eggbutt sides this could be changed to a loose-ring or wire-ring bit; similarly, a change from a half-moon shaped mouthpiece to a jointed one, particularly the Dr Bristol type with two joints and a flat piece of metal between them, often does the trick. A Dr Bristol bit is often preferred by horses with mouth problems (or rider problems!) because it has a less extreme action on the mouth.

Other ways of encouraging saliva flow are to offer the horse a wet feed with the bit in place to teach him to manipulate it better, to smear black treacle on the bit or to warm the bit in the hands before putting it in the horse's mouth. Needless to say, a gentle, conversational give-and-take down the reins on the part of the rider, rather than a steady, 'dead' contact, also encourages the horse to play with the bit.

Eat, refusing to

See *Drink, refusing to*, because many of the same reasons apply in the case of horses who will not eat, such as dislike of the container or of neighbours, excitement or sickness. Of course, strange food could put off a finicky feeder although if the Golden Rules of feeding are observed, and all changes made gradually with the new food added a little at a time to the normal rations, this should not cause problems. If the horse's teeth are hurting him, this could obviously be a good reason for his not eating (see *Quidding*). Sore mouths from bit injuries etc can certainly be a cause.

Horses who are fed large amounts of concentrates when they are in hard work may refuse food because of corn sickness (as horsemen, but not veterinary surgeons, call it). This means they are simply getting too much of a good thing and could have slight chronic indigestion, just like humans who constantly eat either too much or too rich food. Leaving food in front of such horses in the hope that they will eventually eat it is not a good idea if taken to excess as it is calculated to put off a shy feeder even more (this does not apply to hay, only concentrates).

A good way to avoid corn sickness in a horse on high concentrate rations is to give him one twenty-four hour period a week with no more than a single handful of his normal concentrates at each feed time, making up the feed with, say, molassed chop and soaked sugar beet pulp, coarsely grated carrots, a turnip or whatever the horse likes. This will give his system a chance to clear itself out, but the tiny amount of concentrate given will keep the digestive bugs going until normal service is resumed the next day.

It is often recommended that a single 'cornless' feed (usually a mash) be given the night before a rest day, and that concentrates are halved on that day. A mash containing just bran is no longer considered good for the horse, because bran contains phosphorous which can block the absorption of calcium from other foods when fed to excess. The mineral imbalance it causes can produce osteoporosis, which is weakening and enlargement of the bone. If fed at all, bran should comprise no more than one sixth (by weight) of the concentrate ration or, at the most, one quarter. This means that if 2.7kg (6lb) oats are being fed no more than 450g (1lb) or 675g (1lb 8oz) bran should be given. A better balanced 'false' feed of the ingredients mentioned above, plus, perhaps, dried grass or lucerne meal, is preferable.

If such feeds are given for a full twenty-four hour period, then the concentrates gradually restored to normal over the next twenty-four hours, the horse's indigestion will be lessened considerably. Glaubers' salts or charcoal (probably in granules) also often help horses with slight chronic indigestion, although this should be discussed with either a veterinary surgeon or equine nutritionist.

Even if the correct amounts of concentrates are given the feeds themselves may be too large and the ration could be split into more feeds, so the horse is not over-faced. One very fussy feeder I knew was helped by his owner throwing into his manger (which was near the door) a handful of his total daily ration every time she passed his box. The horse came to regard this as a game and his owner always maintained she got him to eat many more concentrates than she would have otherwise.

It is well known that many horses eat better at night. The last feed of the day is normally recommended to be the largest so the horse has time to eat and digest it in peace, and sometimes this does work. If you invested in an automatic feeder (at the time of

185

writing, there is none on the British market, but watch the equestrian press for the launch of a new product), you could feed the horse yourself last thing at night and set the feeder to deliver another feed in the small hours of the morning.

Although it is not good for the horse's digestion to give completely different ingredients in each succeeding feed, with the shy feeder who might get bored with a monotonous diet, it might be a good idea to make the predominant ingredient of each feed different while still including small amounts of the others. For example, breakfast could be mainly cubes with a few oats, lunch could be mainly oats with a few cubes, etc. Just adding a different succulent to each feed could also make a difference, especially where a ready-blended coarse mix is being used. Carrots could be given with the breakfast feed, sugar beet pulp with the second feed, apples with the third and so on. There are also many goodies that can be added to a horse's food to provide variety and interest, such as boiled linseed, boiled barley, molasses and so on, and some horses develop a liking for things such as honey, stout, milk and even eggs. Even a constant, gradual change from one type of feed to another can often maintain interest in meal times. Quality of food is paramount – no horse can be blamed for turning up his top lip at sour, mouldy or musty food.

Sometimes, putting a finicky feeder next door to a greedy horse has a great psychological effect and encourages appetite. Also, of course, some horses do best in a bustling atmosphere while others prefer peace and quiet.

Trying and considering all the above methods will usually help to improve a shy feeder, if not reform him altogether.

Escaping from field

Some animals, notably ponies, seem to have a knack of escaping from whatever field they are put in, to the extent in extreme cases where their owners/handlers simply stop turning them out. This is a great shame because being allowed freedom and grazing is of great benefit to the horse.

Obviously, the inmates of a field will not be able to get out if fencing and gates are adequate. Therefore, these must be improved and made high enough and strong enough to resist all attempts to jump out or break through. If a horse has acquired a healthy respect for electric fences, probably by being led up to them and having his moistened nose pressed against the wire to give him a harmless but most uncomfortable shock, these may well act as a deterrent and keep the horse far enough away from the perimeter of his field to discourage jumping out.

Although some animals always seem to find the grass greener on the other side of the fence, most do not jump out without a good reason; usually they are in search of company. Animals turned out alone are the most common escapees, when they make a bee-line either for their own stables or for the nearest field with horses, or even donkeys or cows, in it. Passing horses can also prompt an effort to escape. Tethering can be tried with an inveterate absconder, but not where other animals are loose as accidents can occur with the rope. Tethered animals must also have permanent access to shelter and water and must not be left where vandals or enemies can get at them.

Forging

Forging is where a horse strikes the underside of his forefeet at the toes with the toes of his hind feet, normally at trot but very occasionally at walk. It makes a distinctive clacking noise which warns the rider or whip immediately. It is caused by lack of schooling, unfitness or weakness, poor riding or driving where the horse is allowed to go along unbalanced and on the forehand, by having the horse shod with too-heavy shoes and is also common in horses with very short backs.

Even in the latter, the fault can quite easily be overcome. First, it is advisable to fit rolled-toe shoes to the hind feet and to concave out the front shoes. Young horses usually grow out of the fault with increased maturity, strength and schooling. Such horses should be well ridden or driven and encouraged to pick up their feet and move with a degree of self-carriage. Schooling over ground poles or cavalletti and work at trot over any going which will encourage the horse to pick up his feet – rough ground, shallow water – both help, but fast, unbalanced trotting should certainly be avoided, as with any horse.

Gateway, refusing to pass through

This problem usually arises because the horse has knocked his hips on some previous occasion or the gate has been allowed to

187

swing back onto him. There are cases where a horse has, unwisely, been left tied to a gate and has taken off in fright, lifting the gate off its hinges and dragging it behind him; naturally, he will associate the particular place, and perhaps all gates, as a source of fear and pain.

Gateways should be wide enough for a horse and handler to pass through with at least 30cm (2ft) on either side of them. Gates should be securely held or fastened back while the pair pass through. This may be very difficult to arrange if a single person is trying to extricate one horse from a milling crowd all anxious to leave the field, but it is precisely this situation which makes some horses troublesome at gates.

Help should be sought to enable the process to be accomplished without mishap. Some of the tension can be removed from the situation if a catching pen is constructed in the gateway, as the handler's anxiety is often transmitted to the horse and this alone can be enough to make him difficult. It takes a well-trained, confident horse to allow the handler to open the gate with one hand and guide him through with the other, then to perform on command what amounts to a turn about the forehand, and stand still while the handler fastens the gate again with one hand. Of course, many horses do just this, also when being brought in and out of a stable, and accomplish the manoeuvre like a well-rehearsed dance routine.

With a problem horse, retraining is the answer. In an emergency, turn the horse round and back him through, or blindfold him.

See also *Stable, refusing to enter* and *Stable, refusing to leave*.

Grinding the teeth

This is a sign of distress, annoyance, irritation or nervous apprehension. It is, perhaps significantly, quite common in competitive dressage horses and show horses when they are habitually 'drilled' for over-long periods before a test or class. Such conditions may cause the competitive tension of the rider to be passed on to the horse who grinds his teeth to find a release for his pent-up nerves. Sometimes the habit is accompanied by tail thrashing or switching, as well. It is seen in other competitive horses, too, but does not appear to be at all common among racehorses. Although their work is highly stressful, they are not schooled in a manège and kept 'under orders' like horses in other sports. Also, their work is more herd-related than that of other categories of horse.

There is not a great deal that can be done to stop teeth-grinding except, of course, to remove the conditions that cause it. Many top competitors, in fact, do not work in the manège but school their horses while out hacking. Periods of schooling work should be short and the horse given frequent breaks and praise.

Consideration should also be given to whether the horse is in physical discomfort or pain, perhaps from ill-fitting tack, an unsuitable or badly fitting bit or poor riding.

Grooming, dislike of
A horse who has been roughly handled in the past will almost certainly be difficult to groom. Scrubbing at sensitive areas like belly and head with a dandy brush is a case in point; using a metal curry comb on the body or even a plastic-toothed one too hard, or simply knocking the horse on a bony part with a wooden-backed brush, can all cause discomfort and apprehension.

Fig 35 Be prepared to groom ticklish areas with nothing more than your hand or a stable rubber to accustom the horse to being groomed and to show him it does not hurt

Remember, horses, particularly well bred ones, do have sensitive skin. Groom ticklish areas with a stable rubber or your hand and work gently until the horse, maybe over weeks or months, calms down. Do not subject him to prolonged periods of grooming but do him as quickly and calmly as possible, playing soothing music or speaking gently as you work. Never startle him by suddenly beginning on an area without warning but work gradually all over him, talking before you move. Give him a ration of hay to occupy him, if he is not going to work immediately, so he associates grooming with something pleasurable.

It is better to create trust, if possible, by grooming the horse loose but in bad cases, or where the horse is groomed outdoors, it may be necessary to tie him up to restrain him. This in itself may induce a feeling of being trapped which will not help an already apprehensive horse who may panic if he feels restricted. It may lead to halter pulling; for dealing with this see *Pulling back when tied up.*

Grunting

Grunting is a sign of great physical effort; showjumpers and eventers can be heard to grunt over a particularly taxing obstacle, and draught horses when hauling a heavy load over difficult or uphill going. However, if a horse grunts when performing what appears to be a moderate task there may be something physically wrong.

For example, if a horse begins to grunt over small obstacles it could signify that he is in pain from some injury which is not actually causing lameness, such as an obscure muscle strain, back problem or the like. Elderly animals may grunt on getting up – it is reasonable to suppose that stiffness due to the infirmities of old age, such as rheumatism and arthritis, makes the action very difficult for the horse and involves him in substantial effort, particularly at the moment of heaving up his hindquarters. In such cases, veterinary treatment of the underlying condition is recommended.

Handle, difficult to

Horses who are generally difficult to handle are often so because they are not used to considerate treatment or, having been allowed to run more or less wild from birth, have never had much

Fig 36 Young animals which have not been handled properly from birth are both difficult and dangerous to deal with

to do with humans and regard them as aliens, not as part of their everyday lives.

To ensure a well-mannered, easy-to-work-with horse, the animal should be handled correctly and frequently from birth. He needs to develop a total acceptance of mankind and of being handled by humans, as well as respect for them. It is comparatively easy to develop respect in foals as, at least with young foals, physical strength is on our side, as well as intellect. However, foals even a few months old have already developed to the extent that they can quite easily win a straightforward test of strength.

When faced with handling an animal who is obviously stronger than we are, it is best to avoid a battle beginning in the first place. If possible, at least two handlers should be available who are familiar with the various methods of restraint discussed in Part I of this book (see pages 97–107).

With animals which have been badly frightened, for instance

191

native ponies who have been captured off the moors in the annual drift or those who have been brutally treated in the past, much time will have to be spent just being present near the horse or pony to accustom it to the presence of a human who is not going to beat or otherwise hurt it. A calm, soothing voice, confident, knowledgeable people and neighbours who will set the horse an example (horses usually take cues from one another), will help in this process.

Stable manners should be taught from birth, when possible, or in the case of older animals as soon as possible, as an excellent rapport is built up between human and horse in the stable. A horse should feel secure in his stable, yet it is just this situation – a confined space with a potential enemy – which can frighten a horse not used to being handled. If anything is done to alarm him, his flight-or-fight response comes into action and, being unable to take flight, he may well kick, bite, crowd or whatever to protect himself.

The handler should speak before moving, in a calm, low voice, so as to let the horse know what to expect. The horse will soon learn simple commands such as 'over' (when we want him to move over) accompanied by a push on the side or quarters, 'up' (when we want him to pick up a hoof) accompanied by the correct method of lifting the foot, and so on.

Handling a horse who knows very well what is wanted but who just does not feel like complying, or wants to exert his authority over his handler without actually being vicious about it, calls for a slightly different approach. Firm authority, no-nonsense handling and an air of supreme confidence which tells the horse that we fully expect him to do as we wish often works like a charm with such a customer. The odd slap on the belly or shoulder is not out of place, but beating the horse up is surely calculated to turn a slightly difficult horse into a savage beast with a justifiable hatred of all mankind.

The whole business of handling a horse comes down to knowing the individual or being able to assess him or her quickly, and starting correctly from the beginning, in a way appropriate to that particular animal. It is a fascinating topic as every horse is different and each one can teach us something new about himself and his kind, if we want to learn.

See also *Bad manners in work; Stable manners, bad.*

Head banging
This pitiful habit is normally a sign of great or continual pain, or severe psychological distress. The horse leans with, usually, his forehead against the wall of the stable and presses on it or moves backwards and forwards banging his head with each movement.

Physical causes could be infection or injury to any part of the head (ears, brain, sinuses, teeth, etc). In cases of neglect, it can be caused by a headcollar being left on a growing youngster without being adjusted as the animal grows, resulting in its becoming embedded in the head.

A psychological reason could be, most notably, the stress of being confined, particularly in very claustrophobic animals which are not given enough work and are never allowed any freedom. Zoo animals kept confined exhibit many neurotic responses to their predicament also shown by horses in the same situation, such as pacing, weaving and chewing their enclosures. One reaction very much akin to head banging in horses is where the animal rubs its head back and forth or up and down against the wall in a seemingly pointless action, often wearing away the hair on the head and, indeed, the skin, too. As explained on pages 13–16, recent research at the University of Utrecht leads us to believe now that such repetitive actions cause the release into the bloodstream of substances called endorphins, the body's own pain and stress relievers and akin to morphine often administered, of course, for such relief.

Any horse afflicted with this problem should have a thorough veterinary examination to ascertain whether it has a physical cause. A veterinary surgeon should also be able to discuss the animal's living conditions and would have a good idea if these, too, were causing it sufficient stress to bring on head banging/ rubbing. In any case, such a horse is obviously extremely disturbed and must have everything possible done to help him. Apart from physical treatment, where appropriate, the horse should be kept in as natural conditions as possible, with plenty of space, activity (not merely work but natural social intercourse with other friendly horses at freedom in a paddock) and human handling and leadership he can trust and respect. His needs for food, water and shelter should obviously be met adequately to ensure his physical comfort as far as possible so as not to add further stress in this direction.

Horses have many ways of reacting to stress. Not all badly upset horses use head banging as some sort of release from tension, indeed it is probably fairly rare, but it should be remembered that any particularly stressful time in a horse's life can cause reactions of one kind or another. Apart from birth itself, the first real trauma in many horses and ponies' lives is weaning, particularly when, as is often the case, it is carried out too early and very suddenly. Being sold to a new home is much more stressful than we realise, particularly if the horse's routine, diet and work are changed in addition to his surroundings, companions and human attendants.

Severely depressed horses, like their human counterparts, need very sensitive handling over a long period, plus a natural, easy lifestyle but even then, complete recovery is not guaranteed.

Head shaking/tossing

Head shaking is one of the most frustrating problems because in most cases there seems to be absolutely nothing to be done about it. There are the obvious cases where a horse shakes or tosses his head because of a badly fitting bridle – the browband may be too tight and be pulling on the headpiece, causing pressure round the base of the ears, the noseband may be too high and rubbing on the sharp cheek bones, or its supporting pieces may be rubbing the corner of the horse's eye; anything like this can cause quite marked and persistent head tossing. The bit, too, can obviously cause it, plus excessive champing and frothing if it fits badly, is worn or damaged in some way and so causing pain, or is roughly used by rider or whip. Some Arab horses and their crosses do sometimes perform a 'circular' head-tossing movement which appears to be characteristic of the breed and is usually simply a sign of excitement or high spirits.

There are, however, several medical reasons why a horse may shake his head about. Sometimes the tossing appears to be intended and controllable by the horse; at other times it seems to be involuntary. The shaking is usually up and down, and in severe cases the rider can sustain facial injuries from contact with the horse's poll. As the head shakes about, also, the reins can be jerked from the hands and make control of the animal very difficult.

The movement is often a violent jerk, when pain may be the cause – earache or toothache, for example. Nerve disorder such as neuralgia, which is a sudden, stabbing pain, could also cause it. Parasites in the ear, or foreign bodies such as bits of bedding which have found their way down into the ear can certainly cause head shaking. This is one good reason not to clip the hair out of the insides of horses' ears; it is their protection against this sort of happening.

For such possible causes as sinus trouble, throat problems or infection of the guttural pouch (part of the inner ear), a veterinary surgeon can examine the horse with a fibrescope (fibreoptic endoscope), an instrument with a built-in light which passes 'pictures' of the area being examined up flexible fibres, and can reveal infection, growths and other abnormalities.

Unfortunately, many causes of head shaking seem to remain a mystery and so do their cures. It is noted that many horses are affected only in warm weather. Some specialists believe that certain light conditions cause the problem as some horses are affected if stabled in, or worked/exercised in, a sunny area, but improve when put in the shade.

A simple remedy which has been effective in some cases is to fit an ordinary fly fringe to the bridle – either to the browband, or to the noseband so that the fringe hangs over the nostrils. Although there seems to be no satisfactory scientific explanation for its success, if it works and does no harm it is well worth trying.

Some people recommend fitting a standing martingale and fixing inside the noseband something which will inflict discomfort or pain on the horse, such as a strip of stiff bristles, but this smacks of the old-fashioned kind of 'punishment training' rather than the more enlightened 'reward training'. It is better to try to be a little more understanding and to stop the horse wanting to throw up his head in the first place.

See also *Headshyness*.

Headshyness

A horse is described as being headshy when he dislikes anyone handling his head in any way. Often, the horse will do all he can to prevent handling by holding his head high up out of reach. If his handler tries to force him to submit, often a battle ensues, which, of course, does nothing to solve the problem or improve the condition. It will simply confirm the horse's fears, for that is the problem with a headshy horse – he is frightened.

Many such horses have been beaten about the head, not simply with a sharp slap to the muzzle which may have been administered for biting but really knocked about, probably with a stick or whip. Headshyness can also be caused by pain in the head from ear, tooth or sinus infections, or by the horse having been roughly bridled in the past or forced to wear a bridle when bridle sores were present through neglect.

Every step should be taken to remove an existing cause, such as injury or infection, and the horse must be gradually retrained to accept having his head handled. With a frightened horse this may take a long time, but great gentleness, care and patience will usually win through in the end.

When bridling the horse, it is often necessary to take the bridle to pieces and put it together again as quickly, unobtrusively and gently as possible actually on the horse's head. Start by carefully sliding the headpiece, minus cheekstraps, up the neck to the poll, thread the browband carefully on and attach the cheekpieces. Fasten one side of the bit and ask the horse to accept the bit as you bring it up between his teeth (maybe tickling his tongue with your thumb through the corner of his mouth). If you can manage without a noseband, do so, as the less there is to fiddle with the better. The reins should be fastened individually to the bit rings, passed up the shoulders and buckled above the withers. It might be necessary to have an assistant to help you, and to have a box to stand on.

Advantage should be taken of the grooming procedure to establish trust and rapport with the horse. Start grooming at the shoulder or back, and when the horse is settled gradually work up to the neck as far as you can without upsetting him. If you cannot groom the head without his becoming unduly worried, even with a cloth or your hand, leave it. If he will let you eventually gently sponge out his nostrils and eyes, this is a good sign and you can slowly take things from there.

Use your voice in a low, calming tone all the time. Never do anything sudden near the horse, do not raise your voice and do not throw things around, such as rugs or tack. When rugging and tacking up, keep your equipment as low as possible. Do not throw rugs, blankets, numnah etc, over his back like a tablecloth, but put them on unobtrusively and sort them out deftly and quickly without in any way giving him the impression you are in a hurry. Horses hate to be rushed and tension will add to his fraught state.

Considerable improvement can be expected in due course if you are careful never to frighten a headshy horse – but one unpleasant incident, such as an accidental poke in the eye or knock with a wooden brush, can ruin weeks or months of careful work.

See also *Head shaking/tossing; Tack up/harness, difficult to.*

Injections, fear of

When you watch a veterinary surgeon slapping a horse and then 'slapping' in the needle on the last blow without the horse batting an eyelid, you tend to forget that many horses are, in fact, quite nervous of having injections. Although, in Britain at any rate, horse owners rarely give injections to their own horses, at least without instructions from their vets, some horses and ponies do take exception to needles despite their having been expertly inserted. An ordinary injection usually causes less trouble than the rather different procedure needed for a blood sample, where the needle is inserted into the blood vessel.

Most veterinary surgeons are so expert at handling horses that they can get round the problem with persistence and a confident air. In some cases, however, for the safety of all concerned, some form of restraint is needed. If the horse is still, the needle will hurt him less than if he is jigging around.

A simple form of restraint is to lift one foreleg, which is enough for many horses. Where it is not, a neck twitch (where the vet takes up a fold of skin and pinches and slightly twists it) often keeps the recalcitrant horse still. Gripping the upper lip tightly in the hand often works, but sometimes it is necessary to actually twitch the horse (see page 121) before he will stand still.

Rather than resort to these methods, it is better to try and distract the animal while having him under reasonable control. These days, most vets prefer to inject in the quarters rather than the neck, which horses find less objectionable, anyway. If you have the horse wearing a lungeing cavesson or a bridle (both of which give more control than a headcollar, physical as well as psychological) and his head in a bucket of his favourite food, this will distract him. Stand close to his neck, blocking his rear view with your body so he cannot see the dreaded vet/needle, and it will probably be all over before he realises what has happened. A bridle with blinkers, or a racehorse-type blinker hood can be worn, if available.

Jealousy

This emotion is more common in horses than is often imagined. Many experts say horses do not possess emotions in the way that we do, but this is a moot point. Jealousy is certainly exhibited plainly in some circumstances and can cause a problem to humans and other animals. Unfortunately, there is very little that can be done about it.

Jealousy can obviously be shown by a horse when a neighbour is being fed titbits and he is not, when one animal is being trotted up and having attention paid to him and another is not, when one horse is being taken out for exercise and another is kept in. I have seen a yard where several serving stallions were kept together (a common and most unnatural practice which would never happen in the wild) and in which one particular horse, who regarded himself as the top horse, would sulk terribly – sulk, not fret – when another stallion was taken out to serve a mare. His face, normally proud and kind, would become incredibly sour, with ears back, mean eyes and nostrils drawn back, and no amount of attention would change him until a good half hour after the other horse returned. The only thing which consoled him was to have a mare of his own, so the owners of the yard tried their utmost to ensure that he was used at the same time as, and in a different place from, his rivals. He was taken from his box first and returned last; this fooled him and there was never any more jealousy on that score, although he continued to demand the bulk of the human attention if he could possibly manage it.

Some horses are jealous of their owners. If one particular horse is used to being ridden by one particular rider with whom he has a close and strong rapport, it is not unknown for him to show jealousy when his rider takes out another horse.

Where the jealous horse becomes nasty and starts biting or kicking the rival horse or the human who is causing the problem,

198

a reprimand must obviously be administered to prevent the behaviour getting out of hand, but one must not expect to prevent the feeling. The best course of action is to avoid the situation, if possible, or get round it in some way (as in the case of the stallion mentioned previously). It is silly to provoke the animal (to teach him 'to get used to it') by letting the situation continue; this will simply sour his temper and upset him more.

Do not stable obvious rivals next to one another or even within sight, sound or smell of one another, if possible. At feed times, feed the jealous horse first to keep him quiet. When it is impossible not to provoke his jealousy, such as when his neighbour is receiving attention, and if he is expected to react violently perhaps by kicking the stable, an effort should be made to take him away, either for his exercise or grazing period. If this is not possible, closing his top door temporarily may help; alternatively, he could be tied up so that his heels cannot reach the wall.

Jealousy in the field is more difficult to control, apart from simply not turning out susceptible horses with those likely to cause the trouble. Certainly at feed times, if horses are fed together in the field, at least one more container of feed than there are horses must be put out. Horses should be watched to see that some poor individual is not being kept out of a shelter area by a jealous companion. The 'cure' for situations like this is to remove the jealous horse for the sake of all the others.

Jibbing/Napping

There have probably been more remedies recommended for jibbing than any other single vice, partly because it is fairly common and partly because the reasons for it and the characters of the horses involved, not to mention their riders or drivers, are so very varied.

Nappy horses simply refuse to go forward, although the term is not used for a horse's refusal to take a jump. A napper or jibber will either root himself to the spot, forelegs braced and a stubborn-as-a-mule look on his face, or he may run back, buck or kick on the spot or, worst of all, develop the habit of rearing. Some horses try to nap with any riders just to test them, some only nap with experienced riders as a sign of resentment of their authority and others with novice riders because the horse knows they are too weak to do anything about it.

199

Many nappers are unhappy horses who have been mistreated in the past and have had enough of being ridden or driven in an unsympathetic or brutal way. Nappy horses come in all characters, from riding school plugs to sensitive, high-couraged animals who have not had handlers to match. They may nap because they are confused, insecure and worried, or because they are bossy, lazy and ungenerous – and before a suitable remedy can be found the reason has to be discovered by a sympathetic, competent horseman. Young horses often go through a phase of trying it on as they mature and find their feet; it is part of their growing-up process to test those in authority over them to see just how far they can go. Most animals do it with their own kind and with their human associates, too. A certain amount of tolerance is usually shown, but when they go too far, the youngsters are put smartly in their places, and often return to the older animal or human to apologise and make up, restoring the status quo for the sake of peace and psychological security.

So it is with horse and handler. A horseman who insists on absolute obedience at all times may, in fact, make, rather than cure, a jibber, but equally a weak, over-sentimental person can do just the same.

With the horse who has been mistreated under saddle or in harness, retraining, practically from scratch, by a competent and sensitive trainer will often do the trick; however, should a less talented handler take over, the vice may well return because a confirmed, mature jibber is more or less impossible to cure.

If the horse is a youngster trying out his handlers, and they are sure the horse (a) understands what is wanted, (b) is not tired or sick, and (c) is not sore or aching from strenuous work when unfit or from badly fitting tack or harness, firmness with leg and voice usually has good effect. If the horse is really insistent, one good crack with the whip behind the leg or a sharp flick on the quarters usually makes him think twice about repeating his efforts. If the trouble seems to be taking hold, his training should be taken back a step to re-establish obedience to the aids. Many authorities claim success with long reining, as opposed to lungeing, particularly the school where the trainer is very close to the horse rather than the old English method which more resembles lungeing with two reins, one round the horse's quarters.

I have had success with long reining, but with a rider as well. The rider uses the normal aids and the trainer walks close behind the horse with the long reins passed through the rider's stirrups. Vocal encouragement, a competent rider and the presence of the trainer immediately behind the horse seem to combine to do the trick.

With a really stubborn jibber who is simply lazy and has learned he can get away with it, first 'uproot' him by moving him to the side, just to get his forelegs moving. Circling fast and tight often works, then driving on in the desired direction before the horse has time to realise what is happening. If the horse is running backwards, *make* him back faster than he wants to, preferably into something unpleasant (a holly bush is ideal!) or solid, then drive him on at once, circling as described if he still refuses. Should the horse buck on the spot, remember he cannot buck effectively with his head up, so get it up, sit up yourself and kick on, maybe in a circle, but anywhere but on the spot.

One method which worked successfully for me in a few cases was to have an assistant behind the jibber with a stiff stable broom. When the horse began his tricks, he was scrubbed none too gently under the tail with the broom, which usually resulted in a prompt jump forward.

Another method, suitable for those working alone, is to take a lungeing rein or other long rope and fasten it to the front dee on one side of the pommel of the saddle. Pass it under the saddle flap, behind the horse under his tail, forward under the other saddle flap and hold the rest in the hand on that side. Be sure to keep the rope short enough to prevent it falling near the hocks but not so that it is tight round the thighs. When the horse shows the first inkling of napping, pull forward, hard, on the rope (in addition to normal leg and voice aids) and the horse will, perhaps after a couple of sharp tugs, normally go forward. A few sessions of this often make a jibber think twice and become co-operative.

There is a similar method for harness horses who jib. The rope is fixed like a crupper, round the root of the tail, passed forward to the pad, put through one of the terrets and passed back to the driver's hand. When the horse naps, the driver pulls back on the rope, which obviously gives the horse an unpleasant jerk under the tail, and prompts a speedy response to the request 'walk on'! Harness horses may nap justifiably when asked to pull too heavy

201

a load, if their shoulders are sore (as mentioned earlier) or if an incline is too steep. Relieving the weight on the collar by moving the vehicle forward by the wheels often helps.

Sometimes, simply having a foreleg lifted and moved forward by an assistant on the ground is enough to shift a nappy horse into forward gear – perhaps his physical block, in such cases, is on a par with his mental one, and when the connecting 'link' is broken by the leg being moved, it breaks down the resistance.

In cases where a jibber seems to be developing that most dangerous of vices, rearing (see under that heading), he should be reschooled by a thoroughly competent trainer who can get to the bottom of his resistance. In any case, if the habit of napping has occurred more than once, it is becoming established and steps must be taken quickly to prevent it becoming ingrained into the horse's behaviour patterns. Often, horses only nap in one place – where they have done so before – as in shying, because they then come to associate that particular spot with napping.

It is essential to use an appropriate approach for the horse concerned. Even with a mean, lazy horse, beating him up simply embitters the animal and makes him worse; it will not 'show him

---

(top left)
A simple technique which can help keep a horse quiet during noisy operations such as clipping or spraying on fly repellant is to stuff cotton wool in the ears. This deadens the noise, which is what frightens many animals. There is an international show jumper who always jumps with cotton wool in his ears as otherwise the music and the noise of the crowd, particularly the applause, distract him too much. This technique has also proved helpful in some cases of headshaking

(top right)
To protect yourself when pulling the tail of a horse who is likely to kick, get someone to hold the horse inside his box and pull his tail over the door like this. If the horse is too small for his tail to go over the door, a wall of straw bales can be constructed instead

(below left)
This is a three-quarter shoe which has also been set in slightly on its inner branch. Such shoes are helpful in preventing injury in horses who brush or speedy cut (*Peter R. Sweet*)

(below right)
A crib-biter will take hold of any convenient projection with his teeth, in this case the top of the stable door, to help him arch his neck to form the essential vacuum which enables him to gulp down air into his digestive tract. Removing projections and shutting the horse in are not the answers to this problem!

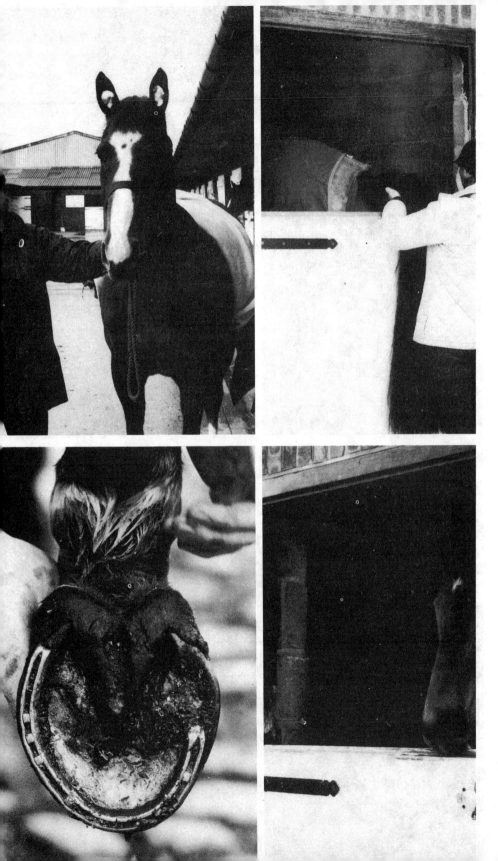

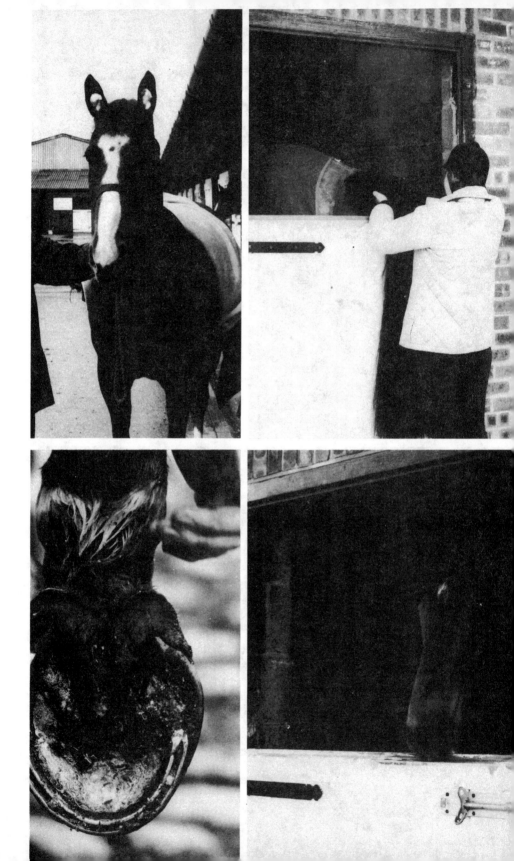

who's boss'. If a battle is unavoidable, it must be a long (if necessary), firm but quiet one to wear him down. I am not the only person who has sat on a horse for a few hours because he refused to pass a certain spot in the lane, and found that he never napped there again.

See also *Leave other horses/home, refusing to.*

Jogging

Horses who persist in jogging around are usually of the naturally energetic type. The habit is not only tiring for the rider, not to mention nauseating if you are that way inclined, it is also annoying when performed in harness and can upset neighbouring horses.

Working in the company of a very staid, somewhat lazy animal often improves the situation (interestingly enough, it rarely works the other way round), and cutting down the concentrate feed, giving a lower energy feed, allowing plenty of liberty in a paddock and giving plenty of work also help. If the problem still persists after all this, then retraining should have some effect.

Some horses take up jogging when they have been made to walk out faster than they comfortably can, or been asked to trot too slowly. A rider who constantly nags with the legs can definitely cause it – some animals go 'dead' to unremitting leg aids but others, more sensitive, simply start to jog out of confusion or annoyance.

Put the horse back on the lunge and make quite certain that he fully understands what the command 'walk' means. Under saddle, use the command with normal slowing-down aids the instant the horse jogs. Do not pull roughly on the reins or command in a rough voice as this will upset him and put him on

---

To instil discipline, start young! This foal is being effectively and harmlessly taught that he cannot escape human discipline and also that he is not going to be hurt. The soft stable rubber round the neck restrains him from the front, hands on the quarters restrain him from behind, and Mum is close by to give moral support and set an example, led by a third person to leave the other two free to teach the youngster

Soon, the foal can be led by one person direct from the foal slip, with a guiding hand on the quarters. Eventually, one person can lead both mare and foal, one in each hand

edge, when he is more likely to jog, not less. Calmly bring him back to walk and insist absolutely that he walks. When he obeys, do not push him on at a fast pace, but rather let him go slowly and do not use any leg aids until he gets the idea that walking is peaceful and relaxing.

It is up to the rider to stop the jogging so that the horse eventually gets the idea that it is not wanted. Do not let the horse jog on for a little way and then bring him back to walk, as he will think periods of jogging are acceptable. It must be either walk or a proper trot. Sensitive aids, persistence and consistency are the answers.

Jump, refusing to

This is a very common problem indeed, and one normally caused by poor initial training and/or subsequent bad riding.

If the horse's initial schooling has been hurried so that he is asked to tackle obstacles before he is ready, if he has been jumped when too young, particularly on hard ground, and has, as a result, had his immature bones and feet jarred, the pain will obviously put him off jumping, then and in the future – horses have elephantine memories! An over-heavy rider, particularly on a young, immature back, will also cause physical stress, injury and pain. An impatient rider, and especially one who loses his or her temper when a horse shows uncertainty, is sure to create a refuser out of a normally willing jumper. If, every time the horse jumps a fence, someone socks him in the mouth or bangs down on his back or loins, it is no wonder that he starts refusing. Over-jumping (too high, too wide and too often) is also an obvious cause.

This book, obviously, is not intended for highly competent or professional riders; they will have their own remedies. But there must be many of us who have been behind the scenes at some big show or other and watched the Grade A or international competitors schooling. Particularly after a refusal in the ring, the horses of such competitors are often seen being put time and time again at a fence similar to that at which they refused to make sure they do not repeat the fault. These horses have to earn their riders' livings for them, and are working horses in the truest sense. If they are off the road for any reason (and a showjumper who refuses is no use at all) their stable loses a lot of money in winnings and maintenance costs. However, one cannot help thinking that a complete rest from jumping for a few months would be a good idea for a horse who has begun to refuse. Top-level jumpers who are in the business for many years are normally those who are not over-jumped, or asked to jump when injured or unwell. Others appear in a flash of glory and disappear just as quickly, over-faced and sickened.

Ordinary mortals faced with a horse who is refusing are often beset with the problem of knowing whether the horse is saying 'I can't' or 'I won't'. It is no easy decision to make, even for very experienced horsemasters, and it is hoped that Dr Moyra Williams' contribution to this book (see pages 110–114) will help here.

To jump a fence successfully, of course, the horse must be given every chance by being brought in correctly. Most horses jump best, particularly if they themselves are not expert, if brought in on a straight line rather than at an angle. They should be under control, moving with impulsion and not held back by a rider who is afraid of jumping the fence, as if this apprehension is transmitted to a horse he will almost certainly refuse. The old saying 'throw your heart over the fence and the horse will follow' seems true and it has worked for generations of children and adults up to date.

Too tight a hold on the reins is as bad as no contact at all. Most horses like to know that their riders are in touch but not hanging on like grim death. The ability to 'see' or judge the horse's stride is a great help to the rider so that he can fold down at the correct instant and help the horse rather than hinder him by jerking him in the mouth. It helps both horse and rider if the rider thinks of the track to be followed ahead and not so much of the obstacle, treating the latter like a minor hindrance in his path which will simply be stepped over. The jump is quite incidental to the track.

Psychological factors apart, it has to be admitted that it can be impossible to cure a confirmed case of refusing, but given expert advice and sympathetic (not necessarily soft) treatment, many horses can be reformed.

Starting off again with trotting poles, walking the horse through the empty wings of a jump (ie with no pole present), schooling in the presence of jumps but not actually taking them, and having cavalletti scattered about the schooling area to be trotted over nonchalantly and occasionally, can all help the refuser. The horse's tack should obviously be above reproach, very comfortable, and the bit should not be misused by the rider – and nor should whip or spurs. If the horse refuses to walk over a cavalletto, have an assistant standing on the other side (and one on each side of it) holding out his favourite titbit as an instant reward when he crosses over.

Very gradual raising of the poles, particularly little cross-poles, should be adopted. Always be sure to bring the horse in straight with a light, even contact on the bit, and a well-balanced rider; verbal praise should be given at every successful or courageous try, and the sessions should be very short. Popping over logs out hacking also creates fun rather than fear, particularly in company when another horse can give a lead in an informal atmosphere.

Things to be avoided are thrashing the horse, hard spurring, yelling, punishment with the bit etc. These 'crimes' are guaranteed to make a refuser worse. As mentioned, it does take expert judgement to decide when a horse is afraid, in pain or just being awkward, but with experienced help where available, a competent rider, sensible reschooling and time, great improvements can often be made.

See also *Running out at fences*.

Kicking

Kicking is basically a defensive action and most horses do not do it unless their other methods of defence (running away/ avoidance, nipping/biting and, according to the individual, striking out with the forefeet) have been removed or are inappropriate, ie when the threat, real or imagined, is from the rear. When horses kick for no apparent reason, they are usually trying to protect themselves from an attack or other discomfort which they think is imminent. It is unlikely that they have the mental aptitude to do it as a warning.

A really confirmed kicker may well be impossible to cure and although an improvement in his (or more usually her, for most kickers seem to be mares) behaviour may be achieved, such a horse can never be relied upon not to kick and should always be thought of as a kicker and handled accordingly.

I have consulted many people as to the best way to deal with this behavioural problem, and while some experts say there is no real remedy others have offered a variety of correctives and preventives which may interest readers. Almost everyone consulted agreed that to hit a riding horse on the flank as a punishment for kicking under saddle would have only one effect, and that would be to make him much worse. A sharp vocal reprimand is recommended but further punishment, even a crack down the shoulder with the whip, is not generally advised as kicking is normally brought on (particularly in a horse who is normally good natured and not prone to aggressiveness) by ill-treatment. Further pain in the form of physical punishment will merely encourage the horse to defend himself in the way he has chosen – kicking.

When under saddle and in a situation where kicking might be likely (hacking in company, out hunting etc) the horse must be ridden well up to his bridle and encouraged to bring his hocks under him; in other words, to go in as reasonably collected a manner as possible. Horses cannot kick effectively without relieving their hindquarters of weight, which allows them to raise the leg to kick, so riding and schooling which trains and encourages a horse to 'bring his hind legs under him' makes kicking more difficult.

In harness, a kicker can quickly demolish an expensive vehicle and, here again, a sting with the whip does not appear to be the answer. Instead, a kicking strap (see Fig 37) is a definite discouragement as, in order to raise the quarters to kick, the horse must also raise the weight of the vehicle. A horse who kicks other horses with impunity should be driven only in single harness and/or used for riding, because he can easily break his colleagues' legs.

It is obvious that, in addition to putting a red ribbon in the tail of a kicker and warning those who come close to him or her, the person in charge of the horse should do all possible to prevent the horse being put in a position where he can, or wants to, kick. In a crowd of horses, for example, the horse should be kept on the edge and behind when possible. If standing 'coffee-housing' on any occasion, the horse's quarters should be kept directed away from companions. If dogs are running loose, try to avoid them, and to warn their owners that your horse could kick the dogs. Out hunting, it is a heinous crime for a horse to kick a hound,

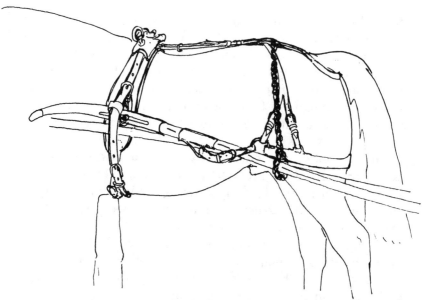

Fig 37 To discourage a horse from kicking in harness, a kicking strap can be most effective. A rope is attached to the crupper, and on each side to the shafts, making it extremely difficult for the horse to kick unless he also lifts the weight of the vehicle with his quarters, which he is unlikely to manage

and although it may not always be easy, the rider should be constantly alert for potential trouble and keep the horse's quarters away from hounds.

Horses who kick others when loose in a yard or paddock should preferably be turned out alone and should, in any case, never be turned loose with other horses unless the hind shoes have been removed. It is sometimes recommended that such an animal be turned out with an equally determined kicker, but the potential damage and the unlikelihood of a cure make this course of action a doubtful proposition.

Horses who kick out at humans either when loose or in the stable are a real menace. It is normally better to stay on the other side of the paddock gate and get the horse to come to you for some favourite titbit, then catch hold of a short rope or loop of binder twine attached to the ring under the headcollar, than to go into the field and risk the horse's turning on you with his heels. If, for some reason, this is unavoidable, treat it as an emergency and take in with you a strong cutting whip. Avoid the horse's quarters like the plague and do all you can to get him to approach you, probably for a bucket of whatever he prefers. But if you find yourself faced with his quarters, summon up all your agility and get round to his front end as quickly as you can, or simply forward and away. Horses who kick often back into their victims, kicking as they come, so get out of the line of fire. As a last resort, if you find yourself in the frightening position of being cornered by him, thrash his quarters as hard as you can with the whip, repeatedly, and yell at him fiercely. Unfortunately, this goes against the 'no further punishment' idea mentioned earlier, but it is probably your only choice in what has become a dangerous emergency – standing there quietly will do you no good at all! Avoidance behaviour on your part is by far the most effective method of protecting yourself against a kicker.

Fig 38 Habituation to a stimulus can help retrain a horse. Here, a kicker is being gently stroked with a long stick and allowed to kick out to his heart's content. The general idea is that once he realises that kicking does no good, he will stop. But care must be taken not to torment the horse and tease him. Use your voice in a calming way

If faced with a horse who kicks in the stable, a good plan is, again, to get him to put his head over the door for a titbit, get hold of his headcollar, open his door with your free hand, walk in, still holding the horse, and tie him up before you do anything else. Then, when working on or around him, keep out of the way of his quarters. If the horse cow kicks (sideways or forwards), be ready for it and gauge the reach of his kick so that you can keep out of the way.

In many cases, ignoring the kicking altogether and not even telling the horse off verbally has resulted in the horse giving up the vice as he finds it has no result and does not prevent your handling him. Talk to the horse normally and change neither your tone of voice nor whatever you are doing, and the horse might well eventually give up, although the inclination to kick might remain. Tie him up in such a way that his hind hooves cannot reach the wall behind him, as if he hears a lovely crash when he kicks he might realise the kicking does have some effect after all and carry on doing it.

As many horses who kick in the stable (but possibly at no other time) have developed the habit through rough or even vicious handling, it pays to treat them gently but confidently at all times. When grooming, for instance, it would be extremely foolish to scrub at them hard with the dandy brush, particularly in sensitive places and/or when they are tied up (as kickers should be when you are working in the box) as they will naturally want to retaliate. Be considerate of their feelings and remember that kicking, unlike biting, is more a defence than an act of aggression, therefore do not give them reason to wish to defend themselves. In time, gentle but firm handling will probably bring about a great improvement once they realise that you are not going to give them cause for complaint.

If you do notice a kick coming (ears back, head down and tail up are the usual signs, not to mention a wavering leg), and you cannot get out of the way, quickly get as *close* to the quarters as possible so that you will only receive a push rather than the full strength of the kick at leg's length.

Handling a kicker's hind legs and feet can present problems. An assistant is helpful, to keep the horse's head slightly up. If you can manage to pull fairly hard down on his tail while picking up the leg (and, of course, face his tail all the time, as detailed in any good horse-care book), you will find it a lot easier. The head up/tail down business does discourage kicking. If the horse attempts to kick while you are holding his tail, jerk it hard and give it a twist, too.

A technique called 'habituation' often wears out a kicker's desire. Simply take a long cane or stick (long enough to keep you out of reach of his hind hooves), stand with your back to his head and gentle him all over, starting at the shoulder, with the cane. Just stroke him with it and talk all the time, gradually working to his quarters and down the hind legs; let him kick out as much as he wants but do not reprimand him. Eventually, after perhaps a few lessons, he will get thoroughly tired of his useless kicking, realise you are not hurting him, and give it up. Finally, you can use your hand to gentle him and handle him without his kicking at you.

Horses sometimes kick their box walls when they want attention or food (feed them first at feed times as making them wait reinforces the habit), when they are in need of freedom (turn them loose somewhere as much as possible), when in need of exercise/work (again, supply their need and more, if possible), when they are stabled next to an enemy (move one of them), when there is vermin in the stable (get a cat or two), when they have an irritating skin condition of the legs (call in the vet if you cannot cure it yourself), if their clothing is uncomfortable or bedding has become worked up under it and is irritating the skin, or because they have got used to the habit and like the noise they make. In the latter case, padding the walls of the box to deaden the sound prevents the desired result and the horse sometimes stops doing it. The padding can consist of stuffed sacks (which the horse may start biting and tearing) or tough rubber or synthetic material.

There are various anti-kicking devices which comprise arrangements of straps round the pasterns leading to a roller, or from forelegs to roller to hind legs, various types of hobbles, straps round the upper leg with a length of chain, or a lump of wood hanging from a piece of string (which is supposed to hit the horse's leg and so 'punish' him each time he kicks but which, in practice, makes many horses worse, as can be imagined). There are also various schooling techniques involving the above, all of which meet with varying degrees of success according to the

Fig 39 Here, a rope is attached to a hobble round the pastern and when the horse is standing normally, will be fastened to the bottom D of the head-collar. Then, when the horse kicks out, he will give himself an unpleasant jab on the nose – another example of self-inflicted punishment. The handler should remain present, perhaps grooming or generally handling the horse, and ensure that a foreleg does not get over the rope

temperament of the horse in question. These methods are not detailed in this book as they are the province of the expert. If you cannot solve a kicking problem by any of the more conventional methods, consider sending the horse to a professional for expert advice and handling.

Lead, refusing to

It is most important that a horse should learn to lead obligingly in hand from an early age. The longer the task is left the more difficult it becomes because, of course, it is completely unnatural for the horse. No wild or feral animal would allow itself to be haltered or would walk calmly along beside an alien being, yet this is one of the first things a foal must learn.

With mature horses who have never been properly taught to lead, we can surely have problems. They should not be led from another horse until they have been re-trained as, obviously, they can create a most dangerous situation by hanging back or playing up. They must be taught to obey instantly the vocal command of 'walk on'. A competent rider may use a whip on the quarters of the reluctant horse but must be ready and able to cope with two horses should one start playing up and affect the other one too. Foals are much easier to handle, but even one who has been allowed to run free beside its dam for the first few weeks of its life can begin to cause trouble for its handlers, so most good studs never permit this practice. The foal begins to learn from a few days old, by having a foal slip fitted and by being manoeuvred along with an arm or soft rope behind its buttocks and a stable rubber round its neck, that it must go where these two-legged things tell it. If the handlers are wise, they will use the co-operation of the dam as an example and let the foal be led alongside or just behind Mother at first. Gradually, the arm and stable rubber are dispensed with and the foal walks along quite happily being led by his own personal handler, near Mother. Pretty soon, one person can lead both mare and foal together, and then, within a very few weeks, you have a horse who has been properly taught to lead and will remember the lesson all his life.

With a more mature animal, arms and stable rubbers will do no good at all. For the not-too-bad case, a brick wall and a schooling whip are helpful. Have a bridle on (more control, physical and psychological, than a headcollar and certainly more than a rope halter), and lead the horse along, with you on one side and the wall on the other. In the hand away from the wall carry a long schooling whip held behind your back. Standing at the horse's shoulder and exerting no restraining pressure on the bit, give the command 'walk on' and at the same time flick his flank with the whip behind your back. This makes most horses jump to it, so be ready for that. Praise him when he walks forward. A few sessions of this and you will be able to lead the horse away from the wall. If he is reluctant, have an assistant standing behind him with a stiff-bristled stable broom. At the instant you say 'walk on' and flick him, the assistant scrubs him under the tail with the broom. For those who feel that this constitutes 'punishment training' with all the undesirable connotations that entails, try the 'carrot-on-a-stick' routine – which, in

215

my experience, works with only a few horses.

Another good solo method is to take a lungeing rein and fix one end firmly to the horse's saddle (probably to the girth tabs under the flap), pass it round his thighs like a fillet string, up the other side and through the run-up stirrup to keep the line up, through the headcollar ring (the headcollar being put on top of the bridle if you wish) and thence to your hand. When you give the command 'walk on' give a good, firm forward tug on the line which will probably urge the horse forward. I have used this method successfully several times.

If the horse really starts playing up, rearing in hand and so on, it is advisable to call in expert help. Quiet, but very firm handling from an expert will often improve matters, particularly when the horse is misbehaving rather than being genuinely ignorant of what is required. In no circumstances should you allow the horse to be thrashed because, as in most problems, this will probably make him much worse. On the other hand, if a less-

Fig 40 A rope looped under the tail, knotted over loins and withers to prevent it dropping down dangerously, with both free ends passed through one of the Ds of the headcollar and thence to the leader's hand can be pulled forward at the same time as the command to 'walk on' is given. This will encourage most reluctant horses to stride out

than-expert owner/handler lets such a horse get away with refusing to lead, he or she will also make the problem much worse.

Leave other horses/home, refusing to

The desire to remain with companions or in familiar surroundings obviously stems from insecurity and affects all horses to some degree. However, it is overcome in most by means of instilling confidence in and obedience to the rider/driver/handler, usually when the horse is young.

During foalhood, especially if the foal is shown, which is an excellent way to introduce him to the world and extend his education beyond the normal handling and obedience/habituation training given at home, the foal has to learn that his dam will be a little distance away for a short time, being stood up or trotted out. Foals used to this rarely become 'barn sour' or a 'barn rat', as Americans call it.

Animals who have not had this experience when young, or who have always been kept and worked in company, can become a serious and dangerous problem when eventually required to work alone. Some animals at poorer riding schools will not even leave the line during a ride, eg if they are leading file they will not canter to the rear of the ride or leave it to jump. It is not uncommon for a school client to purchase a favourite mount from the school only to find that when it is required to hack out alone carrying its new owner it refuses to leave the yard.

Training a horse to be independent when a foal begins with correct lead training which, in itself, centres the foal's attention on its handler rather than its dam. When the foal is used to more or less obeying the handler, the foal and dam are gradually led out further and further away from each other, one is led past the other and so on, until the foal willingly goes where the handler tells it rather than hanging on to Mother's tail all the time.

This independent obedience should be carried on as a yearling. It is common, especially on Thoroughbred studs, for yearlings to be taught to lead well in hand and to trot up in company, but it is better for at least some individual leading to be done out of sight of the others.

With an adult horse cursed with this problem, training can be difficult, and knowledgeable, strong (not vicious) handling and

217

riding are needed. Many youngsters of three or four years go through a phase where they 'try it on' with their human handlers and get a bit nappy just to see how far they can go, even though they have been perfectly obedient before this. The lunge line arrangement described under *Lead, refusing to* can be usefully adopted here.

A schoolmaster horse should be employed to assist in retraining. If a manège ride is going on, the horse should join in and, with a strong and competent rider up, be made to stand or walk while other horses pass to the opposite end of the manège; then the problem horse should be made to pass them in turn. When riding out, the horse should similarly be made to take his turn in leading or going last, to go past the schoolmaster and then gradually be ridden further and further apart from his companion. When a fork in the road is reached, provided the horse has shown a reasonable degree of independent work, the two

Fig 41 Horses who refuse to leave their colleagues or familiar home ground are an absolute nuisance. Sympathetic, strong retraining is essential

should be taken by different routes. It is particularly helpful if the problem horse can be taken on a route heading towards home and with which he is familiar, at least for his early excursions, as this will concentrate his mind on getting home rather than on the companion he has just left.

Gradually, with strong handling and retraining like this, the horse will accept being alone. It should be remembered that if anything happens to hurt or frighten the horse while he is alone (such as being given a thrashing by his rider or being involved in a motor accident) this will serve to reinforce his conviction that working alone is definitely something to fear, so safe routes and strong riders who are not whip-happy are called for.

Should a horse develop a 'sticky patch' at one particular place, such as refusing to go down a certain road or past a certain building, he may, in his own mind, have a perfectly good reason for this behaviour. He may be terrified of something he can hear, see or smell which we can't, or which we do not connect with his fear. As mentioned in other parts of this book, one of the horse-master's greatest difficulties is deciding whether the horse is afraid or stubborn. When this occurs in a horse who has just left company or who is being asked to leave the yard, a 'quiet fight' may be needed. In other words, the rider may simply have to sit it out until the cows come home or the moon rises over the cow-sheds, if necessary, particularly if he has no help. This very time-consuming remedy does work, and usually once the horse has, perhaps after hours, given in and proceeded in the direction in which he is pointed, he rarely does it again. Profuse praise should be administered no matter how angry or exhausted or bored the rider is!

Backing the horse past a sticky spot often works. Just take a few steps to get some movement going again, then turn round and the horse may well carry on as if nothing had happened.

It is not so easy to remedy this fault in driving horses, but basically the same principle should apply. A horse used to pair work may refuse to go at all in single harness, and this is only one reason why it is so useful for driving horses to be also broken to saddle. If they are not, however, again simply leading a horse near them and then gradually taking him further and further away is the most logical way to proceed.

See also *Jibbing/Napping.*

219

Lie down in stable, refusing to

This habit stems mainly from insecurity, though it could be due to injury or disease (see also *Shivering*). Perhaps the horse has had an unpleasant experience, such as being cast, or has had a stable frequented by rats (many horses are afraid of rats), or has never been given enough bedding so he has bruised himself on the floor and found lying down uncomfortable. Horses brought to a new home or those previously kept out sometimes refuse to lie down in the stable, particularly if they feel it is too small for them to do so in safety.

Such a horse should be given the largest and most pleasant box available. It should be bedded down exceptionally well and kept clean as although horses do lie in their own droppings (they often have no choice, of course), most horses find them objectionable and a sensitive animal may well refuse to lie down in a dirty box.

It is a good idea to keep the horse in fairly hard, or long work, within reason, so he is tired and will want to lie down. Once the horse finds peace and security and a measure of happiness in his stable or new home, he will probably eventually discover the joys of lying down flat out to sleep and, even if he is grey, you will be overjoyed to see stable stains on him in the mornings!

Some horses will not lie down when wearing clothing, particularly the old-fashioned type of rug with a belt-like surcingle round the girth and, more especially, the rarer type with a second surcingle around the belly. The modern rugs with crossed surcingles or leg-strap fastenings are much more comfortable and less discouraging to this type of horse. If a restricting rug does seem to be the reason for his remaining standing, try putting him in a warmer stable, upping his feed and leaving him without clothing, and see if that teaches him that if he does get down nothing awful is going to happen.

Do not be tempted to force the horse down in his stable. 'Throwing' a horse is best done by a veterinary surgeon as it is fraught with dangers for all concerned, not least the horse, if inexpertly performed. In any case, the last thing you want to do is give the horse another nasty experience to reinforce his belief that lying down in the stable is associated with fear, stress and maybe pain.

If he is settled, with neighbours he likes, handlers he trusts and all his physical comforts catered for, the day will probably come when he does finally lie down. After that your problem may be getting him up again (see *Lying down during work*)!

Lying down during work/Refusing to get up in stable

If your horse remains lying down when you go into his box (provided you are sure he is not ill or injured), you can take it as a compliment. Many disciplinarians will be thinking: 'Well, I'd take it as an insult!' But although mutual respect is important in a horse/human relationship, I would rather have a friendly relationship as well, than a boss/subordinate one. I do not particularly like horses jumping to their feet when I go into their boxes; it tells me they are worried by my presence and feel safer on their feet. If, however, the horse has been trained to do this by a previous owner, and particularly if he is the bolshie type who takes a yard if you give him an inch, then it is both understandable and desirable.

If the horse must be made to get up for some reason (visit from the vet, time to go out, stable needs mucking out) and requests and pushes have no effect, one method which usually works is to splash cold water on his neck, or, if you must, on his face.

The horse or pony who lies down during work can be a real and dangerous menace. Horses of ungenerous nature might be prone to this but some animals who have been driven mentally or physically to the end of their tether also do it. Azoturia can also cause a horse to lie down, in which case veterinary attention should be obtained at once. If a horse has learned that he can escape work or obedience by lying down, he may well do it regularly, so, provided you are sure your work or schooling demands are genuinely not too much for him, you must be on the watch and stop it happening in the first place, if at all possible.

Horses lie down front end first, so the first signs are the head going down, the horse pawing and/or buckling at the knees. Be on your guard for this, either under saddle or in harness, and use your voice, legs and whip, as the case may be, to keep him up and moving forward. Be sure to get his head up quickly.

If the horse actually succeeds in getting down, it can be very difficult to get him up again. If you have any cold water handy, pouring it on him, near his head, may well work. Kicking, thrashing, yelling and even laughing at him are variously recommended, but I have found the cold water treatment more effective than any of these – it does not hurt, just frightens him. Making rude noises down his ear has worked for me on more than one occasion!

See also *Rolling*.

Load, refusing to

Readers are first referred to Dr Sharon Cregier's contribution to Part II of this book, on transportation problems (see pp 123–32).

At the time of writing, it is extremely difficult to find trailers in Britain which enable horses to be transported in a balanced way, tail to the engine. Most horseboxes, also, do not permit this, although many allow for horses to travel either diagonally or sideways, both of which are a little better than facing the engine.

The type of transport most available in Britain necessitates the horse walking forward up a ramp and into the vehicle, rather than being backed in as recommended by Dr Cregier. Whether the entrance is at the side or the rear, to the horse it is all the same, the ramp has to be negotiated and the 'cavern' has to be entered.

Most horses are difficult to load because they are frightened, although a few might just be contrary. Although many horses and ponies enter vehicles readily and apparently without apprehension, others do show some anxiety and a few actually do so to the point where they refuse to enter. Often, a horse simply needs a few seconds to weigh up the situation, to muster his faculties and go in. Others can be induced to enter by means of just lifting a forefoot onto the ramp and being shown it is not going to collapse under them. A few can be tempted by a bucket of feed or by a companion being loaded first (even if the companion is subsequently taken out again). Horses are naturally claustrophobic and may be afraid of the closed-in space presented to them, particularly in the case of a trailer.

Positioning the trailer so it presents the least difficulty to the horse is one of the best ways to help him make up his mind to enter, apart from a positive mental attitude on the part of the handler. Face the vehicle downhill if at all possible so that when the ramp is lowered it will be reasonably level and not a steep incline. It helps to cover the ramp and the floor of the vehicle with familiar bedding material and to make sure it is light inside so that the horse can see where he is going.

It is abuse during loading which makes many horses progressively difficult at this time, therefore it is never recommended that a horse is hit when he hesitates or refuses to enter the vehicle. The familiar trick of pushing the horse in by means of two lunge lines crossed behind his buttocks should only be used as a last resort. Very often, an assistant standing behind and slightly to one side with a stiff-bristled stable broom can help the horse make up his mind by brushing him under the tail, although even this is abuse, if mild. Unfortunately, there are occasions where needs must, such as if the horse is already away at an event and has to go home.

Many experts maintain that horses are unable to 'think ahead' and do not, therefore, associate the act of loading into a vehicle with the process of actually being transported, ie with the vehicle in motion. In other words, the way in which the horse is driven can make no difference to his attitude to loading. This has not been my experience. I have found that horses subjected to rough driving or some other frightening experience during transit can certainly become subsequently difficult to both load and travel.

The most difficult times for the horse in transit are during braking, accelerating and cornering. Roundabouts are particu-

Fig 42 Site the trailer on a slope so that the ramp is almost level, make sure it is light inside, keep the horse straight and employ positive thinking!

larly bad if the driver does not go really slowly as the horse is swung first to one side then to the other. When transporting horses face-to-the-engine, the main points to remember are to brake very gradually (and keep your distance from the vehicle in front so that you have plenty of time to slow down), accelerate equally slowly and corner at snail's pace.

Careful driving and lack of abuse during loading are the best ways of improving the horse's behaviour when being boxed.

Men, dislike of

For some reason many horses dislike or are frightened of men in general. I cannot remember ever meeting up with a horse who disliked women in the same way although, of course, any horse can take a dislike to an individual, man or woman, who has mistreated him.

It may perhaps be true that men, having 50 per cent more physical strength for their size than women, do exert it more, despite the fact that even a small pony is far stronger than any man and will always win an out-and-out test of strength. Women have no hope whatever of dominating a horse by strength alone, and many experts agree that it is women's gentler and more tactful approach which brings them, in general, such success with horses, although for either sex there are exceptions.

Unfortunately, if a horse has an ingrained hatred of men, there is little that can be done about it. Those with whom the animal does come into contact should, obviously, do nothing to hurt or frighten the horse if they wish to win his trust and co-operation, and try to persuade him, by kind treatment, that not all men are going to browbeat him into submission.

Mixing gaits

This is normally caused by the horse finding a particular gait, or way of performing it, physically difficult. Horses who have a habit of breaking uninvited into trot from walk have often been made to walk too fast. Those who perform a sort of hop, skip and a jump in trot are perhaps being asked to extend before they are able; and being trotted too fast or in an unbalanced way are other causes of mixed gaits, both prompting the horse to try to canter and avoid an uncomfortable action while still providing what he may believe you want – more speed.

Impure, mixed gaits can also be caused by unfitness, unsoundness, confusion as to what the rider wants, lack of schooling and balance particularly or, in a few cases, reluctance to work as required through sheer laziness.

To avoid the problem, and prevent its becoming a habit, the horse should be ridden by a competent rider, and preferably by one person only to avoid any confusion over various riders' slightly different (and, to the horse, inconsistent) aids. The horse should be checked for soundness of limbs and back, should be made fit, progressively and correctly schooled, and not asked to do more advanced work than he is ready for. Overwork and unreasonable demands should be avoided. As the horse matures or becomes more experienced and stronger, the problem often disappears.

Correct, consistent riding is also the answer with the lazy horse who prefers to slip into another gait rather than perform the required one correctly. It should be said, however, that if a poor rider on a well schooled, sensitive horse causes the horse to go badly by making him feel uncomfortable, sitting incorrectly, being unsteady, jabbing him in the mouth, etc, the horse may be so upset, confused or simply physically unbalanced that he resorts to another gait out of confusion, objection or misunderstanding.

Mounted, refusing to be

Fidgeting or walking off while being mounted is a particularly tiresome habit and can deter the rider from dismounting during a ride out for fear of not being able to get back on again! A horse who refuses to be mounted is badly trained but he may have a very good reason for his behaviour, apart from the fact that he just does not want to work.

If the process is made uncomfortable or even painful for him, it is no wonder he objects. Riders who do not or cannot spring up but rather drag themselves up by hanging on to the saddle, kick the horse's hip or croup on the way over, wrench the saddle over and stress the horse's back and maybe even pull him off balance or haul on his mouth during mounting, adding a heavy plump into the saddle for good measure, are guaranteed to make any horse or pony difficult to mount.

If a rider is stiff, or not so agile because of advancing age or

Fig 43 No wonder this horse has become difficult to mount. His owner is pulling him in the mouth, jabbing him in the ribs and yanking the saddle uncomfortably over his back

physical disability, there is nothing wrong at all with using a mounting block. It is, of course, more or less essential that most riders and their horses are accustomed to the mounting process being accomplished without 'artificial aids', but in cases such as those mentioned above, a proper mounting block or even a sturdy box or strong upturned bucket can help lessen the discomfort for both rider and horse.

The horse might, of course, have some kind of back injury which makes mounting painful for him, although he would usually show some sort of prior resistance such as shrinking down when being saddled. The phrase 'cold backed' is quite common in the horse world but it seems unlikely that most horses flinching from the saddle are, in practice, afraid of the feel of cold leather on their skin. It is almost certainly pain they are afraid of and any horse showing such symptoms should have a thorough veterinary examination, as to ride him in that condition will only make matters worse.

If it has been determined that pain is not the cause of apprehension, a reassuring retraining programme will improve the majority of horses. A horse should stand stock still while his rider mounts, so any deviation from this needs to be corrected.

The rider should try to make matters as easy for the horse as possible, especially in the early stages, so some kind of mounting block should be made available. The procedure is to mount calmly, taking steps to ensure that nothing happens to upset the horse – no undue pressure on the reins, no twisting round of the saddle (indeed, most mounting blocks make it possible for the right leg to be swung over the horse's croup while the left foot is still on top of the block, enabling the rider to settle down gently in the saddle) and no kicking or even touching the horse's hip or croup, certainly no digging in of the left toe as the rider swings up.

Assuming that care is taken over the above points, proceed as normal but stop the instant the horse moves; refuse to continue until he is standing absolutely still, and back where he was if he has stepped away. It takes a lot of patience on your part, but the next stage of the process should not be undertaken until you have complete obedience. In bad cases, the whole process may not be accomplished on the first day. Ten minutes a lesson is enough. Talk to the horse reassuringly throughout and say, in a reproving but not harsh tone of voice, 'no' or 'stand' if the horse moves.

The positioning of the horse can help, too. If his normal evasion during mounting is to move away sideways, place him with his off side against a wall; if he usually steps back, set his quarters against the wall and so on. An assistant to block routes of escape, but not to hold the horse, would also be helpful.

With patient retraining like this, most horses improve greatly and remain good provided nothing happens to worry them again.

Napping see **Jibbing**

One-sidedness
A horse may go easily and well in one direction (usually to the left) but stiffly and perhaps not so willingly to the other. Like people, horses have a favourite 'side'; most humans are right-handed, most horses seem to be left-footed, for want of a better expression.

There are usually two reasons offered for this. One is that this must have been the way the foetus was positioned in the womb (not really valid in view of the amount of movement a foetus makes); the second is because it is traditional to lead horses from the left (near) side and they become accustomed to being handled from this side and so tend to 'think left' all the time. But this does not really explain why so many horses show a distinct preference for the left rein when under saddle or in harness, or even on the lunge or long reins.

In any case, one-sidedness does create problems when schooling. Apart from schooling more to the difficult side to make the horse 'ambidextrous', efforts can be made to accustom the horse to being handled from his non-favourite side and to thinking in that direction. He can be lead from the 'wrong' side (and maybe persuaded to flex his head and neck to that side by being offered titbits as he walks along), and mounted and dismounted from that side. If the horse favours his left, he must certainly be taught to lead from the right as if he is ever led along a public highway (in the UK), his leader will have to be on his right between him and the traffic, with him walking on the left side of the road. If he is not used to being led from the right he may play up, and the last place you want him to do that is in traffic.

There are many harsh methods detailed in old (and not so old) books aimed at making the horse bend the way he does not want to go, which I do not propose to explain or recommend here. Suffice it to say that competent schooling straightens up most horses, even though a small preference for one side or the other might remain all the horse's life.

See also *Stiffness; Turn, refusing to.*

Overbending

An overbent horse moves with the lower part of his head (muzzle/chin) tucked in towards his chest. To the uninitiated this often looks proud, but the experienced horseman knows it is not only incorrect and uncomfortable for the horse but causes difficulty in controlling the horse and maintaining a light, communicative contact.

Horses overbend because they are afraid of the bit. It is an individual reaction, because some horses, equally afraid of the bit, show their fear in other ways, such as sticking their noses up and out or even, strangely, leaning hard on the object causing their discomfort. Some horses are encouraged, in fact, to overbend, according to their trainers' school of equestrian thought,

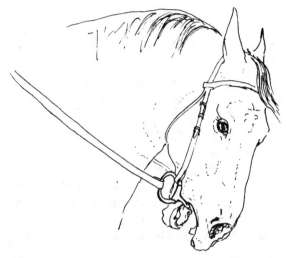

Fig 44 A horse overbends, maybe opening the mouth as well, because he is afraid of, or resents, contact with the bit

when it is called 'going deep', although many experts dislike this way of going. In so-called classical equitation, at any rate (on which all modern equitation methods claim to be based) it is regarded as a serious fault, showing that the trainer has not succeeded in giving his horse confidence to accept the bit and to 'bridle' to it.

Overbending can be caused by too severe a bit (and this can apply to various snaffles, particularly twisted ones, as well as long-cheeked, high-ported curb bits), by any bit, even a rubber snaffle, roughly or erratically used, by the rider exerting too strong a contact through the reins, or by sore bars (the toothless gum area in the mouth where the bit rests) or tongue. The soreness may be caused by an infection, by an injury from previous rough handling of the bit, or by teething in a youngster.

Whatever the cause, the mouth and teeth should first be checked and put right, the horse should be worked in as mild a bit as possible and the rider or driver should use it properly and humanely. Patient reschooling to give the horse confidence, perhaps in a bitless bridle for a while, helps most horses overcome the problem.

Over-reaching

Over-reaching is caused by faulty action, when a horse injures his own fore pasterns, heels or the sides of his coronets with his hind feet. Depending on the horse's action, the wound (always a bruise wound and often with a flap of skin hanging down from it) may be on the back of the area, or, quite commonly, on the outside. In severe cases a deep wound is sustained which cuts into tendons and/or ligaments.

Over-reaches occur in fast work and jumping, fast and tight turns, sudden stops or checks in pace or in deep going and uneven ground. Horses most prone to these injuries are those with short backs, sickle hocks, over-long hind legs (often combined with being croup high) and those who are young, unschooled and unbalanced, weak or fatigued. Over-long or unevenly trimmed hooves and unsuitable shoes can also contribute to over-reaching.

Prevention, apart from avoiding the conditions mentioned above, consists of better schooling and riding or driving, resulting in a better way of going, and the fitting of set-back shoes with rolled toes and/or feather-edges, depending on where exactly the injury usually occurs.

Over-reach (bell) boots are commonly available but do have disadvantages. The conventional rubber sort can turn inside out (up and over the fetlock) when they not only flap about and annoy the horse but can interfere with his action. They can also rub the pastern skin of a sensitive horse. However, at the time of writing a design has appeared on the market with flaps of synthetic material suspended from a padded pastern band; this appears to be an improvement on the traditional sort, and can be more easily put on and taken off, too.

Pigs (and other animals), fear of

It is a widespread belief that horses are instinctively frightened of pigs. In practice, it will be found that horses brought up among pigs in fact have no fear of them and only show a normal young foal's curiosity about anything strange. The fear of pigs extends to any animal with which a horse is unfamiliar. Many horses are terrified of donkeys, town horses are nervous of cattle and so on, and while most horses are accustomed to dogs, others are not only frightened of them but positively detest them, probably because they have been harassed or bitten by one in the past. Marauding packs of pet dogs can be the bane of a suburban horse's life (and his owner). Although it is considered a heinous crime for a horse out hunting to kick a hound, one cannot really blame the horse if he has had a bad experience with a dog in the past.

Attempts to overcome this fear, or dislike, have variable results. Sometimes a cure can be effected by simply putting the horse into contact with whatever animal is causing the problem. Stabling him next to pigs, for example, turning him out with them and having them wandering about the stable yard can be tried, but it should be remembered that if the horse is truly petrified he may develop a blind panic and either smash his box to pieces or take off in a headlong bolt and seriously injure or kill himself. It is reasonably common for an equid of any kind to run headlong into trees or walls and kill itself when panicked; it seems to be a trait of the species, so the horse should not be put into a position where this could happen.

In some cases fear may be converted into hatred. I used to own a horse who, when I bought him, quite liked dogs. Unfortunately, he put his nose over his stable door to greet one and it bit him sharply on the nose. Ever after, the horse bit first and would go for any dog he could with his teeth, but never with his heels. Some horses whom their owners feel are cured of their fear also unexpectedly develop hatred. Where a horse cannot be cured, or comes to hate the offending species, it seems that little can be done to improve the situation and a sensible horsemaster will try to avoid contact with whatever species of animal is causing the problem.

Plunging in harness

This can be a very unpleasant habit. Horses do it when their load is too heavy, the going too deep or a hill too steep, or simply from impatience or excitement. They also plunge when in fear of the whip.

Steady, calm handling, much soothing use of the voice and work on the level at slow paces help stop the habit, plus retraining from the ground. Long reins should be used to start off the horse from scratch, gradually working up to pulling a tyre, log or something similar and then, with the trainer still on foot, the

231

horse can be put into a light vehicle. The trainer can stand on either side of the vehicle about level with the seat, the far rein passed first under a rail above the dashboard and the near rein direct to the hand. If necessary in bad cases, an assistant, if possible one at each side, should be at the horse's head to guide and steady him.

Much work should be done at the walk until the horse is quite quiet and calm. The driver can then sit in the vehicle normally and, initially, remain in walk, with the assistants at the horse's head. Very gradually, work at a steady trot can begin, always ensuring that the horse is not overburdened by a heavy load, overfaced by a hill, and so on until he is established in his work. The voice should be used in a calming tone, and it is useful to accustom the horse to the word 'no' and to say it at the first inkling of plunging, provided he does connect the word with wrong-doing. Reward by some term he understands, such as 'good boy', should immediately be given when he ceases to offer to plunge.

As in any kind of schooling, work should gradually progress to normal trotting pace and varied terrain, and the habit will usually stop if patience and consideration are used.

Fig 45 Plunging in harness is both dangerous and frightening

Fig 46 Definitely not a remedy for the novice, but one which can be most effective when carried out by experts. The horse is deliberately brought to his knees by means of ropes attached to hobbles round his fore pasterns and to the harness, thence to the trainer's hand. The horse is fitted with correctly adjusted knee pads and the lesson is only given on soft ground. For inveterate 'plungers', one or two such experiences can usually cure the habit

Pole, leaning against

Leaning on the pole is a habit some harness horses develop which can make life most unpleasant for their partners and also the whip. It can be caused by laziness on the part of a horse who simply does not wish to pull honestly, by fatigue (when it is done for support), by badly fitting harness (which provokes leaning as a resistance in the horse), by driving with insufficient skill and consideration (for instance, asking the horses to go too fast or to perform manoeuvres beyond their capabilities), and by over-excitement or panic on the part of the whip transmitting itself to the horses. Leaning can also develop in young or inexperienced horses seeking leadership from a more experienced partner.

It is difficult to keep the horses straight when one is continually leaning against the other and, in fact, the other may start leaning in opposition. This can cause the horses to slip, and can also cause uneven pressure on the harness which can in turn create sores. In severe cases, one horse pushing against another can bring the innocent horse down, with disastrous results.

Apart from reprimanding with the whip, one way to break the habit is to change the position of the horse (for instance, if he is used to going on the near side and is leaning to the off, put him on the off side). It is also a good idea to work the horse in single harness for some time and also in tandem, if possible, and/or to ride him out to give him a complete change. This may help prevent the habit becoming confirmed; once it is, it is almost impossible to cure.

A rather uncomfortable remedy (which does not always work) is to fasten dandy brushes along the side of the pole so that the horse leans on them. This may be used as a last resort, but every effort should first be made in other directions to cure the habit, particularly as regards finding the reason for the horse's leaning and trying to ensure that the cause is removed.

Pole, pulling away from
This habit has very similar causes and effects to leaning against the pole. The pair often learn to pull away from each other (one trying to balance himself up against the pull from his partner) with the result that they become very unsteady on their feet, give themselves harness sores and are most unpleasant and difficult, not to mention unsafe, to drive.

Again, the best remedy seems to be in practice to change the horses about from side to side so that they never get so used to one position that they pull away almost automatically. Riding out, working in single harness and also in tandem are recommended. A thorough assessment of the cause is essential so that matters can be put right at the very first sign of the habit developing.

Pulling
It takes two to argue and it takes two to pull. Pulling is most unpleasant. It is uncomfortable to ride a horse who is constantly heavy in hand or maybe pulling your arms out, difficult to give sensitive rein aids and does not make for good horsemanship or a harmonious relationship between horse and rider.

Some horses begin to pull because their riders use a system of equitation which requires a firm contact on the bit. Others develop the habit because they are used to riders who steady themselves by means of the reins and yet others pull because it is a means of supporting themselves in movements they find difficult, so they lean on the bit for balance. Driving horses pull for similar reasons. Horses sometimes develop the habit if fitted with a bit they do not like. For instance, some horses much prefer a bit which can be easily moved about in the mouth, such as a sliding-cheek bit or a loose or wire-ring snaffle. If fitted with, say, a fixed-cheek bit or an eggbutt snaffle, they are unable to mouth the bit to the same extent and develop a 'dead' mouth, which leads to pulling and heaviness in hand.

The habit should be stopped because, apart from being unpleasant, it can easily lead on to running away in appropriate circumstances.

The horse cannot pull against a loose or unpredictable rein or bit contact, so a slight give-and-take often shows the horse he cannot rely on the bit for support but will have to learn to carry himself. Youngsters are sometimes allowed to lean on the bit for balance (depending on the school of equitation being followed) but as training progresses the practice must be discouraged if the horse is not to be put in danger of becoming permanently heavy in hand.

Riders and drivers must make sure they are not encouraging, even teaching, the horse to pull by taking too heavy a contact. This, combined with a steady, as opposed to slightly intermittent, pressure, is an almost sure way of creating a puller.

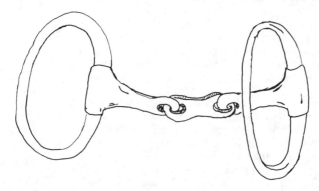

Fig 47 A Dr Bristol snaffle is often helpful as it has a less extreme action than a conventional single-jointed snaffle

Pulling

In mature horses who may have developed hard mouths, a slightly more severe bit may be the answer, tactfully used, although generally resorting to gradually more and more severe bits makes the problem worse. Sometimes even a simple change of bit works, say from a mullen-mouth snaffle to a jointed one, or from a single joint to a double, such as a Dr Bristol snaffle. Alternating from bit to bit works with some horses as they never know what to expect and have to get used to a different feel and action in their mouths each time, and tend rather to 'back off' than pull on an unfamiliar mouthpiece.

If the horse pulls through excitement, as many do, this can be very difficult to cope with, but again, a give-and-take contact often helps as it does not give the horse a reliable object to pull on.

With horses which have been positively encouraged to take a firm hold, such as racehorses, serious problems can ensue for their new riders if they are retired to another equestrian discipline after racing. As these horses have never been taught to go 'off their back ends' or in any way collectedly, complete reschooling is usually needed. Much patient work at slow paces, plus a total refusal on the part of the rider to give the horse something to lean on, is normally the way to overcome the habit. Faster paces should only be introduced when the horse is going

---

Many horses are easier to deal with if they cannot see what is going on. A blinker bridle can be used to block rear view, or the handler can stand close to the horse's neck, incline the head to the side where the vet is working, and have a distracting bucket of food. The injection will be done before he knows it!

The combined technique of long reining *and* riding can often overcome resistance in a nappy horse. Obviously, this method would not be safe to use with a horse known to kick

A simple and effective technique for encouraging a horse to walk out in hand is shown in this photograph. The handler is on one side of the horse and there is a fence on the other. In her outside hand she has a long schooling whip. When the horse hangs back, she puts her hand behind her back and gives him a flick on the flank or thigh which almost always results in free forward movement! The fence prevents the quarters swinging away from the whip. After a short while of this training, the horse needs only to see the leader's hand going behind her back, whip or no whip, for him to step out smartly. A verbal command such as 'walk on' should accompany the aid with the whip

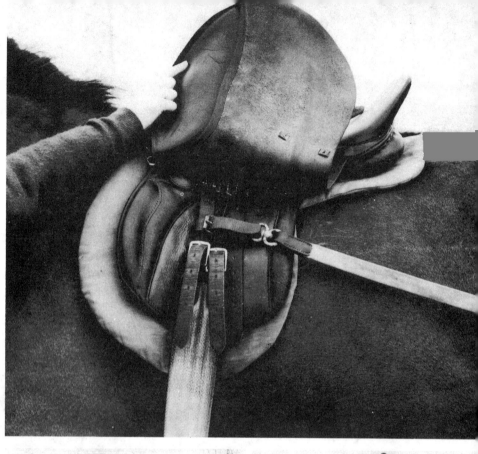

kindly at the slower ones, although it is usually only at fast paces that ex-racehorses pull, anyway.

Bear in mind that the horse may associate a particular bit with galloping and jumping (if he has hurdled or chased) so a change of bit may well help. An acquaintance of mine says that her ex-racehorse was always raced in a loose-ring snaffle and if the bit is used now he automatically reverts to his racing mentality, but if ridden in the German eggbutt she normally uses he knows he has to go calmly and not pull. (This psychology can be applied to the serving stallion used for other work – if he always wears a stallion bridle and bit for serving and a completely different bridle and bit for his other work, he will normally work well and not be preoccupied with mares in season, even if near him. However, if his serving 'outfit' is put on he becomes, naturally, highly excited and associates that headgear with stud work.)

See also *Boring; Raking.*

Pulling back when tied up

Horses are tied or racked up for many reasons; if kept in standing stalls they are tied up most of the time, but horses are also tied up in loose boxes – for grooming or other attention, when their boxes are being mucked out, when the door is to be kept open for any length of time – and outside in the yard.

We take the practice of tying up horses so much for granted that we tend to forget how potentially troublesome or, indeed, dangerous it can be. Take, for instance, the horse tied up outside his box on a nice day to be groomed. He is not known to pull back and his groom or owner leaves him for a few moments to get something from the tack room. Something frightens the horse, maybe a stable rubber or a piece of paper blowing about, a

---

Another useful method for dealing with a nappy horse, particularly if you have to work without help, is shown in these three photographs. A lunge rein is fastened to the girth tabs on one side of the saddle . . .
. . . it is passed round behind the horse like the fillet string on a rug . . .
. . . and then to the rider's hand. When the horse naps, a tug on the rein often induces forward movement. Leg and voice aids should also be used at the same time. As with many remedies, what works for one horse does not work for another. A few horses will react to this treatment by either sitting down or offering to rear, but they are in the minority

sudden strange noise or a dog snapping at his heels. He pulls back on his rope in panic until something gives – either the ring comes away, or the rope-clip, the ring on the headcollar, the headcollar itself or maybe the rope, breaks. One point must be remembered; a horse should never, under any circumstances, be tied up by the reins. Apart from the fact that reins and bridle can break more easily than a headcollar, being of finer leather, the pull exerted moves the bit out of position in the horse's mouth and can cause considerable pain which causes the horse to panic even more than he may be doing already. A mouth damaged temporarily or permanently can also result. But the horse is now free and a panicking horse loose in a stable yard can obviously injure not only himself but anyone nearby. If a gate is open the horse can get onto the road and cause a traffic accident.

Something else has also happened; the horse has learned he can get free by using his considerable physical strength. The next time he wants to get free, it may not be in panic but just because he does not want to be tied up – and he will use the same tactic repeatedly until he is not safe to be left for a moment. In fact, once a horse is confirmed in this habit, it is best to tie him to a loop of ordinary string which will break if much pressure is put on it. This is generally regarded as preferable to having the horse struggle, maybe losing his feet and ending up suspended by the head and injuring himself.

It has to be admitted that many 'old-school' horsemen, particularly in heavy horse circles, it seems, purposely tied up young horses in such a way that they could not break free. As youngsters will invariably lose their feet in their struggles, this method acquired the name 'swinging' as that was exactly what happened to the unfortunate animals. Such horsemen claimed, probably rightly, in fact, that once a horse had been 'swung' he never again pulled back at his halter. Fortunately, such 'break rather than make' methods are becoming rarer in the horse world today and more humane and intelligent methods are gradually taking over in many spheres.

It is far better to teach a young horse to stand patiently when tied up. For a start, he should be held by an assistant rather than tied, and placed with his quarters not far from a wall. If he attempts to move back, he should be restrained calmly but firmly and taught the command 'stand', and praised when he does so. If

240

he insists on going back, his quarters will bump into the wall and he will realise he cannot go any further. In a young foal, this lesson is easily taught. If he decides to go up instead, his head should be brought down (a horse cannot rear effectively with his head down), he should be reprimanded and then praised when he behaves.

Older animals, who have found their strength but who have never been trained at the stud to be tied up, can be taught effectively by the following method. Instead of a normal rope, take a lunge rein or similar long rope, fasten it to the usual headcollar ring, pass it through a firm ring or bracket on the wall and then to the trainer's hand. Groom the horse with the free hand, then whenever the horse pulls back, let out a little rein so that he does not feel a pull on his headcollar, at the same time commanding him calmly but firmly to stand. If his quarters bump into the wall, so much the better; then gently 'reel' him back to where he was before. Keep doing this until he realises that he has to stand and that he is not going to be hurt by what you are doing. The

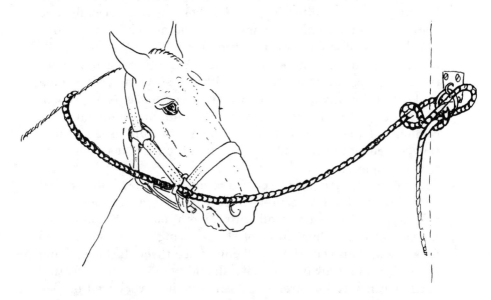

Fig 48 Here, a rope has been clipped to the near side D, passed up over the horse's neck, through the off side D and fastened to the ring. Again, the horse will pull against himself in a way he finds hard to resist. A doubled rope can be used, if you have one long enough, the middle being placed on the neck, each free end passed through the side Ds and thence to the ring

letting out of the rope helps reassure horses, who are naturally afraid of being restrained, and gives them more of a feeling of freedom.

Although this training method works well, the time will come when the horse has to be tied normally, but it is often found that, having been taught as described, he adapts to it well and causes no problems.

With animals who have learned that they can break free whenever they wish by pulling back hard enough, it is often more effective to fit a broad neck strap, rather than an ordinary headcollar, as they do not seem to pull so hard against the pressure on their necks. If an animal is genuinely frightened by something, it is probably better that he be allowed to break free rather than involve himself in a possibly dangerous struggle, and to this end many experts believe in tying a loop of string to the metal ring in the wall, as mentioned previously, so that the string breaks if undue stress is put on it.

The following method of stopping horses who pull back just to be awkward is also often helpful. The horse is tied normally, one person attending to him and another standing behind and to one side with a stiff stable broom at the ready. When the horse pulls back, the groom commands him to stand and the assistant gives the horse a scrub under the tail with the stiff bristles, keeping well out of the way of any kick which might ensue. A few repetitions of this often makes horses think again and frequently the command 'stand' is enough to stop them in future as they think they are going to get scrubbed, which, although it does not hurt, is very unpleasant.

A method I have used to cure a really confirmed halter puller is as follows. Find a securely fixed ring or bracket, preferably bolted through a strong wall with a metal plate set against the far side of the wall in front of the securing nut to spread the pressure and prevent the bolt being pulled through the wall and the ring coming away. (The site should not be on hard footing such as concrete but preferably earth or in a very well bedded loose box.) Fit the horse with a strong, broad neck strap with a very strong steel ring under the throat. The strap should fit round the top of the neck comfortably but not be so loose as to slip down the neck.

Take a lungeing rein or similar length of rope and use a half

242

bow (slip knot) to fasten one end to the ring in the neck strap so that it can easily be pulled undone in an emergency with one tug on the free end. Pass the rope behind the horse's quarters (like a fillet string) and thread it back through the ring in the neck strap, then tie it with another half bow to the ring in the wall. The horse should be so tied that he is a normal distance away from the wall. Although the rope should not slip down when he is in this position, it must not exert any pressure on the backs of his thighs unless he pulls back. When he does, he will in effect be pulling against himself; the harder he pulls the harder the rope presses on his thighs. If he resists this pressure (and few horses do) and decides to rear, the rope passing through the ring on the neck strap exerts a downwards pressure and firmly discourages this, too. The beauty of this method is that it takes only one person, who does not even need to touch the horse but simply command him to stand and let him realise that not only can he

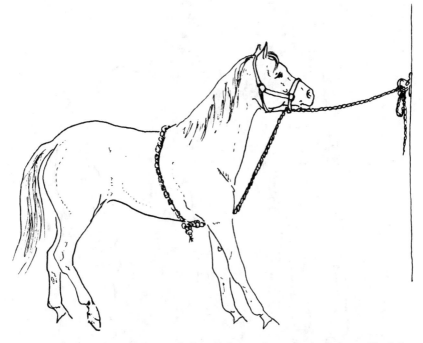

Fig 49 A rope is fastened round the girth, up through the bottom D of the headcollar and to a firmly fixed ring. When the horse pulls back he will effectively be pulling against himself. The rope being passed through the bottom headcollar D also discourages any attempt to rear, as firm pressure will be exerted on the poll the instant there is any upward movement

not break away but that it is much more comfortable to stand quietly.

An alternative method is to tie the rope round the horse's girth (as illustrated), securing it with a non-slip bowline knot, passing it through the headcollar or neck-strap ring and to the ring in the wall. Again, the horse is pulling against himself all the time and usually learns to stand quietly.

With both the above methods, there is no danger of the horse being swung, as there is plenty of length in the rope for him to get to his feet if he does fall; in practice, I have not known horses lose their feet. However, use these procedures only where there is soft footing, just in case; and never use them to train a youngster, only to retrain a confirmed halter puller, and preferably under expert supervision.

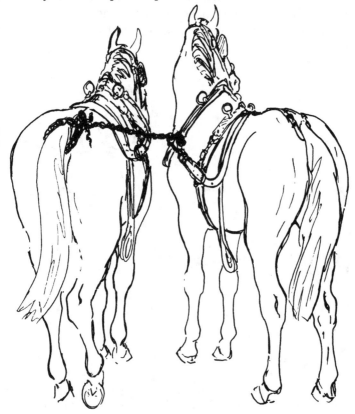

Fig 50 Where a collar harness is worn, the rope should be fixed to the partner's collar, or to the tug

Pull in harness, refusing to

Many harness horses, particularly those used in pair harness or as wheelers in tandem or four-in-hand, learn that they do not need to pull their weight as their colleagues will do it for them. Their reluctance to pull may be due to ill-fitting harness causing sore shoulders, so this point should first be checked and time allowed for any rubs or strains to heal.

If a horse persists in the habit, remove the crupper and replace it with a rope loop, carrying the other end of the rope to the driving pad of the horse's colleague (who must be a hard-working, honest puller) and fastening it securely to one of the terrets. The rope should be adjusted so that if the two horses are level it does not come into action but if the reluctant one drops back the rope pulls in no uncertain manner under his tail. This has cured many a horse, and should be accompanied with flicks of the whip on the quarters and the command to 'trot on', with the horse's name.

Often a spell in single harness improves such horses.

Quidding

Quidding is the forming of balls of partly chewed food which the horse lets fall from his mouth instead of chewing them thoroughly and swallowing. It is normally caused by dental problems or a sore mouth, bit injuries or some infection.

A veterinary surgeon should be called in to check the horse's teeth thoroughly and prescribe treatment if an infection is found. In the case of bit injuries, the horse should be used in a bitless bridle or rested until the mouth heals. From then on, great care should be taken to see that the bit cannot cause any further damage, by examining it for any roughness and putting it right, by reverting to a smoother, milder bit or by ensuring it is not used in a heavy-handed manner.

The horse should be fed soft food until the condition improves. Hay, in particular, should be soaked thoroughly in hot water, which softens it better than cold (a bucket of water just thrown over it does virtually no good at all).

Raking at reins

When a horse makes a habit of firmly stretching out his neck and pulling or jerking at the reins with outstretched muzzle, it is

245

termed 'raking'. The habit is a nuisance because it makes good riding or driving very difficult.

It is a symptom of the horse's being unhappy with his bit or with the amount of contact put on it by his rider or driver. Even if the bit does not hurt, some horses just do not like the feeling of restriction which a significant contact places them under. With some animals, however, the lightest contact, even on a bitless bridle, can provoke raking. It can also be brought on by an uneven, jerky contact, which confuses and can hurt a horse.

The usual remedies consist of a light, steady (but not dead) contact being given. Correct riding, with impulsion and consistent rein aids (so as not to confuse the horse), also helps. Some horses who rake in a snaffle stop doing so if ridden in a pelham or double bridle. I have known a few horses who disliked any contact on a snaffle or bridoon but went very kindly with a featherlight contact on the curb only.

Trying to remedy the fault by fitting a standing martingale or by keeping a firm contact on the bit, or even riding in side reins so that the horse jabs himself in the mouth when he tries to rake, can easily make the problem worse, or convert it into something else.

See also *Boring; Pulling.*

Rearing

This is one of the most dangerous vices a horse can have and it is not one with which a novice, or, indeed, any but the most competent and nerveless of horsemen should attempt to deal. The remedies given here, therefore, are largely for information only, as this book has been written mainly to help not-so-expert riders and drivers.

If a rider finds himself or herself on a horse who is going up, the most important things to remember are *not* to pull on the reins to maintain one's balance, and *not* to lean back. The rider should lean forward and, if possible, put both arms round the horse's neck or hold the mane, staying as still as possible so as not to put the horse off his precarious balance and bring him over backwards on top of his rider or onto his side, causing serious injury.

As soon as the horse lands the rider should urge him forward at once, and strongly, to prevent a repetition. It is important,

Fig 51 Do not pull on the horse's mouth or he might come over backwards on top of you. Get well forward and try to get your arms round his neck. The instant he starts coming down straighten up, and kick on the moment his forefeet touch the ground

Fig 52 Another practice for experts only. Quit your stirrups and, when the horse is at the highest point of his rear, dismount! If you are agile and quick thinking, not to mention without nerves, this enables you to show the horse that rearing will not stop you riding him. You simply keep getting on again. This method is best suited to horses who purposely throw themselves backwards as it stops you being crushed under the horse. However it must be stressed that this is strictly a technique for only the most competent riders

however, not to punish the horse when he has landed as he will interpret it as punishment for coming down. Horses have to stop in order to rear, so if the rider feels the horse slowing down, stopping and 'bunching himself up' (gathering his weight on to his quarters) to rear, he or she should get him moving forward again as quickly as possible. Once the horse's forefeet have left the ground, vocal reprimands only should be given as physical action can, as mentioned, put him off his balance.

A remedy an expert horseman might use with a rearer is to bring one rein hard down and to one side, to get the head down (the horse cannot rear unless his head can go up). A similar remedy is to bring one rein under the rider's foot and, using a pulley effect, again get the head down and to one side, quickly releasing it when the horse lands. Alternatively, the head can be kept down and the horse urged round and round in circles with the other leg to discourage him from going up again.

Remedies should always suit the cause of the vice. If a horse rears out of laziness and stubbornness because he does not want to work, sickening him of his own habit may have some effect. An expert might achieve this by riding the horse without stirrups and jumping clear as soon as the horse rears, keeping hold of the reins, and remounting immediately the horse comes down, perhaps with a quick leg-up from a helper. Bringing the horse over (making him fall) is very risky, even on soft ground and is not recommended, generally; in fact, some horses even throw themselves down on their riders on purpose. However, re-peatedly jumping clear and getting on again has often worked by making the horse realise that rearing will achieve nothing.

Many rearers have very sensitive mouths and have been made to rear by painful use of the bit. In this case, expert and sensitive reschooling, possibly in a bitless bridle for some time, can be very helpful. A simple rubber bit may be used or, in truly expert hands, a curb bit or double bridle, with a weight-of-the-rein contact, guiding the horse mainly by seat and legs. I have known three rearers be cured through being ridden in a pelham using only the curb rein, or Weymouth only, and, in one case, with a leather curb instead of a chain. It takes a very competent rider with a secure seat and perfect control of his hands, but it is certainly possible.

Rearing in harness is lethal and the general consensus of

opinion is to get rid of a horse who does this. Some experts would first try to reschool the horse on long reins. Some recommend getting the horse's weight on to his forehand by teaching turn about the forehand and asking for it whenever (and the very instant) the horse offers to rear. Others equip the horse with tack which keeps the head low (draw reins, standing martingale etc) and reschool in a mild bit, stressing forward movement and avoiding work which puts the horse's weight on to his quarters (collection, rein back etc). This has proved successful in certain cases, when expertly carried out, and applies to horses intended for either riding or driving.

Relapse in behaviour

It is most frustrating to have 'cured' a horse of a problem only to find it recurring some time later. This usually happens when the horse has a new owner or when a groom is changed, but it can also happen with the same person who effected the cure in the first place. It usually means that retraining was not complete or that the situation which originally caused the problem has recurred, bringing with it the undesirable behaviour.

The answer is to go back to the drawing-board and start further retraining. It should also be remembered that because horses have phenomenal memories and are creatures of habit the roots of the problem behaviour will probably always remain in the horse's brain and will surface if conditions permit. Some vices and other problems are impossible to eradicate completely and a few, such as crib-biting, may not be able to be improved at all in certain individuals.

Rolling

Although rolling is normally a good thing for a horse to do, being his natural way of cooling off when hot and sweaty, or of scratching his back or giving himself a good coating of mud as protection from the weather, it cannot, of course, be tolerated during work. Rolling under saddle or in harness breaks saddle-trees, riders' legs, harness, shafts and vehicles.

As he does when lying down, the horse will give warning by lowering his head, pawing the ground and buckling at the knees. Urge him on at once, get his head up, use voice, legs, whip, as appropriate, but get him on and moving.

Rolling

If the horse has become hot and sweaty from working in a long, thick coat, it is understandable that he should want to roll, particularly if he is young or has learned that his rider or driver cannot stop him. Children's ponies are particularly prone to it. I learned to ride on the beach when tiny, and was taught at a very tender age to get my pony's head up, kick on (whip and spurs not being allowed) and adopt a stern note in my voice. Sand, particularly soft sand, is very tempting to any horse or pony, hot and sweaty or not, and the same goes for outdoor manèges, indoor schools, dusty patches in fields, although probably not to the same extent, and also water, whether sea, river or puddle. Violent pawing in water may be hilarious to the uninitiated – until they find themselves down in it and maybe under their horse or pony, which can, of course, be extremely dangerous. Very firm encouragement to keep going is called for in these circumstances.

See also *Lying down during work*.

Fig 53 Horses and ponies often like to roll, in water or soft going such as sand. The rider should sit up, get the head up by means of jerks on the reins, and kick on

Rubbing

Horses who rub their heads all over their handlers when their bridles are removed, or just because they have an itch somewhere, can be either a source of endearment or annoyance depending on the handler's attitude. If you don't mind it remember to warn others who may about the habit, particularly if they are fussy about their clothes. If you do object, simply get out of the way if a horse tries to rub, and say a firm 'no' with maybe a slap on the shoulder.

It would be considerate of you to rub his head if he is obviously feeling itchy and sweaty after work, particularly round the ears and noseband areas, especially if he has been wearing a drop noseband or some other type which causes pressure anywhere. Many horses like their backs being slapped or scratched after the saddle or driving pad has been removed, as evidenced by the number who roll after work.

Another type of rubbing which is much more objectionable and, indeed, dangerous, is where the horse tries to rub his rider against a fence or wall. It is hard to see any other reason for this except sheer vindictiveness although the horse must, one pre-

Fig 54 The point of no return! Once the horse has got to this stage, you are unlikely to stop him getting down. Quit your stirrups and step off, or you will not only get a wetting but be crushed as well

sumes, have been given a reason at some time for wanting to get rid of his rider.

The rider of such a horse must be on the alert when riding near fences, walls and in enclosed spaces such as a manège, trying to ride off the track in the latter situation. With a determined, persistent horse, spurs should be worn but only used when the crime is committed. Such horses sometimes try to knock their riders off by rushing without warning under low tree branches. This kind of action does appear to demonstrate reasoning ability in the horse as it shows premeditation and knowledge of the results. Constant vigilance is needed on horses of this type; there must be a permanent schooling campaign to make the horse absolutely obedient to the leg (so that you can give him the aid to move away as soon as you feel him sidle up to a fence) and immediate, short punishment if he manages to achieve his aim.

Rug-tearing/chewing

The price of clothing being what it is these days, rug-tearing is a very expensive habit. It can be stopped effectively if you soak the parts of the rug within reach with old-fashioned bitter aloes from the chemist. This tastes absolutely foul and works better than any other method I know. It does stain clothing brown, so make a habit of buying brown clothing in the first place! However, one taste of aloes is usually enough to put a permanent stop to the habit.

Of course, some thought should be given as to why the horse is tearing his clothing in the first place. Obviously if it is irritating him this is his way of trying to do something about it. People who habitually put clothing down on the bedding and do not bother to remove every scrap from the inside of the rug or blanket before putting it back on the horse can only expect the poor creature to be uncomfortable. If the horse has some kind of irritating skin condition he may take to tearing his clothing while trying to relieve the itch. A few horses just do not like wearing clothing at all so if they really have to (for instance, if they have to be clipped for work in winter) try at least to make the clothing well-fitting and comfortable.

Skin irritations can be caused by the clothing itself if it is washed in harsh detergent, particularly biological washing powders. The safest and most effective thing to wash horse clothing with, if your horse is susceptible to skin complaints or rather allergies from detergents, is washing soda. It should be rinsed out very well; resist the temptation to use fabric softener.

The horse can be fitted with a bib hanging from the headcollar so that when he turns round his teeth make contact with the bib and he cannot get hold of the rug, yet he can still eat and drink normally. It is still best to try and eradicate the cause, if at all possible.

Youngsters teething (up to four years old) sometimes chew things, including clothing, so consult your vet for some remedy to rub on the gums to alleviate the soreness. (See Dominic Prince's contribution to Part II.)

Running away *see* Bolting

Running back
A very dangerous habit which can result in serious accidents, running back is a form of napping and jibbing and is a very effective evasion. It can also occur out of fear, if the horse is confronted by an object or situation he simply feels he cannot face. Because of the difficulty in dealing with this behaviour, it is stressed that the rein back should not be taught to horses before they are fully confirmed in the habit of free, forward movement on command in all situations; this is unlikely to be achieved before the age of five years. Resisting the temptation to rein back too soon can help prevent the thought of running back as an evasion ever entering the horse's head.

If the rider is able to steer the backing horse into some solid object such as a wall or fence, or something prickly such as a hedge, this can easily result in the horse jumping forward like lightning and may well prevent the practice in future. Another method is to keep the horse backing, by aids and verbal command, long after he has offered to give up; go either straight back or twisting and turning and then, turning him round, push him *forwards* energetically which will probably take him by surprise. I do not approve of backing the horse into a ditch as this can cause a severe back injury as his feet drop away from him and he tries, by the use of his back muscles, to heave himself upwards again.

If you can arrange it and have a fairly brave, nimble-footed and sensible assistant, arm him or her with a stiff-bristled stable broom and have it applied under the tail as the horse is backing. This often works a treat.

With the horse who runs back out of fear rather than temper, more tact is needed, although he must still be shown that he is not allowed to do this, no matter what the circumstances. Praise and a calming voice should be used the instant he stops. Exercising or working such a horse in the company of a calm, reliable schoolmaster horse can be invaluable.

Running back in harness is obviously very dangerous. Work in pair harness, particularly using the type of equipment described under *Pull in harness, refusing to*, namely a rope loop round the horse's tail attached to the collar or driving pad of his colleague, usually stops the habit.

Running out at fences

Weak riding and overfacing are the commonest causes of this habit, plus the obvious one of the horse not wanting to jump because he associates it with pain or unreasonable physical effort – such as when he is unfit or tired, or simply sick of jumping because he has been asked to do too much too often.

Fences with long wings and also jumping lanes high enough to prevent the horse jumping out over the sides are most useful when dealing with running out. They should be combined with fences known to be well within the horse's capabilities to avoid any possibility of overfacing. Patient retraining over this type of obstacle is a big help, and also loose schooling which many horses love once they realise they are not encumbered by the weight of a rider or a rider who actually hampers them by poor riding – catching the horse in the mouth, banging down on his back, hitting him after he has taken off (it does happen even at the best of shows), or expecting him to take off at a difficult angle or on a wrong stride before the horse is clever enough at jumping to look after himself.

If the horse makes a habit of running out to one particular side, the whip should be carried in that hand and be used down the shoulder the second the horse tries to run out. The main idea, however, is to remove the reason for the horse's wanting to run out in the first place which, apart from being certain the horse is

254

not in pain, usually means patient retraining to show the horse there is nothing to be afraid of.

It is more common than might be imagined to find horses who just will not jump at all, despite any amount of reschooling and patience. We cannot be successful at reforming all problems, and such horses are best kept for work on the flat and hacking where they will not be expected to jump.

Competent riding obviously makes a big difference to any retraining programme. Correct, supportive use of the legs is important, backed up by appropriate rein contact. For instance, if the horse habitually runs out to the right, try bringing him in angled very slightly to the left, use the right leg more strongly than the left and have a little more contact on the left rein. As with any jumping problem, it helps to modify the jumping position of the rider so that the seat is more in contact with the saddle, rather than adopting a more up-in-the-air position, as this makes for better control and extra security in case of emergency. Too-short stirrups also are not conducive to control, especially in situations where the leg is instrumental in giving extra direction to the horse.

See also *Jump, refusing to.*

Rushing at fences

Strange though it may seem, rushing is a sign of nervousness and insecurity rather than eagerness. Anxiety over jumping can be caused by all sorts of things – slippery ground conditions; fences too high, strange looking or too numerous, causing the horse to hot up; bad riding of any kind and too tight a contact on the reins during the approach, which may cause the horse to feel he cannot get up enough speed or achieve enough freedom to make the height and width.

Once the cause has been analysed and corrected, then schooling methods can be used to steady the horse down as well, such as grid jumping on a bend or circle; the use of placing-jumps before the fence at roughly 2.7m (9ft) often helps. All work should initially be undertaken at a calm trot with a rider who can sit still and not restrict or worry the horse, and who can keep a light, even contact on the bit, neither taking too firm a hold nor 'dropping' contact at take off.

Work on circles should be undertaken, just missing jumps so

that the horse never knows when he is going to be asked to jump. The circle can be enlarged to take in the jump when the horse is calm, and diminished to bypass it when he is excited or pulling. Also, work the horse in the presence of jumps without asking him to take them, or in an area where he normally jumps, say out hacking, but don't ask him to do so. The emphasis should always be on quietness and calmness; when the horse is excited simply do not jump.

Savaging

Horses which savage people, other horses or other animals are obviously extremely unpleasant to handle and those who cannot be cured of savaging humans may well have to be put down as they are usually considered too dangerous to have around. It is to be noted that most really savage horses are stallions rather than geldings or mares. This may well be due to the inhumane and unnatural treatment some stallions are still subjected to on studs. They lead isolated lives and are denied normal social company. They may have been cursed in the past with handlers who, perhaps because they were afraid or were bullies by nature, constantly beat the horses or jabbed them in the mouth at every tiny excuse, and may have been managed badly by being kept in dark closed-in stabling or even tied up within the loose box.

It is usually only in cases of very valuable Thoroughbred stallions that vicious behaviour is tolerated. Many remain vicious all their lives, although there are stories of formerly savage brutes gradually becoming reformed characters when managed in a more natural and humane fashion – being given freedom in a paddock with a view or a light, airy loose box in which there is room to move around, attendants who do not yell at them or brandish big sticks, and a generally more pleasant existence.

It is, of course, a time-consuming process reforming such a horse. I know of a few cases where it has been done (always by women, incidentally) and the people concerned always took on the horse (usually cheaply because no one could handle him) without any deadline approaching such as the stud season. For weeks (months in one case) no one touched the horse because they simply dared not. He was kept in facilities where he could go from his box straight into an exercise paddock – well-fenced but with a view. Feed and hay were either given through hatches or watch was kept until the horse was at the far end of the paddock, then someone would nip into the box, shut the back door, muck out, feed etc and, on being assured the horse was still nowhere near, open the back door again, go out and close the front door behind them.

In each case, emphasis was placed on giving the stallion complete freedom to go in and out of his box to the paddock as he wanted, on giving plenty of hay and few concentrates (and then of a low-energy nature), and on talking soothingly and quietly to the horse over the fence or box door, staying out of reach, of course. Someone would be placed outside his box cleaning tack on a fine day, perhaps with a radio playing, other animals could be seen around, the family dog, stable cat etc, and very gradually the horse calmed down and became interested in his new home and people. Only one of these horses retained a propensity to have a quick nip now and then.

The stud groom at one establishment told me:

I'll never forget the day I gave him his first apple. He'd been here two months and no one had been able to lay a finger on him in all that time. We were getting worried because his feet needed trimming, although he had no shoes on when he came, and I just thought progress was going to *have* to be faster because of those feet. His mane and tail were in a right old state as you can imagine but, surprisingly, his body wasn't that dirty. Anyway, I was washing my car in the yard and he was just watching me, real interested like. I had an apple in my pocket and I took a short break and had a bite and went to talk to him.

Well, his nose started going, you know how they do, and he reached his head out to the apple. I said 'Do you want a bit, old boy?' and just held it out as though there was nothing unusual, and he just took it from me, quiet as a lamb. I didn't try and touch him, but later that day I tried him with some Polo mints. I don't think he'd ever had any – he spat them out at first and then wanted to try again, so I gave him half a dozen and as he took them in his lips I curled my fingers up and cupped my hand under his muzzle and he never bothered at all, and we just took it from there. I rasped his feet myself within a week and now he's firm friends with the farrier and everyone else. Fortunately, I've got a good staff here and everyone's quiet and kind with him – I wouldn't like to be the first person to upset him though! They'd have us both to deal with!

Not all horses may be reformed like that but there is little doubt that, with correct management and handling, a vast improvement can be made in many cases if enough time is taken.

There is always the possibility of a brain disorder, such as a tumour, in the case of a vicious horse and it may be necessary to consult a veterinary surgeon as to the best way of finding out. Perhaps an anaesthetic dart would have to be administered, as is done with animals in safari parks, then the horse X-rayed and blood samples taken, or whatever the veterinary surgeon felt was necessary.

What is certain, however, is that so-called 'firm' handling rarely does any good in improving the behaviour of truly vicious animals – this is usually what made them vicious in the first place. So, whereas one might give a horse a sharp pinch on the muzzle for the odd, intentional bite, or a crack on the nose if he rushed at one with teeth bared, with the type of horse we are considering here this will not work and will be quite insufficient to protect the handler. Ill-treatment begets ill-feeling. Novices must not attempt to handle dangerous horses and should take expert advice from sympathetic, competent horsepeople if ever they find themselves in the situation of being faced with such an animal. See also *Biting, nipping or 'snatching'*.

Shivering

Shivering is more a subject for a veterinary book than one on problem behaviour. It is a nervous disease arising from some disorder or abnormality of the nervous system/spinal cord and affects the hind legs and often also the quarters and tail. Very rarely it occurs in the forehand. The hind legs and quarter muscles will tremble and appear tight and the tail will be raised and quivering. If you notice this behaviour in your horse, call the veterinary surgeon. Long periods can occur between bouts, and it cannot apparently be detected during examination for sale or general health. Affected horses often do not lie down indoors and may take to resting by leaning their quarters on a convenient ledge such as the edge of the manger. If they do get down they often have difficulty in rising again. There is no cure for shivering and although being kept outdoors greatly alleviates it, the disease eventually results in wasting away of the muscles of the hind legs and quarters.

Like us, horses also shiver when cold and (particularly) wet. Some horses tremble, particularly in the forelegs, from excitement such as before a competitive event. Of course, both these sorts of shivering should not be confused with the disease described above.

Shoe, difficult to

This is one of the most trying problems with which an owner has to cope. Horses who are bad to shoe almost invariably have had a painful or frightening experience at the hands of a rough, impatient, bullying or incompetent farrier – and by all accounts these abound. Indeed, in some parts of the country a good farrier is impossible to come by. The Farriers' Registration Council and the Worshipful Company of Farriers are working to improve the situation, but shortage of good farriers is still a major problem in many areas.

Unfortunately, farriers good and bad often refuse to shoe difficult horses at all and some owners have been driven to keeping their horses without shoes and rasping their feet themselves, not a difficult task to learn with the help of a good book on the topic, such as *Farriery* by John Hickman (J. A. Allen), and quite lawful – it is the nailing on of shoes by an unqualified person which is unlawful.

It is significant that many horses who are bad to shoe allow any amount of handling, foot-scraping and so on by almost anyone other than a farrier – they can obviously detect farriers just as many can detect veterinary surgeons.

There does not seem to be any one part of the shoeing process which causes the most trouble; what does cause the problem in many cases, however, is the length of time the horse is expected to stand on three legs and the resultant tiring and aching muscles, especially in the opposite hind leg. When the horse asks to put his leg down for a while, some farriers shout and hold the required leg in a vice-like grip, preventing the horse from relieving his discomfort. A 'fight' often ensues or the horse simply suffers and the psychological damage is done.

Another fault in shoeing is that so many farriers in my experience hold the hind leg too high and, worst of all, force it outwards from the hip, increasing this movement if the horse struggles and therefore making the situation even worse. This movement is completely unnatural for the horse as the hip joint is not constructed for outward-sideways movement at all, only backwards-forwards. Therefore, to force the leg out and up causes the horse considerable pain, discomfort, stress and fear. No wonder the horse resists and comes to dread the process. If a horse has suffered any kind of muscular injury during shoeing, such as a back strain, or, say, injury to the tendons or ligaments due to being held in an enforced position, it should be remembered that it may take a very long time for the injury to heal. The horse will not be able to reassume the position that caused the trouble, due to pain; and even after healing, a recurrence is always likely once a structure has been injured.

Fig 55 This method is often useful with horses who will not stand still to be shod. There is a pair of front hobbles to which a rope is fastened and run to a single hobble on the back pastern of the foot not being worked on. With a very resistant or nervous horse, this method could result in injury should the horse struggle and come down. You must certainly know your horse before using any method of restraint. Other horses will simply give up and stand still. This would also discourage kicking with the hobbled hind leg, say during first-aid treatment

Obviously, if a horse has been hurt or frightened in any way during shoeing it is to be expected that he will kick up a fuss, perhaps literally, on future occasions. He may have been pricked with a nail; or perhaps the hot metal (in hot shoeing) was held against the horn too long and the heat penetrated to the sensitive tissues if he had particularly thin feet; and he may have been frightened by the smell, heat, noise, shadows on the wall, the fire or by the farrier himself.

It only takes one unpleasant experience for the horse to be made, and branded, bad to shoe, and it can take a very long time, a great deal of patience and tact and a thoroughly competent, sympathetic and professional farrier to put the problem right. Professionalism in farriery covers not only the physical ability to perform the job but the intelligence to understand the horse and treat him accordingly; psychology is every bit as important as physiology – and the latter should also cover that hip joint!

Getting the vet to tranquillise a horse might work for clipping but it is not recommended for shoeing because of the need to stand on three legs – many tranquillisers disorient the horse to the extent that his balance is affected.

Many horses, as mentioned earlier, allow their owners to handle them but dislike strangers. One young lady solved this problem with her horse by, at the farrier's suggestion, putting a blinker bridle on the horse so that he could not see behind him. The girl picked up the horse's foot and started tapping it with a hammer for a little while, then the farrier himself quietly took over, the girl talking to the horse all the while, and he was no more trouble. The bridle was removed and the horse seemed to realise that this man was not going to hurt him.

Training a horse when young, or retraining a difficult one, should take the form of making the experience of foot-handling enjoyable. His handlers should proceed very gradually and not force him at all, but persuade and have someone at his head giving lots of his favourite titbit every time even a little progress is made. It is not necessary for the foot to be lifted properly to be picked out; the toe may rest on the ground and the job completed, then a great fuss made of the horse. Little by little the foot can be lifted and held longer and longer, the hoof tapped, eventually quite hard, with the hoofpick and finally a hammer to simulate shoeing, and all the time, quiet, confident handling, talking, fuss and titbits (which both reward and distract) should be administered.

Even if you have to transport your horse out of your area and pay twice the normal amount for shoeing, the first shoeing process after the retraining must be undertaken by a quiet, confident, competent farrier and, just as important, one who is quick. It is natural for a farrier not to wish to shoe a difficult horse as the risk of injury is great, but if you explain that you have done as much at home as possible to train or retrain the horse and that the farrier has been highly recommended, a good man may well agree. Your farrier is so important to you and your horse that you may consider it well worth while staying with such a man – if he will take you on as a regular customer! It may also be advisable to cold shoe your horse, certainly at first, if not permanently.

Horse owners should be able to remove a shoe themselves if necessary. This is best done with the proper tools, but a stout screwdriver placed under the clenches and a strong household hammer will sometimes do the job. If the clenches are straightened out thoroughly the shoe may lift straight off, particularly if it is ready for coming off anyway. If not, lever it off carefully from the heels.

When you are fortunate enough to find a good farrier with a professional attitude to his job, for goodness sake treat him properly if you want to keep him. Paying on the nail before you wave him goodbye should be regarded as essential, unless you have an invoicing arrangement. Discussing your ideas and plans for your horse will create interest for him, and asking for advice and suggestions on your shoeing or trimming ideas rather than simply telling him what to do is bound to bring better results and an improved working relationship between you. You will all benefit, especially your horse.

Shy feeder, the *see* **Eat, refusing to**

Shying
Shying can be an extremely dangerous habit and nerve-racking for riders who are less than confident. Done in harness it can, in bad cases, break shafts and tip over vehicles. In traffic, whether ridden or driven, a shying horse can land himself and his rider or

driver right in the path of a vehicle or down a ditch at the side of the road.

Two main causes should first be considered. One is that the horse is simply over-fresh due to too much feed and/or too little work. A lower energy feed should be used and more work given. The second cause could be defective eyesight. If a horse only half sees something or sees something he does not recognise or which looks frightening, self-preservation in the form of a shy away from it is almost inevitable. If the habit occurs frequently a vet should be called in to examine the eyesight.

If neither of the above is the cause, the horse could simply be playing up the handler. Perhaps that particular handler does not instil confidence in the horse, or is weaker than the animal needs and the horse is just taking advantage and inventing an excuse to mess about.

Once a horse has shied in a particular place he almost inevitably shies at that spot for ever after. It is interesting to note, however, that a horse who shies at one place often, indeed usually, does not do so when passing it in the opposite direction. For example, if a horse shies at a certain spot in the hedge when travelling north on a lane, he will almost surely not do so when travelling south. This bears out the fact that vision is closely linked with shying because horses, it is believed, see and 'register' an object with one eye only in such situations. If something, such as a piece of paper blowing in the road or caught in the hedge, is seen with the left eye it registers and is remembered, but when that place is passed in the opposite direction and the paper has gone, no shy occurs. Passing the place again and seeing it with the left eye, even though there is no paper any more, induces a shy because the horse remembers the view with that eye and expects to see a piece of paper. The horse will probably never forget this, and the rider must beware of tensing up and transmitting his tension to the horse who will be doubly certain of shying if he senses that his rider is on the alert and that there must, therefore, be something to worry about.

Even the most confident of riders or drivers can become a bag of nerves, particularly in traffic, when exercising a horse who constantly shies. Whether the horse is over-fresh and full of natural *joie de vivre*, or simply taking advantage of you, or is genuinely afraid of something, it is not usually a good idea to punish him with the whip as this often makes matters worse.

If the horse is scared of something, depending on road conditions (if you are on a public highway), it is a good plan to let him look at it and talk calmly and soothingly to him. I do not agree with the advice given by some experts to dismount and lead the horse up to the object, perhaps touching it yourself. Horses do not appear to reason that if a human touches something it is all right (although they often do if another horse sets the same example). If you are on your feet holding the reins and the horse is unable to control his fear, he can very easily break away from you, and a loose horse on the road can turn a risky situation into a positively dangerous and maybe tragic one. You have much better control on his back.

Talk reassuringly, yes, but do not pat him and tell him he is a good boy, because he isn't – though he may easily believe you are pleased and think this is the thing to do. After all, in all your training and handling you have praised him for doing what you want. How is he to know you are now praising him for something you do *not* want?

When he has passed the object as calmly as can be expected, *then* praise him. If he does not, continue to speak soothingly and ignore it for the moment. Obviously, home training, if this can be arranged, or excursions with a schoolmaster horse to the same spot, should be undertaken.

If you can get him to go up to the object and examine it for himself, all well and good, but do not force the issue or you will confirm his belief in the unpleasantness and fear of the situation. Strong riding or driving past the object, if he is simply playing up out of habit or a little naughtiness, is the answer. No praise and no punishment.

Slipping on roads

Young, inexperienced and unfit horses, particularly those unused to hard roads, are often unsure on their feet. As they become stronger and more experienced they often right themselves, but the condition can be helped by shoeing.

Studs are not recommended in front by most farriers because they restrict the little bit of forward slide which occurs when the horse puts his forefeet down and so permanently affect the horse's action. Studs behind can be put on both heels, if the studs are small enough, without fear of the horse hurting himself, unless his action is such that he is likely to tread on or hit himself. The tiniest studs possible should be used, perhaps what my farrier used to call 'needle' studs which were simply hardened projections about ⅛in (4mm) long permanently welded into the heels of the hind shoes. As the horse for whom they were used matured, they became unnecessary.

If you are on a slippery road, give the horse his head and quit the stirrups if you are riding so that he can balance himself and you are able to dismount quickly in an emergency. Working such horses in knee pads is a good idea. In frosty conditions it may still be possible to take the horse out if you explore the possibility of fitting frost nails to the shoes. These are just ordinary nails with a little blob of hardened metal on the ground surface. They are used extensively in countries such as Switzerland and Canada, where racing takes place on frozen lakes. They were in common use earlier this century when horses *had* to go out to earn their owners' livings, and are in use by some breweries and similar companies today.

Speedicutting

The term speedicutting is used to describe self-inflicted injuries of the forelegs on the inside of the cannon high up, maybe even as far as the knee. The horse hits himself in motion at the faster paces with the inside of his opposite hoof, eg he injures his off fore with his near fore.

This is caused by physical weakness, lack of general fitness, faulty trimming of the hooves or bad conformation. It happens mostly when the horse is changing legs or leading with the wrong leg on a bend or circle. The conformation which is most prone to it is that termed 'base narrow' where the tops of the forelegs are very close together rather than the normal distance apart, in narrow breasted horses. Horses with large feet and those of pigeon-toed conformation (turned-in toes) sometimes show this fault.

If the cause is due to weakness, immaturity and physical unfitness the condition will often improve as the horse matures, becomes stronger, fitter and better schooled. If conformation or previous faulty trimming is a cause the farrier can help considerably, first by carrying out a certain amount of corrective

265

trimming (although the extent to which he is able to do this on a mature horse whose bones are no longer malleable is very limited), and secondly by advising on a suitable type of shoe. Often, feather-edged shoes or special speedicutting shoes are fitted to such horses. The idea is to reduce the risk of the metal knocking the horse, so the inner quarter of the offending hoof's shoe is usually straight rather than following the outward curve of the hoof. The shoe must be adapted to suit each individual horse's pattern of injury and action, so detailed assessment is necessary by the farrier and also discussion with the owner.

It is advisable for such horses always to wear special speedicutting boots to protect against injury. Obviously, particular watch must be kept on the inner clenches of the shoes of the forefeet as a very serious injury could occur should a clench tear open the opposite foreleg.

Stable, refusing to enter

See *Stable, refusing to leave,* as the principles, and the remedies, are basically the same.

Refusal to enter the stable can have two other possible causes. First, if the interior of the stable is dark the horse may be afraid to go in because he cannot see clearly where he is going. Even though it is his familiar box, he likes to be sure that there are no monsters waiting for him. Second, if the horse is more claustrophobic than most or is the type who does not do well in confined situations, this could certainly cause him to be reluctant to enter his box. It helps to make the stable very light and to give him the largest stable available, and also never to close the top door except in dire emergency. Such horses are normally happier kept out with a shelter, and rug when needed.

See also *Gateway, refusing to pass through.*

Stable, refusing to leave

Although perhaps not as common as refusing to enter the stable, this problem can, in fact, cause more trouble. It certainly needs delicate handling because a horse in a confined space, if handled wrongly, may panic due to being restricted by the walls of his box, and make matters more dangerous than if he were on the outside refusing to come in.

Knowledge of the horse involved always helps when dealing

with any problem and here, too, it helps to know whether or not the horse is just being stubborn or whether he is genuinely frightened for some reason. If the former, a sharp slap on the belly and a firm command to walk on often does the trick, perhaps combined with an assistant standing behind and to one side and backing up your efforts with a firm hand on the quarters or buttocks. If the horse still resists, it often works to turn him round and back him out, taking care to back him straight so that he does not bump into the door jamb.

Although occasionally attempted, it is not usually a good idea to haul the horse out with ropes crossed behind his quarters and fastened to each door jamb; this often causes plunging and half-rearing, when the horse is in danger of banging his head on the lintel, or the roof of the stable if it is low. Such an injury would simply compound the problem. Similarly, whipping the horse's quarters rarely has the desired effect of getting him to move smartly forward; in practice, this often provokes the horse to kick out violently and if the assistant administering the whipping is in the way, a serious injury could result. The last thing one wants is a horse either panicked or angered, particularly in the confined space of a loose box.

If backing out is not working, blindfold the horse (with a proper hood, if available, or simply with a jacket over his head, slid up from behind), lead him round his box a couple of times and straight out of the door, talking calmly to him all the time and being very careful that he does not touch the door jambs on the way out. If the horse will not stand while the blindfold is being put on, have someone cover his eyes with their hands until the blindfold is in place. Do talk calmly to the horse all the time to avoid any panic or tension.

It is necessary to find out why the horse has this problem, if at all possible, so that steps can be taken to alleviate matters. A common reason for a horse refusing to pass either way through a doorway is that it is too low and, possibly from a past experience, he is afraid of banging his head. If it is narrow, he may be frightened of knocking his hips.

If you are not in a position to dismantle his stable to redesign the doorway, try to retrain and reassure the horse by leaving his door open and letting him wander in and out at will. Tempting him out with a feed is a well-known ploy, of course, but it often works better if you wait until feed time and then leave his feed outside the stable, make sure he knows it is there, leave the door wide open (and fastened securely back), then go right away and let his appetite get the better of him.

See also *Gateway, refusing to pass through.*

Stable manners, bad

As with bad manners in work, poor stable manners often result from a horse's never having been taught how he is expected to behave when humans are present. Even affectionate animals who are, in turn, loved by their owners need a code of conduct so that they understand, for example, that although they are allowed to nuzzle a welcome they are not allowed to nip, often a sign of affection between horses. It should be remembered that nervous animals may regard the human as having invaded their personal space; and they may feel that aggression is the best form of defence against an expected unwelcome or painful act from which, being hemmed in by four walls, they will be unable to escape. This explains why some horses are quite amenable in the field but 'turn nasty' in their stables. Fear or apprehension are often manifested by defensive or aggressive actions such as nipping or kicking.

An owner or groom who is less than expert should take advice before handling such a horse. Individual actions such as biting and kicking are dealt with under the appropriate headings in this Problem Dictionary. For general insecurity in the stable, provided the horse is not actually dangerously vicious or aggressive, there is much to be said for spending as much time as is available in the stable with him, showing him that the expected aggression on your part is not going to materialise.

Many such horses have been treated roughly, often by grooms who are simply unthinking or are afraid themselves and are using the same defensive policy as the horse – attack before you are attacked. Rough grooming, particularly, for example, with a dandy brush on sensitive areas such as the belly, quick, bustling movements, loud or shrill voices, buckets and other equipment being clattered and clanged around, can all upset an animal as sensitive as a horse. Let the horse know that from now on he can expect gentle, confident handling, no shouting and, as far as you are able to manage it, a quiet, peaceful atmosphere in the stable-yard, or a quiet corner of it if that is what he wants.

Try sitting in his box and reading a book – don't do anything to the horse at all, just be there. Have a few pieces of carrot or nuts to give the horse occasionally so that he comes to associate your presence with pleasure rather than unpleasantness. It is true that some horses will begin to nip out of spite when the titbits run out, but not all, and you must assess each horse individually. With the defensive, nervous horse (which is what most of them are) the above method often works. If you treat him with respect he is likely eventually to treat you the same.

Of course, some horses require definite correction if they are ill-mannered to the point of becoming dangerous. Some horses are always 'quirky' in various environments and will always need careful handling. It is often their way of showing their personalities or, more likely, their dislike of an artificial environment.

See also *Barging; Biting, nipping or 'snatching'; Crowding.*

Stargazing

True stargazing, where the horse goes with his head up in the air and carries his neck with a downward (concave) curve to it (known as 'ewe necked') is usually a fault of conformation. It is not to be confused with the high head carriage shown by horses who have been abused in the mouth by bad riding and severe bits, when it is a defensive posture against the pain.

Whatever the reason, this way of going makes control very difficult, particularly in bad cases where the front of the face may be carried almost horizontally (often seen in those tourist photographs of Arab horses ridden by the Bedouin in their native land), because the pressure of the bit is transferred from the bars of the mouth to the corners of the lips. Pain will still be felt if the rider is rough, of course, because of the stretching of the skin, but the horse apparently feels it is more bearable than on the bars of his mouth. Control is jeopardised and should such a horse decide to take charge in earnest it can be extremely difficult to stop him and bring him under control again.

The horse will inevitably go also with a hollow back and trailing hind legs; indeed, the fault is sometimes seen in horses with painful backs caused either by injury, a skin problem or a badly fitting saddle or harness. Rugs secured by the girth type of surcingle rather than the modern crossed surcingle or leg-strap arrangements can certainly cause a sore back, as can a separate roller if incorrectly padded. The anti-cast, iron arch rollers must also be used with caution because every time the horse does try to roll wearing such a device he gives himself a bang right next to his spine on the very muscles on which the saddle (and therefore the rider's weight) rests.

The first thing is to see if pain rather than general conformation is the reason for stargazing and this means careful examination by owner and veterinary surgeon. If the bit is the cause, the horse could be ridden for a period in a bitless bridle, which will give time for the injury to heal but still keep the horse in work if necessary, and allow him to realise that he is not going to suffer any more abuse to his mouth.

A mild bit such as a half-moon rubber snaffle or a rubber or leather-covered jointed bit (depending on what type the horse prefers) should then be used and, indeed, may be all that is needed for a horse with a very sensitive mouth. Many horses with mouth problems go kindly in some kind of curb bit, which may sound surprising, but, provided the hands on the other end are truly competent and sympathetic, the much lighter touch used on such a bit is more to their liking than the heavier contact often used with a snaffle.

One of the things which cause horses to be difficult to shoe is that some farriers often seem to hold up the hind feet incorrectly and for extended periods of time. The horse's hip joint is only structured to allow the leg to move backwards and forwards; it permits very little sideways movement. When the hip joint is forced out of its natural position by the foot being held too high and out to the side, as shown here, pain or at least severe discomfort is caused

If care is taken to keep the hips level and to lift the foot up directly underneath the hip joint rather than out to the side, and no higher than necessary (say, level with the opposing hock), pain will not be caused, unless the limb or joints are already injured, and the horse will be able to tolerate standing on three legs more easily

Leaving a bucket of feed outside the open stable door like this may well tempt the horse to come out in his own good time. Putting the bucket on the ground and directly outside the door, as here, encourages the horse to come out straight and with his head low. Banging his hips through being led out crooked, or knocking his head on the lintel, are what may have caused the horse to be afraid to leave his stable in the first place

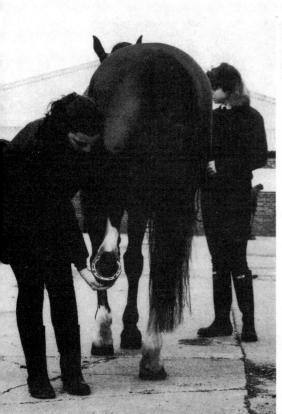

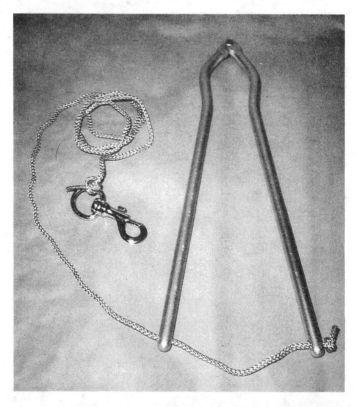

Standing martingales are sometimes put on stargazers but in practice they give horses a significant feeling of constraint and do not generally improve the problem, not least because the horses lean on them and develop the wrong muscles during the process. Controversy exists as to the use of so-called gadgets, but some experts do report considerable success with stargazers equipped with a chambon. This consists of a simple arrangement of a cord, straps and metal rings. There is a ring positioned just behind and below each ear; these rings are linked by a strap over the poll. Running up from the girth between the forelegs is a leather strap with a ring on the top end, reaching to about the point where the horse's neck meets his breast. These two pieces of equipment are linked by a cord attached to the top of one bit ring, passing up and through the ring at the ear on the same side, down through the ring on the strap running from the girth and up again through the other 'ear-ring' on the opposite side, from where it runs down and is attached to the top of the other bit ring. The chambon is adjusted, by means of lengthening or shortening either the strap from the girth or the cord, so that if

---

When the horse holds his head up out of reach, hook it down with the headpiece, like this. Alternatively, unbuckle the reins, pass one up each shoulder, buckle them again over the withers, pass them up to his poll, and gently bring his head down that way

Putting the bridle together piece by piece on the horse's head is often simpler than trying to bridle a resistant horse in the conventional way. Here, the handler has fastened the off side cheekpiece which is attached to the bit and is passing the bit gently up into the pony's mouth, after which she will buckle the nearside cheekpiece – and the job will be done. If the pony will not open his mouth, she will put her right thumb into the corner of his mouth and tickle his tongue, which works ninety-nine times out of a hundred

This is a humane twitch which simply clamps on to the horse's top lip and has the same effect as a rope twitch without the danger of cutting the skin (which can happen with a carelessly applied or too tight rope twitch). The same precautions should be taken, however, ie do not leave it on for more than a few minutes, ensure the edges of the lips are not curled up but under to avoid any possible chance of injury to the mucous membranes, and massage the lip to restore circulation after use. Also, allow a few minutes for the endorphins to circulate and start to work before doing whatever it is you have to do to the horse for which he needs restraint. This device is available from Horse Requisites Newmarket Ltd, Black Bear Lane, Newmarket, Suffolk, CB8 9BA

the horse raises his head too much or tosses it about, he feels pressure on the poll and also the bit. The idea is that he learns that when he goes with his head down in the desired position, he escapes the uncomfortable pressure.

Reschooling these horses is largely a matter of having gentle and steady hands so that they can rely on an even contact and will gradually realise that pain is a thing of the past. Unfortunately, horses do have very long memories and a little inadvertent movement resulting in a jab or too harsh a contact can undo months of good work and send the horse's head flying up again in fear and lost confidence.

Training the horse on long reins or lunge to obey the voice, and adopting a school of equitation which places more reliance on seat and legs than on hands are both methods which can help produce good results from horses afraid of their mouths. Driving horses are normally trained to obey the voice in any case.

Where a back problem has been the cause of this fault in going, healing must obviously be complete before the horse can be expected to carry or pull weight again. Then a light rider with a good seat, or a light load, as the case may be, can be introduced.

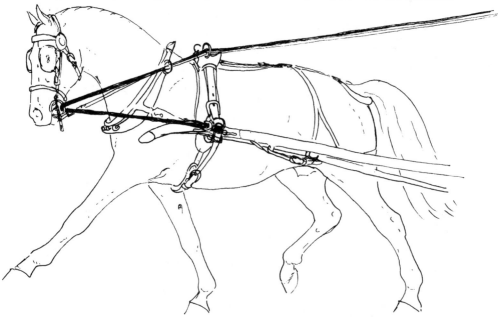

Fig 56 Stargazing in harness can be dealt with by a driving version of draw reins

For harness horses, a 'driving draw rein', for want of a better expression, can be used by fastening a long rein (maybe a lunge rein) to the driving pad, passing it through the bit rings and the terrets on the pad and thence to the whip's hand. This would be in addition to the ordinary rein and would only be used by applying light pressure when the horse raised his head and hollowed his neck. (See Fig. 56.)

Both this arrangement and the chambon mentioned for riding horses are intended to persuade the horse to drop his head. When he does drop his head nicely, even if he does so from the 'wrong' vertebrae in the neck, he should be praised unmistakably so that he gets the idea that this is what is wanted.

Stiffness

As with humans, some horses are naturally more athletic than others. Apparent stiffness affects some more than others despite their being given the same amount of schooling. Stiffness is not only the result of natural physical make-up but can be the result of injury or of disease such as arthritis or rheumatism, and not only in elderly horses.

Cases of stiffness resulting from physical disorder should obviously be subject to veterinary attention. The use of pain-killers of various sorts to help horses overcome the effects of injury is still the subject of much discussion, even though the problem seems now to be more under control than in the past. With elderly horses or those stricken with arthritis or rheumatism, there seems nothing at all wrong with the judicious administration of medicines to help the animal feel more comfortable. Phenylbutazone (bute) has been banned for use in humans but is still permitted for animals.

Whether such animals should be expected to work or not is a moot point. Many horses are not happy living a life of complete leisure; many, on the other hand, love it. If stiffness is caused through disease, the animal must obviously be kept in conditions which do not exacerbate it, such as outdoors in cold, wet weather, except for short spells for exercise and probably then wearing a New Zealand rug. Common sense is called for in management. Horses are flesh and blood like humans, and sufferers of both species can be treated basically the same!

See also *One-sidedness; Turn, refusing to.*

Fig 57 If you are a quick thinker and reasonably agile, you could try this method to puzzle a striker. Standing just to one side, when he strikes grab hold of his foreleg and keep it there for a few seconds or as long as you can. When the horse finds his action has been foiled and he is only 'shaking hands' with you, he may well give up the habit

Striking out

Striking out with a foreleg is a sign of excitement, aggression or competitiveness among horses and is almost always used by stallions and rigs, although geldings who were cut late or 'proud' can also do it.

Horses rarely do it to humans, but mainly to other horses. Strange horses should never be stood nose to nose for fear of injury to one if the other strikes out. They should be kept under control, side by side, certainly until they appear to have introduced themselves. If the victim were also wearing some kind of martingale, schooling rein or even a breastplate, the hoof of the horse striking out could become caught and cause a nasty accident.

Mares will sometimes strike out when being tried at stud, so handlers should not stand directly in front of them or position them in such a way that they might hit the stallion. On good studs, a solid, padded trying barrier is used so that if the mare or stallion strikes out, or the mare kicks out behind, they cannot possibly make contact and hurt each other.

276

This action is quite natural to the horse and there is little point in reprimanding him for doing it to another. If he (or she) does, a verbal reprimand can be given but the best course of action is to move the horse into such a position that he can do no harm. If the animal persists, he should be taken right away from the animal causing the excitement until he has settled down. As it is usually a temporary action until the horses feel they know each other, gradual familiarisation with each other will normally result in it stopping naturally.

Should a horse strike like this at a human a quick rap on the cannon bone with a stick or, failing a stick, an instantaneous hard slap on the belly will correct the horse. Prolonged punishment, or more than one blow, is pointless and stupid. Horses who have been ill-treated sometimes do it, but improve once trust is established.

Stubbornness

This can be a difficult problem to overcome because it invariably involves judgement on the part of the handler as to whether the horse is being stubborn out of wilfulness or because he simply does not understand what is wanted, or is afraid perhaps of what he is being asked to do or of being punished. Readers are referred to Dr Moyra Williams' contribution to Part II on the recognition of emotions in the horse.

We are usually told that no horse is born bad but is made so by humans, and this is almost always the case. However, the following story on the subject of general stubbornness (which was written for *Equine Behaviour*, the journal of the Equine Behaviour Study Circle, in the Winter 1982 issue) was told to me by the elderly stud groom of a top-class Thoroughbred stud:

We had a foal born to one of our mares a few years ago. His sire was a Classic winner and his dam winner of several important races. We had had several foals from this mare and had used the stallion, too, on many occasions, but had never mated the two together.

Anyway, the mare was sent off to the stud where she was to foal down and be mated to the resident stallion. It's a good stud, very reputable and we know them well. She foaled all right, and was mated, held to her first service and came home with her foal. Right from the very first day he was a bad 'un. He didn't want anyone to touch him for a start, and if you went near him when he was suckling his dam he'd try to kick you. He didn't like wearing a foal slip, was

277

never pleased to see you or inquisitive about you like most foals, but he didn't actually go for you.

When it came to teaching the foals to lead well in hand for the foal sales, all the others would be walking round in a nice circle, well up in hand, and he'd be skulking along with his ears back and tail down, wouldn't come up level and scowled all the time. Quite honestly, I was glad to get rid of him. He was a stubborn little pig.

The next year we were down at Newmarket for the yearling sales, and I saw he was being offered for sale again to go into training for racing. I walked along the lines and found him all right, and the stud groom was in the box with him. I asked him 'Is this So-and-So?' and what have you, and he said 'Yes sir', and touched his cap and started going on about him, you know. 'Lovely young colt, this', he said. 'Classic bred, dam a winner, beautiful action and well grown. He can't fail to do well . . .' Anyway, I said to him: 'Come on, now. I'm stud groom at the stud that bred him and I *know* this colt. Tell me what you *really* think of him.'

He went to the door of the box, looked to the right, then to the left, and came back to me and whispered: 'Well, between you and me I'll be glad to get rid of him. He's an absolute pig!' Now that horse had never been ill-treated in his life in any way. He had always had expert,

Fig 58 'When it came to being taught to lead, he'd be skulking along with his ears back and tail down, scowling all the time'

correct handling and been brought up as well as any other foal but he *was* a bad 'un. I followed him on the racecourse, as well, and he never won a single race, and even his places were in mediocre company.

I think horses are just like humans. They make excuses for all this vandalism today, and there may *be* excuses in some cases, but some people *are* born bad. They *like* doing bad things, and they're bad all their lives, and I'm sure the same goes for horses, too.

That *doyenne* of horse breeders, Marguerite de Beaumont, has maintained, and others have expressed the same opinion, that if a mare is forcibly mated with a stallion before she is ready, or even mated when she is ready but subjected to unnatural stresses like having a foreleg strapped up or hobbles put on, the resulting foal is likely to have an uncertain and ungenerous temperament because of the mare's state of mind at the moment of mating.

It may well be true, therefore, that general stubbornness may be due to natural inclination (some breeds such as the Cleveland Bay and the Akhal Teke are noted for it), to congenital reasons, to fear, poor health or actual sickness, lack of understanding or confusion. It is obvious that some of these causes offer hope for improvement, but others may not.

Stumbling

Stumbling can be a most unnerving habit for the rider, mainly because it can result in a very unpleasant fall, even at the walk, with the horse often ending up on top of or trampling on you after you go over his head, but partly because it usually occurs without warning. With other things likely to cause you to part company, such as bucking or rearing, you get at least some warning as the horse physically prepares himself for action, but with stumbling you usually get none at all – suddenly, his head and neck disappear, you are thrown forward, and probably off, right into his path as he struggles to regain his feet.

There are several reasons for stumbling: poor conformation and faulty action; straight but low action (ie with little knee flexion, known as 'daisycutting'); physical weakness or general unfitness; faulty or unsuitable foot trimming and shoeing; asking the horse to perform intricate movements for which he is not ready; giving him too much weight to pull or carry; and carelessness in the horse himself, for instance, failure to look where he is going.

279

The first point in overcoming the fault is to ensure that the horse's feet are in good condition and that he is suitably shod for his action and work. Often, horses prone to stumbling are shod with rolled-toe shoes, with hardener such as borium or carborundum welded into the toe for improved wear if they are prone to toe-dragging as well. Heavy shoes should be avoided for this type of horse.

Secondly, have his general fitness and health checked and take steps to improve them, if required. Ensure that he is not asked to carry or pull more weight than he reasonably can and see that he is well ridden or driven at all times, going up to his bridle and not being allowed to slop along.

Schooling over cavalletti and little obstacles teaches horses to pick up their feet and watch where they are going, as can work over rough ground, plough and in water. If the horse stumbles because he habitually goes on the forehand or relies on the bit for support, schooling can improve this fault. Using a different (not necessarily more severe) bit teaches him not to lean on it as he will be unfamiliar with its action and feel in his mouth. If he uses your hands for support out of laziness, make a habit of suddenly dropping your reins, either one or both, to teach him he cannot rely on you to prop him up. If you are a competent and confident rider, take the horse over rough ground and when he stumbles, be ready to give him his head and throw your weight back to show him he really must take care of both of you if he wants to stay on his feet, as most horses do. It is advisable to ride the horse in knee pads while the fault continues.

There is a possibility that a horse will stumble because he has been de-nerved to relieve some serious and painful foot condition, such as navicular disease, and has no feeling in his feet. This can come as a nasty shock to a new owner who may not have known of the operation, and it may be that such cases are incurable and unsafe to ride.

See also *Clumsiness*.

Tack up/harness, difficult to

Considering what an uncomfortable process being tacked or harnessed up must be for a horse, it is surprising that so many submit to it without complaint, and not surprising that so many don't.

Difficulty in saddling may well be due to a painful back, and this applies to putting on the driving pad, too. The horse may also object, particularly when being girthed up, because of pain from girth galls, either present or forming, caused by dirty equipment. Putting gear on over dried mud or sweat can rub a sore place and a girth that is too broad for the horse's conformation may cut in behind the elbows.

When girthing up, the forelegs should be pulled out from the knee to smooth out any skin creases behind the elbow and stretch the skin under the girth, which will help avoid galls from pinching. Putting a padded numnah or pad under the saddle or driving pad, and maybe sheepskin sleeves on the girth, can make sensitive-skinned horses more comfortable and prevent rubbing or pressure sores. Of course, any animal with an existing injury must be allowed time for healing, under veterinary supervision if appropriate, before being put back into work again. Remember pressure from a roller can cause injury, too, or even rolling on a stone in the field.

Putting on and taking off the bridle probably cause the most problems. Many horses are difficult in one, but not both operations due to having suffered discomfort or pain at some time.

Some horses do take advantage and use the trick as an evasion because they simply do not want to work. With a tall horse and a small person this is quite easy for the horse who just sticks his head up in the air and looks down at the helpless human with a supercilious expression on his face. This type of animal can be quite easily dealt with by holding the cheekpieces of the bridle, one in each hand, and hooking the headpiece over his nose, enabling you to bring it down. Alternatively, you can unbuckle the reins at the hand end and pass one rein up each shoulder, buckling them again on top of the withers. Then you can bring the reins up to the poll and bring the horse's head down. If you have a horse who lets you put the reins over his head normally but then refuses to co-operate, don't put the reins right back to the withers as is often advised, but keep them at the poll so that you can quickly grasp them together under his throat if he plays up, and retain control.

Horses who are really difficult are normally frightened so you have to reform them by being very gentle, if persistent. Allowing the straps to rub the eyes, letting the bit bang the teeth or press on the gums by mistake, and rough handling in general but particularly of the ears, all make for a hard-to-bridle horse, so watch for these points. If the horse is holding his head up and you are too short to keep control, corner him in his box and stand on a sturdy box or stool. Have your forearm over his poll and bring the bridle up carefully, avoiding the eyes and being gentle with the ears.

Another way, if you are not too out of proportion with each other, is to pass your right arm under his throat and, with your right hand, hold both cheekpieces of the bridle together, resting that hand on the front of his face. Gently bring up the bit to his teeth with your left hand. If he does not open them, put your left thumb into the corner of his mouth and tickle his tongue, which almost always results in his opening his mouth. Slip the bit in carefully and pass your left hand up the front of his face to keep control, using it gently to bring the ears under the headpiece. Make sure the mane and forelock are comfortable and not bundled up under the headpiece or browband, and that the browband is not cutting into the ears or pulling the headpiece forward into them because it is too short. Fasten the throatlatch just so tightly that you can get your fist between it and the round jawbone. It is obvious that the fit and condition of all tack and harness must be good and not likely to cause discomfort or pain.

In really bad cases, where you just cannot get the bridle on in any normal fashion at all, you may have to put it together on the head. Have the reins just behind the ears as already described, then slide the headpiece up the back of the neck. Gently fit the browband on up the cheekpieces and fasten the throatlatch. Buckle on the lower halves of the cheekpieces. It is best to forget the noseband unless it is essential as this has to be threaded up through the browband loops which takes time and fiddling. Attach the bit to one of the cheekpieces and, asking the horse to open his mouth as described, bring it up into position and fasten it to the other cheekpiece. If you are very careful, gentle and persistent, the horse will gradually improve.

Taking the bridle off sometimes presents problems because the horse has been handled by someone who has the stupid habit of snatching the bit out of his mouth instead of allowing him to let go in his own time. If the horse takes rather a long time to drop the bit, just tickle his tongue in the corner of his mouth and he will open up. Hold the end of the bit with one hand and actually bring it out of his mouth, carefully avoiding his teeth (knocking his teeth probably caused this behaviour in the first place).

Another common cause of trouble during unbridling is someone in the past having forgotten to undo the noseband before taking the bridle off; it has become caught round the horse's chin or muzzle, hurt or frightened him, and, once more, the psychological damage has been done.

Common sense, thought, gentleness and quiet persistence over a period of time normally cure difficulties over tacking up or harnessing operations.

See also *Headshyness*.

Tail over rein

If the horse frequently flicks his tail over the rein when in harness it is more of a nuisance than a danger, although it can become the latter if the feel of the rein under the tail causes the horse to kick. The simplest way to deal with the habit is to braid the tail up into a 'mud tail' as frequently seen on polo ponies (to prevent their tails getting caught up during the hurly-burly of the game).

Tail rubbing

Horses do not do this for fun or to pass the time, as they do with some other habits, but because the tail and/or the area around it is causing them discomfort. The skin of the dock may have some irritating disorder or parasite infestation or simply be dirty due to careless grooming; the horse could have worms; or he could rub his tail during transportation because he is travelling facing the engine and is balancing himself with his rump during accelerating and cornering or general rough driving.

The causes of tail rubbing are quite clear and it can be stopped by appropriate action in each case. Skin infections should receive veterinary attention, although benzyl benzoate is a good old-fashioned remedy which usually works (rub well into the skin of the dock twice a day), de-worm the horse with an appropriate anthelmintic (anti-parasite drug), wash and groom the tail and dock more thoroughly and frequently, transport the horse in a more balanced way (ideally tail to the engine) and drive smoothly and considerately.

If the horse is seen simply to sit on his tail in the stable on some convenient ledge or his manger, this could be because he is tired, or has some leg, hoof or back pain he is trying to relieve. Refusing to lie down in the stable (see *Lie down in stable, refusing to*) often results in this 'sitting' posture. Again, investigate the cause and put matters right.

Toe dragging

This habit is an annoyance rather than anything else, although it can certainly mean more visits from the farrier because the shoes or hooves are worn away faster than would otherwise be the case. On rough going, it can obviously result in stumbling and possibly falls.

It is more common for a horse to drag the hind toes than the front and it can be caused by poor conformation, laziness on the part of the horse (or on the part of the rider, not encouraging the horse to use his hind legs actively enough), by nervous disorder which prevents full use of the leg or legs concerned, by weakness, injury or by lack of fitness. Young horses sometimes do it before they have learned to 'use their legs' properly under a rider or when pulling a load (more often the former), and croup-high horses do it (a conformation which is becoming fairly common in American racing Thoroughbreds) but as they mature they often learn to compensate by carrying their hind legs outside the normal straight line of action from front to back.

Work over trotting poles and, later, cavalletti certainly helps during schooling or reschooling to encourage the animal to pick up his feet. Horses who drag their toes in front often have what is known as a 'daisycutting' action with little bend of the knee, which obviously encourages the problem, and can be helped by pole work. Work in water and soft going (judiciously done) also encourages knee action and helps develop the muscles the horse needs to pick up his feet higher than he otherwise might. Round poles and cavalletti should be used, and not square ones which might hurt the horse – one should never purposely aim to hurt, frighten or confuse a horse during training.

If the problem is felt to be due to some physical cause, veterinary attention should be sought and also the farrier consulted. The latter will probably be able to fit rolled-toe shoes (hammered smooth and rounded at the anvil to make it less likely that the horse will catch the ground). He might also be able to weld some hardened material into the toe for extra wear.

Tongue over the bit

The sight of horses going along with tongues lolling out of their mouths is not at all uncommon. This habit seems to be particularly prevalent among racehorses and many people well remember the sight of the superb Derby winner, the probably late and certainly lamented Shergar, coming up the hill to the finish at Epsom with his tongue hanging out as he zipped first past the winning post.

The reason horses retract their tongues and flop them over the bit is probably to avoid pressure and pain caused by rough or firm handling of the bit or by bits which do not leave room for their tongues. Unfortunately, what the horses do not appear to realise is that the bit will cause far more pain by tearing the sensitive flesh *under* the tongue than it probably would on top.

Most horses dislike straight-bar bits (such as are often still used for driving), although if they have a sliding cheek the horse can learn to manoeuvre the mouthpiece upwards a little and relieve the pressure somewhat. Half-moon (mullen) mouthpieces, which are curved upwards, allow more room and are preferable to most horses. Some animals much prefer jointed mouthpieces, particularly those with two joints instead of one, as these again allow more room. When the horse pushes a straight-bar bit up with his tongue, it obviously loses contact with the bars of the mouth, to which some horsemasters would object. Half-moon and jointed mouthpieces make retention of contact more likely and would ostensibly make for more control, although this is by no means guaranteed.

The fact is that if a horse is happy with his bit and has no fear or apprehension about having it in his mouth, he will not put his tongue over it. He will have no reason to and will not think about doing it. If, when he was bitted as a youngster, the bit was fitted too low in his mouth, he might at that age have developed the habit as a way of escaping from the feel of this unfamiliar object. The habit, once learned, may stick for life.

The answer would ideally be to ride or drive the horse in such a way that he did not want to put his tongue over his bit. In some spheres of equitation and driving where fast paces are normal, such as eventing, show jumping, competitive carriage driving trials and, particularly, racing where many horses are actually taught to use the bit for support, it may be extremely difficult to control an excitable horse without exerting more pressure on the bit than the horse would like. Riders and whips should, we are told, treat the reins as though they are silken threads which will break under pressure, but the number of people who seem able to control a horse on such a light contact at a fast pace, and the number of horses who are sufficiently well trained to respond to them, appear to be extremely small!

There is no substitute for good training and riding or driving, but, even so, there are cases where the habit is so ingrained in the horse that it is impossible to cure without resort to some mechanical means of prevention. Many horses respond to a simple change of bit (not to mention rider), such as one allowing more flexibility, a softer feel or more room for the tongue.

The two main methods of prevention are: (a) fastening down the tongue, usually done with racehorses where a strap is fitted over the tongue and round the lower jaw and usually to the bit or bridle, depending on personal preference; and (b) by attaching a tongue port on a separate headstall which is added to the bridle, a method often seen on show jumpers. The port is usually quite high, obviously, to prevent the tongue being drawn back far enough to be replaced over it, but as it is not attached to the reins, no pressure is put on it and there is no danger of its jabbing the roof of the mouth, as there definitely is with a high-ported bit.

Traffic-shyness

It is obviously extremely dangerous to take into traffic a horse who is frightened of motor vehicles and who reacts in such a way that his rider is not in excellent control. Unfortunately, once a horse has been badly frightened on the roads or been involved in an accident, he may well become incurable and have to be kept for work away from traffic. His behaviour may be improved in certain cases by the same method as is used to train horses to become accustomed to traffic in the first place.

He may first be grazed in a roadside field. He can be led up and down the fence, initially with his handler between him and the fence, and then next to it himself. The handler should talk soothingly to him and calmly stroke his neck. So that the maximum possible control can be exerted, the horse should wear a well-fitting lungeing cavesson, possibly with a bridle under-neath – a simple headcollar or halter does not offer sufficient control. The person leading should wear leather gloves; and a knot tied in the end of the lead rope can help prevent its being pulled through the hand. Later, when more settled, the horse should be ridden. If available, a schoolmaster horse should accompany the horse being retrained, initially between him and the traffic, then in front and subsequently behind, finally being dispensed with altogether.

Next, progress to taking out the horse on quiet roads with a competent, understanding rider (do not take out the horse in harness at this stage), in the company of at least one school-master horse and rider, and preferably more. The schoolmaster/s should be used initially to shield the frightened horse from the traffic in the same way as when in the field.

Gradually, the situation may improve to the extent that the horse may once again be taken out alone, initially on quiet roads, of course. However, it should be understood that the outlook for a badly frightened animal is not good as regards a complete cure, and he will probably always remain unreliable in traffic.

Fig 59 Retraining a horse in a roadside field is a useful way of schooling near traffic in relative safety

Trampling

A bully horse showing complete lack of manners is not to be confused with a horse trampling his handler in fear or panic. Horses are, needless to say, very strong, heavy, big animals and although much can be achieved by kindness and sympathy, discipline is most certainly necessary. Horses who habitually trample their handlers are very dangerous, obviously, and a firm tug on the lead rope is unlikely to get through to them.

A useful item of equipment is a stout stick pointed (although not too sharply) at one end. This can be used to give the horse a crack he can feel across his breast if he is producing, shall we say, unwanted forward movement, or a poke in the side or on the shoulder if he is coming at you diagonally or broadside on. Hitting him repeatedly, or on the head, is not likely to instil respect, only hatred and resentfulness.

One so-equipped leader on each side of the horse may be needed at first to get through to him that no matter how he tries to trample his handlers, he is not going to succeed. The instant your blow with the stick, or the poke, has the desired effect, stop at once and do not carry on out of vindictiveness. It would be wise to remove the horse's shoes pending an improvement. Verbal punishment in the form of a vicious growl, but not a shout, will help, as will profuse praise when he leads well and co-operatively and stops coming at you like a wild mustang whenever you go near him.

It should be remembered that it is natural for stallions to 'walk all over' their opposition and this is sometimes their way of asserting their authority. They do not differentiate between humans and horses and have to be shown that they must, while retaining mutual respect and regard. See also *Barging*.

Trimming, dislike of

Trimming, when it involves pulling out hair by the roots, can be quite painful for the horse. Many textbooks warn that this should be done only a little each day for fear of causing soreness. Most horses simply tolerate having, for example, their manes and tails pulled; it is debatable whether or not they genuinely do not mind. Although some horses will put up with having their fetlocks and jawlines tidied up by pulling, many find it too painful and scissors and comb, or clippers, have to be used.

288

It is easier to pull the mane and tail at times of year when the coat is changing and hair is less firmly embedded in its follicles. Therefore, spring and autumn are the best times to do major tidying-up jobs; also, it is easier to pull when the skin is warm and pliable after exercise rather than when it is cooler and stiffer.

Manes and tails should be pulled a very few hairs at a time, three or four only. The hairs can be wrapped round the fingers, over a mane comb or pulled out by fingertips if very short, and they should be snatched out sharply from very near the roots. If this is intolerable, consider using a scissor-comb to thin out the mane on the under-layer. This is a device like a pair of scissors but one of the blades is a comb. Alternatively, a razor-comb (available from chain-stores or chemists) can be used. This has a double row of teeth with a sharp blade in between so injury is not possible. Comb the mane hair from underneath at the roots to thin out.

To shorten a mane, normally the ends are just snatched off with the fingertips, if pulling has not shortened it sufficiently; however, the razor-comb can be used – just hold the ends of the hairs with the fingertips of one hand and comb with the razor at the length you want.

The tail presents more problems as the dock is more sensitive than the crest of the neck and the trimmer is directly in the line of fire should the horse kick, although standing right up to the quarters reduces the force of a kick to a rough push. You can protect yourself by pulling the tail over the stable door, having the horse held inside by a helper with a bucket of food. If the process becomes fraught with tension and fear for all concerned, it is best to abandon it and plait the tail for important events – a little more trouble but much nicer looking, and easier on your horse.

Tails, even bushy ones, can be disciplined by having the horse spend some hours a day in a tail bandage or commercially-available tail cover. The hair should be very slightly dampened to make it more amenable, but not too much in case the fabric covering it shrinks and causes discomfort, and even circulatory problems which can result in white hair and the tail dropping off! Incidentally, if a tail bandage is tight enough to stay on overnight, it is too tight. See also *Clipping, dislike of.*

Turn, refusing to

Horses who have never been schooled properly from the start and who have been allowed to indulge in their natural one-sidedness may reach the point where they cannot or will not turn to the 'stiff' side. It should be noted, however, that such horses readily turn to either side when at liberty in the field!

One show jumper's now famous method of getting her top horse to turn to his stiff side (by tying his head to his tail, in desperation, and leaving him in his box for several hours to come to terms with the situation) may well work but most people prefer to rely on a systematic retraining programme. (I have known two people use this method and end up with, on one hand, a fallen horse and a twisted gut due to the impact of the fall, and on the other, a fallen horse again and a broken leg.)

Fig 60 A simple but often effective way of showing a horse he can turn to the side you want is to walk him along and offer a titbit from the saddle to the side you want him to turn. Use your legs to prevent him stopping and don't restrict him with the reins

One fairly simple method I have used is to offer the horse a titbit from the saddle, initially from a standstill and subsequently making him walk round a corner, still holding out the titbit, and, with perseverance, I found it succeeded in convincing the horse that he could, indeed, turn to the right!

Lungeing the horse with the inside side rein (on the offending side) significantly shorter than the outer one can help, although it should not be so short that it pulls the horse's head round too much. When riding, care should be taken not to lose contact with the outside rein while sending messages down the inside one, as this may simply result in the horse 'rubber-necking', ie turning the head and neck but proceeding in a straight line. The outside contact should be firm and steady and the inner one irresistible but consisting of a series of little pulls from the wrist. The legs should support, the outside leg being slightly behind the girth and the inside one on the girth – not to obtain whatever flexion the spine is or is not capable of but to help communicate the rider's wishes that a turn is definitely wanted and expected. The inside seatbone should be slightly weighted as this usually induces the horse to 'follow' the weight out of a natural desire to remain balanced.

Make full use of corners whether in a manège, indoor school or the corner of a field. Use the same tactics when hacking out round winding lanes and be careful always to ensure that the horse does not get away with simply turning his head and neck. Correct rein contact and use of the legs, if necessary under professional guidance, will gradually bring about a great improvement in most horses with this problem, although they may always show a definite preference for one rein over the other.

See also *One-sidedness; Stiffness.*

Vertigo

Vertigo may sound a strange thing to mention in a book of behavioural problems and, because it is usually a symptom of some physical disease, it is, in reality, a case for a veterinary surgeon.

Vertigo is shown by the horse appearing dizzy and unable to stand up straight, not because he is 'saving' a lame leg but because he seems unable to co-ordinate himself. It can be caused by nerve damage, ear infection, poisoning, brain damage, electric shock and various other causes. A veterinary surgeon should be called immediately a horse shows symptoms of vertigo or any other lack of co-ordination such as aimless wandering or circling, staggering, stumbling without apparent cause, etc.

Water-shyness

Unfortunately, many horses show an apparently unreasonable fear of water. It is sometimes claimed that this is due to their natural fear, in the case of horses from wet climates, of falling into a bog, and, in cases of horses from dry climates, because their ancestors rarely saw water! Whether these reasons are true or not, it is obvious that some horses simply do not like getting their feet and legs wet while others couldn't care less. I had a horse who loved going into the sea (and would always take a very short drink!) but hated rivers and streams. He would do all he could to avoid a puddle but would wade happily along a flooded road, would tiptoe disgustedly through liquid mud but roll in it with gusto, and he retained these likes and dislikes all his life.

With so many competitive events these days demanding prowess at going through water, it is almost essential that all horses learn to do so on request. Event horses and hunters must jump into water, trusting their riders implicitly, but show jumpers must not. However, they must not be afraid to jump *over* it. It is a considerable nuisance to be out hacking on a horse who will not go through water. If such a horse avoids a puddle just as a lorry is coming along it could be curtains for you both. It is also infuriating to be stuck at a certain point on your hack because your horse is rooted to the spot refusing to proceed through the dreaded stuff.

It is more often fear than bloody-mindedness which causes horses to baulk at water. It is never a good idea to take a youngster out alone on a route where he will have to tackle water. At least one and preferably two or three schoolmaster companions must be taken along, one leading the way into it, a step at a time, one next to the pupil and perhaps a third giving back-up support behind. It is most unwise to use any kind of force, such as ropes behind the thighs, to drag the youngster, or older renegade, into water. The older horse may have had a very frightening experience involving water and the youngster may become terrified of it for life.

Gentle persuasion works best. Usually when the horse sees his colleagues standing or walking in a stream, he will eventually decide to try it himself and will almost always get used to it and may even enjoy the experience. It may be a good idea to introduce him to water for the first time on a hot day in the hope that he will come to associate it with a refreshing, cooling feeling. If the horse is genuinely frightened, just standing him near water rather than in it will help accustom him to it. On the seashore with an incoming tide, you can, by casual riding, often get the sea lapping his hooves before he realises it.

Splashing the horse does not normally help, rather it frightens and puts him off. Some people claim that the sight of the handler standing in water reassures the horse, but I cannot say this has ever worked for me.

Start off with very shallow water, perhaps little more than a hosepipe-produced pool in the stable yard. Then try progressing to shallow puddles on a rainy day, a shallow stream or the edge of the sea, gradually going deeper until the horse will wade in happily. Trotting in fetlock-deep water can be fun for horse and rider alike. Walking in knee-deep water can be a great help in producing fitness, particularly in areas where there are no hills, because of the considerable muscular and therefore respiratory effort required. Once your horse enters water, even a very shallow puddle, do give him considerable praise and a titbit and stand him there for a minute or so.

Although I have not, throughout this book, normally recommended force, if it becomes apparent that the horse is being dominating and refusing to go through or into water, maybe because he has won such a 'fight' in the past, a little coercion such as with a stiff-bristled stable broom under the tail, often works. He will realise that he is not going to be hurt and that you do expect your requests to be complied with. Again, once in, great praise and fuss, plus a titbit, should be given.

Weaving
Readers are referred to Dominic Prince's contribution on stable vices in Part II of this book.

Weaving is caused by nervous tension and stress from confinement rather than actual boredom, as is often claimed.

Horses are naturally claustrophobic and many more than we

realise or wish to acknowledge cannot stand being confined. Maybe they do not actually panic, but show their distress in other ways, and weaving is one of them. Anti-weaving grilles on doors find a ready market, but the horse often learns to weave up and down instead of from side to side. If a full grille is put on his box, making the caged-in feeling an actuality, he will simply weave inside, and probably more.

The most effective way to 'treat' weaving is to give the horse as much liberty and company as possible. Avoid teasing the horse, such as at feed times, so that he does not experience frustration and resort to weaving as a method of release. Keep him interested in life and take careful note of the stabling accommodation he appears to prefer. An unpleasant neighbour can cause the frustration of not being able to escape from him or her, and this can certainly bring on the habit. Lack of company in the yard ('Why have I been left behind?') can also cause it. In fact, anything which causes tension, fear, apprehension or general unhappiness can start a horse weaving. Weavers usually improve when given a more natural way of life plus work they enjoy.

Wind-sucking

See *Crib-biting*, as wind-sucking is simply an extension of this particular problem, with the same comments applying. See also Dominic Prince's contribution to Part II of this book.

In wind-sucking the horse simply arches his neck and brings in his chin as he, often silently, sucks in air. Like crib-biting, it is almost impossible to get rid of in a confirmed case, and most wind-suckers do best if given a more natural diet, life and management regime than is normally offered to domesticated horses, particularly those kept mainly stabled.

Yawing *see* Raking at reins

Yawning

A sign of tiredness, but also a sign of boredom and of lack of oxygen. Check the ventilation in the stable. Ensure that the horse has sufficient exercise and freedom. As it can be caused by a blood disorder (the blood being responsible for carrying oxygen around the body) consult a veterinary surgeon if the above measures do not improve the situation.

Appendix A

The Equine Behaviour
Study Circle

The Equine Behaviour Study Circle is an international group of enthusiasts from all walks of life who are interested in how horses behave and why they do the things they do. Members comprise professional and amateur horsepeople, veterinary surgeons, research scientists, 'weekend riders', breeders, and, indeed, many people who not only do not have their own horses, ponies, mules or donkeys but who never even associate with other people's – they simply like to observe them from afar or read about them.

The Circle issues a six-monthly journal, *Equine Behaviour*, which is made up almost entirely of members' observations on equine behaviour, both normal and abnormal. Some instances quoted in this book were taken from past issues of *Equine Behaviour*, and many members have found the information in the journal, and the observations and ideas of other members, of particular help in sorting out problems in their own animals.

The Circle organises visits for members and guests to places of interest in the horse world and encourages them to attend its informal and always friendly talks and discussions.

Full details about the Equine Behaviour Study Circle can be obtained from its Chairman, The Hon Mrs Moyra Williams, PhD, Leyland Farm, Gawcott, Buckingham, MK18 4HS, England. For your information, for 1987, the membership subscription rates are £5 for Great Britain; Republic of Ireland IR£6.75; North America/Canada $13.00; and other countries £5 sterling or the equivalent of £6.75 sterling in own currency. The Circle's North American Co-ordinator is Dr Sharon E. Cregier, University of Prince Edward Island, Charlottetown, Prince Edward Island, Canada C1A 4P3.

Back numbers of *Equine Behaviour* are available at £2 sterling each.

Appendix B

Recommended Books

Haworth, Josephine. *The Horsemasters: The Secret of Under-standing Horses* (Methuen, 1983). Deals with the 'old time' methods and horsemen, and some modern ones, too.

Kilgour, R. and Dalton, C. *Livestock Behaviour* (Granada/Collins, 1984). Contains a useful section on equine behaviour and general applicable material.

Rees, Lucy. *The Horse's Mind* (Stanley Paul, 1984). A marvellous book which everyone ought to be made to read and thoroughly digest before being allowed to buy a horse!

Schafer, Michael. *An Eye for a Horse* (J. A. Allen, 1980). How to judge all types of horses and ponies and how evolution and domestication has affected them.

Schafer, Michael. *The Language of the Horse: Habits and Forms of Expression* (Kaye & Ward, 1975). Self-explanatory title. A really excellent book.

Smythe, R. H. *The Mind of the Horse* (J. A. Allen, 1986, reprinting). Now a classic in its field, a worthwhile part of every equestrian library.

Waring, George H. *Horse Behavior* (Noyes Publications, New Jersey, USA, 1983). A truly encyclopaedic work on this important topic. The author condenses the work of researchers and relates them to current thinking. Both helpful and interesting.

Williams, Moyra. *Adventures Unbridled* (Methuen, 1960). Riding/racing without bridle and/or bit. Fascinating, instructional and entertaining.

Williams, Moyra. *A Breed of Horses* (Pergamon Press, 1971). The author's observations on the behaviour and inherited traits of related horses she has bred. Very educational and of great interest.

Williams, Moyra. *Horse Psychology* (J. A. Allen, 1986, reprinted). Often hilarious and usually thought-provoking observations on the author's own horses. Of value to all.

Appendix C

Vices and the Law

The Association of British Riding Schools publishes a very useful little booklet called *The Law on the Buying and Selling of Horses* (available from the Association at Old Brewery Yard, Penzance, Cornwall, TR18 2HY). In it appears a comprehensive list of defects and diseases plus 'problem' habits which can affect the natural usefulness of a horse and, obviously, his saleability. The booklet describes a vice as 'a bad habit, and a bad habit to constitute a vice must either be shown in the temper of the horse, so as to make him dangerous, or diminish his natural usefulness; or it must be a habit decidedly injurious to his health.'

The list of diseases, defects and habits is long and below are given only those relating to what we might call problem behaviour, with their classification:

Backing, jibbing and setting	Vices
Biting and savaging	Vices
Crib-biting alone	Vice
Crib-biting with wind-sucking	Unsoundness
Cutting	Not unsoundness unless wound or lameness existing at time of inspection
Grunting	Unsoundness
Kicking	Vice
Over-reach	Not unsoundness or a vice
Quidding	Unsoundness until cured
Rearing – when unprovoked by bruising or laceration of the mouth	Vice
Roaring and whistling	Unsoundness
Running away	Vice
Shivering	Unsoundness
Shying coming out of stable when chronic	Vice

Shying from shortsightedness	Unsoundness
Slipping the collar	Vice
Stargazing	Not unsoundness or vice
Vertigo	Unsoundness
Vicious to clean	Vice
Weaving	Vice
Wheezing or whistling	Unsoundness
Wind-sucking	Unsoundness and vice

The booklet is well worth obtaining. The price is only 50p, at the time of writing.

Acknowledgements

First of all I wish to thank those very many people who kindly allowed me to interview them regarding their personal remedies for various sorts of behavioural problems in horses and who have added so much to my own knowledge on the subject. What stood out clearly during the interviews was the fact that experts often differ widely in their views of how to handle problems, which just goes to show that experts are as individual as horses! What meets with the approval of one advisor may be anathema to another, just as one remedy may work for one horse but not for his neighbour with the same problem. This all adds to the variety of life and, I hope, widens both the knowledge and experience of those willing to listen to other people's points of view.

Secondly, my sincere thanks go to Joy Claxton for so expertly producing the excellent line drawings. As she is a horsewoman as well as an artist, co-ordination between us was easy and she also added her own contributions regarding equestrian technique.

Thirdly, I am grateful to all the humans and horses at Northfield Riding Centre, Gorsey Lane, Bold, Widnes, Cheshire who so readily helped me stage many of the photographs; to Barrie Hosie for help with photographs and for advice; and to Kit Houghton for supplying the jacket photograph.

Fourthly, I should like to thank in advance all those who read this book with an open mind and are prepared to give the horse the benefit of the doubt.

Index